COSMOS IN MAN

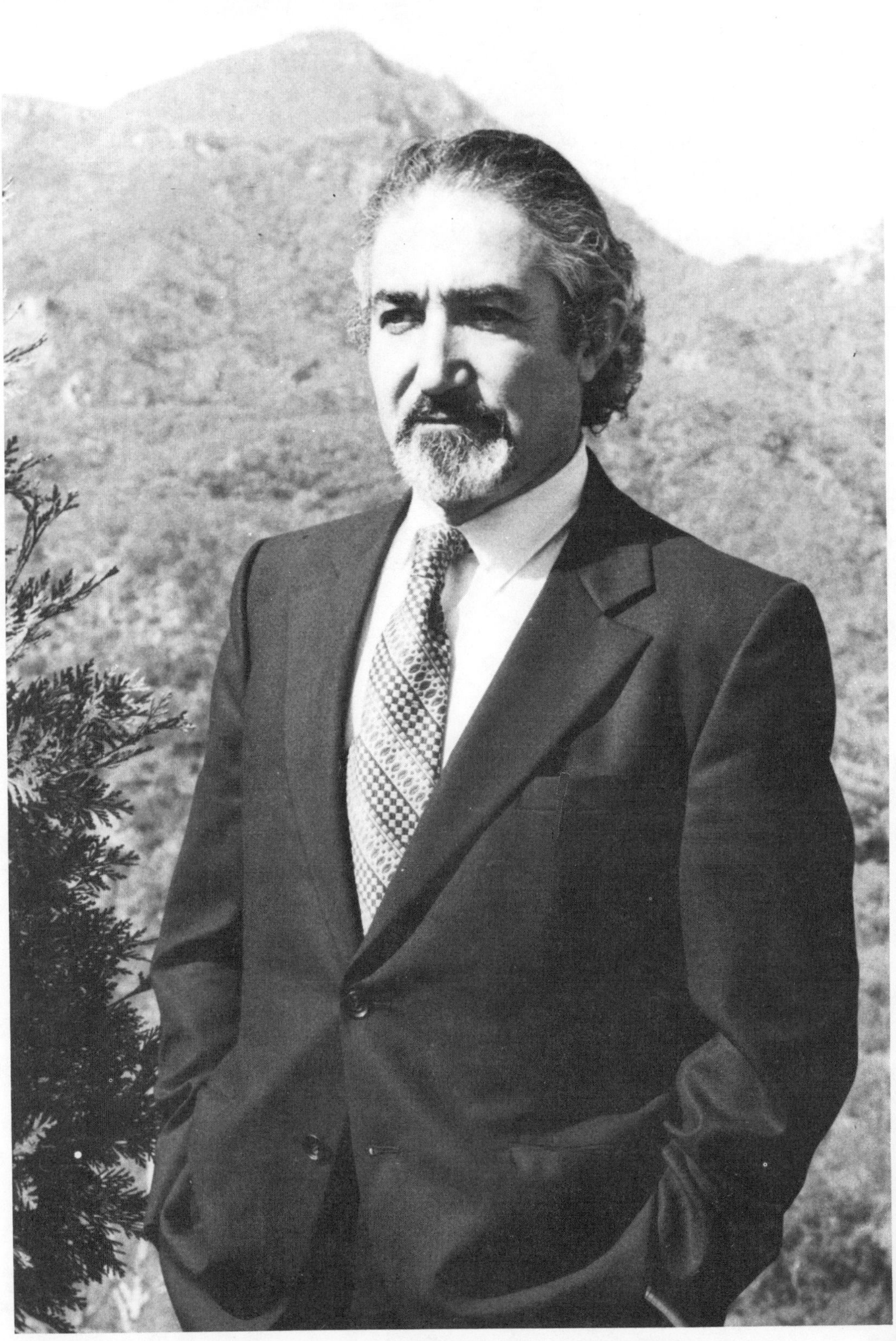

COSMOS IN MAN

By H. Saraydarian

AQUARIAN EDUCATIONAL GROUP
P.O. BOX 267
SEDONA, ARIZONA 86336

Library of Congress Catalog Card No. 73-77838
Hardback: ISBN 0-911794-31-X
Paperback: ISBN 0-911794-32-8

Second Printing 1983
Printed in the United States of America
Typography by Computer Typesetting Services
Book Production by Walsh & Associates, Tempe, Arizona.

Dedicated with gratitude
to
Helena Petrovna Blavatsky

ABOUT THE AUTHOR

H. Saraydarian was born in Asia Minor. Since his childhood he has tried to understand the mystery called man.

He visited monasteries, ancient temples and mystery schools, seeking the answers to his burning questions.

He lived with sufis, dervishes, Christian mystics and with teachers of occult lore. It took long years of discipline and sacrifice to absorb the Ancient Wisdom from its true sources. Meditation became a part of his daily life, and service a natural expression of his soul.

He has lectured in many cities; he has written numerous articles in occult, philosophical and religious publications.

He is a violinist, a teacher, a lecturer, a mechanical engineer, meteorologist, writer and philosopher.

Cosmos in Man is an exploration into the inner space where the mystery of the human psyche is revealed in its entire beauty. The steps toward the inner space are presented in rare simplicity.

Works by H. Saraydarian:

1. The Inner Blooming
2. The Great Invocation
3. The Magnet of Life
4. The Science of Becoming Oneself
5. The Science of Meditation
6. The Fiery Carriage and Drugs

Forthcoming Books:

1. The Avatar of Love
2. The Science of Energies
3. The Bhagavad Gita, translated from the original Sanskrit

CONTENTS

ILLUSTRATIONS

PREFACE

The Cosmos is the symphony of the energies and forces in the Space. Contemplation on the Cosmos calls forth the Cosmos latent in our hearts. The beauty of Cosmos will not be recognized and enjoyed until the Cosmos in our hearts unfolds its petals and expands toward the Cosmos.

Spiritual life is the journey to Cosmos. It is the understanding and identification with the rhythm and harmony of the Cosmos, until man really feels and thinks he is a part of Cosmos.

Spiritual living is a very simple and easy way of living. It is an ever-progressing, expanding way of living which is very natural for the human soul.

People complicate things and make them difficult because they let their personality problems interfere with the progress of their human soul. If they stay as souls and walk the path of life as souls, all will be easy and natural.

The spiritual life is a life of simplicity. People fabricate many things to make it a difficult path. People think that the spiritual life is learning and knowing, whereas the spiritual life is a process of becoming one with the Cosmos.

This Teaching will be difficult for you if you are accumulating knowledge but in the meantime not transforming your life, or actualizing your knowledge and aspirations. Difficulty on the path of the Teaching starts when you reverse yourself and think that you are your body, your emotions, your thoughts, your knowledge, your diplomas, your dollars, your property. This kind of thinking is unnatural because essentially you are a human soul expanding toward Cosmos.

The spiritual life is a very natural life for a human soul. As a child grows and becomes an adult, similarly a human soul must grow and, very naturally and without complications, become an Initiate.

Realize that you are a Spark; you are a ray of Light. Then it will be very natural for you to radiate your Light, to shine your Light and your beauty.

Every day you must have a time of meditation to realize and think that you are essentially a spiritual being; you are a Spark of Cosmic Fire; you are a ray of the Sun. You are not the body, but you are using the body, as you are not your car but you use your car. But if you identify yourself with the car you will complicate your life.

You are not your emotions; you are not your thoughts. If you identify with them, you will lose your control over them and they will complicate your life.

You are not your knowledge. Knowledge is accumulated, used, and thrown out when it becomes obsolete. You are the permanent Self, the Infinity in the human form, the microcosm.

Mental furniture is called knowledge. Do not identify yourself with your mental furniture because as your knowledge changes it will force you to assume that you, the Changeless One, are changing.

One very important thing you are going to do is to **remember** that you are a Spark, a conscious part of the Cosmos. You are going to remember your Home, your originating Source. You must remember that you are a Spark from that Cosmic Fire.

You remember the Prodigal Son, how he turned his face from his father and went into the darkness of matter; he reversed himself. He made himself one with possessions, with property, with matter; until one day he totally forgot his Home. He forgot his true Self.

He went away from himself and became matter, but at the lowest point of identification with matter, suddenly **remembered**. He remembered his origin, his Home, the Cosmos.

The spiritual life starts only when you remember your Home and turn your face toward your Home, toward your true Self. It starts when you remember that you are one with the Cosmos and that there is no other way but to go back to the Cosmos.

There is no other way for a Spark. No matter how long he wanders in the valley of darkness and pain, eventually he will **remember his Home**. In the valley of darkness all is illusion. There is only one important thing: to remember your true origin, your true Self.

Spirituality is the process of remembering your Divine Origin as long as you live in time and space. Spirituality is the result of remembrance of a heavy labor to walk toward Home.

Remember your origin and walk toward your origin through all that you think, speak, and do. If you fail to remember and to turn your face toward Home, you will reverse yourself and increase the duration of your pain and suffering.

All of Nature is proceeding toward Home. You must synchronize your steps with the steps of all those forces who are sailing toward Cosmos.

There are nine steps which must be taken life after life to return back Home.

The first step is **inclusiveness**. The traveler on the spiritual path must expand his consciousness and become inclusive. Any separatism in your heart and mind, or in your actions will create short circuits in the network of your electrical system, and for a while your Light will go out and you will lose your path.

When a man goes toward matter he is separative. When he is going toward spiritual values or toward the Self, toward Home, he is inclusive.

Inclusiveness is protected by the sense of pure discrimination between right and wrong, and between those forces which prevent your going Home and those which help you to go Home.

Inclusiveness is the ability to see the One Source from which all proceeds and to which all returns. Inclusiveness is the ability to accept the Divine Origin of all that exists. Inclusiveness is the ability to evoke the Light from every form and help the Light to increase and shine out.

The second step is **purity**. On the way back Home, it is important to purify your vehicles from all known and unknown impurities. As your speed increases on the path to Home, the small defects in your vehicles can turn into sources of great catastrophes. Only through purification can you stand in the presence of increasing light and increasing energy and transmit it to the sons of men.

Impurity creates inflammation when the tension and pressure of the speed increase. All that can pollute your threefold nature must be repelled or refused.

The third step is **beauty**. Beauty must replace all impurity in your nature. All that you do must be done in the spirit of beauty -- beauty in your manners, dress, words, thoughts, and expressions.

Beauty is a great guide on your spiritual path. Beauty is the presence of the Voice calling you back Home. Beauty makes you think about your Origin. Beauty makes you **remember** the glory of your Innermost Self. Beauty leads you to Cosmos.

Beauty enables you to have contact with the true Selves of others. Beauty leads you to the all-embracing Self of the universe.

Beauty is the call of the leading Center in the Cosmos.

The traveler on the path will reject all that is ugly in his thoughts, emotions, behavior, and deeds because ugliness creates confusion, illusion, and attachments. Ugliness makes you forget about your Home, your destination. Live any way you want, but *make* it inclusive, pure and beautiful.

The fourth step is **goodness**. You cannot reach Home without goodness because Home is the source of all goodness. Only good can reach God.

Once my Teacher told me about the difference between the spellings of "good" and "God." He said that the two o's in the word "good" are the symbols of the personality and the divine Spark, and when they are united man becomes one with God.

Goodness is an ever-progressing transformation within the presence of God. The traveler on the path must develop goodness in his thoughts, words and deeds. Goodness is the mother of harmlessness. Unless one is harmless, he will be caught in the webs of karma and be unable to reach Home.

Goodness must increase in our hearts like a fire and burn out the roots of malice, slander, and selfish, harmful motives.

The fifth step is **truth**. Truth is Light. It reveals reality and makes you see things as they are. Truth is powerful; it never dies. You can bury truth, but soon you see it resurrected.

The traveler on the path must search for truth and try to be truthful to himself, to his family and friends, and to life as a whole. Every time you escape truth or distort truth, you create a short circuit in your spiritual electrical network; you create a short circuit between the Life and your individual existence.

My father used to say that God never accepts visitors who wear masks on their faces. Masks are built by all that is untruthful in your life.

The traveler on the path lives in Light. He does not fight Light. He does not hide from the Light. He does not try to deceive the Light. Your whole room can be full of darkness, but one little match can conquer the darkness. Light is all-powerful. As the traveler ascends, he turns into Light. Light is the song of Cosmos.

The sixth step is **creativity**. The traveler is a creative person. To be creative means to arrange your life in such a way that it runs in harmony with the vision of beauty, goodness, truth, and joy.

Creativity is a transmutation process in which your whole nature, your life, and your surroundings gradually become beautiful. Creativity is the ability to manifest your Divinity in your daily life and relationships. Creativity means to find better ways and means to run your life in harmony with Nature and the universe.

The seventh step is **striving**. Striving is the conscious effort to transform your life and transcend yourself every day. Unless you grow in spiritual light, you cannot unfold the Cosmic Self within you. My Teacher used to say, "Be a better man tomorrow. This is what striving is."

Striving is a steady search for one's true Self. Striving is a steady effort to radiate the discovered Self.

The eighth step is **concentration**. Concentration is the act of mobilization of all your energies toward your spiritual goal, toward Home. Concentration is the moment of conception of the highest vision. It is through concentration that the real seed of the Cosmic Self is conceived within you, nourished, and expressed.

Concentration is a steady communion with the Highest. Concentration is the ability to live as a focused Light in the world.

The ninth step is **joy**. The traveler on the path must try to live in joy because joy transmits wisdom from higher sources and makes it impossible for the traveler to lose his contact with the Heart of the universe.

Joy is the communion with the Heart of the universe, and those who have joy have direction and compassion.

With these nine steps the traveler enters the Temple of Light and meets his true Self.

The spiritual life is a very simple life if you try to live it. It is difficult if you want to know it without living it. The spiritual life leads to simplicity and purity. This is what the Self is. This is what Home is. This is what the path is. This is what Cosmos is.

Sedona, Arizona T.S.

ACKNOWLEDGEMENTS

I want to express my appreciation to
Marcia Barnum, Helen Hall and Mariam Calonne
who typed the manuscript; Julia and Thomas Wade,
Marie Constas, Vivienne Pierce and Asta Klawiter
who read proofs and made valuable suggestions;
Jessie Watson who edited the book;
Jean Brussow who prepared final illustrations;
Mary Potter, Margaret Jenkel and Marlys Cybulski
who indexed; and to
James McHugh who supervised design and printing.

My gratitude to them will never end.

H. Saraydarian

COSMOS IN MAN

INTRODUCTION

Man is Infinity. When we know man we will know the Cosmos. Man is not only a replica of Cosmos, but a living mirror of all that transpires in Cosmos. In the future man will be able to use a living human form to forecast coming events on the planet and in Cosmos. Man is the most sensitive instrument ever created in the Universe—though his mind records only a small part of all impressions that come from Cosmic events and reflect themselves in the mirror of his etheric, astral and mental form. The cells, the atoms, the organs, the glands, the etheric centers, the blood and nervous systems all reflect different events taking place in the Cosmos. All these impressions can be observed in the electromagnetic sphere of a man as in a mirror. Fires and fiery lines can be seen traveling in manifold configurations.

When man achieves initiate consciousness he will be able to translate the language of these fiery manifestations, and thus communicate with the Cosmos, making it possible for the Cosmos to fulfill Itself in man. A man advances in his ability to record impressions coming from Cosmos as he unfolds his consciousness toward Infinity and purifies his nature with the fire of striving.

On the path of Cosmic evolution a moment comes when the Cosmos shines through the man to a great degree and the man says, "I am one with the Cosmos and my heart is the heart of Cosmos."

Man's aura is the screen on which we see the result of the activities of sensitive "electron tubes." . . . Every organ, every system, every gland, every center in man is composed of a set of *tubes*, having different functions in the registering and reflecting of events on the planet, and in Cosmos. Man usually is not conscious of this fact, due to the focus of his consciousness. The consciousness of man is usually out of focus, or focussed upon his "toys", but the beauty of the human being is that he stands as the reflector of the Cosmos, regardless of the lack of his *registering consciousness*. We wonder that the ancients worshipped the mystery of man in the human form!

Many conditions in human life may be the result of Cosmic turbulence over which man has no control. In the future it will be possible to forecast planetary disturbances, fire, famine, weather and epidemics simply by watching the electromagnetic spheres of man on which will be reflected Cosmic turbulences, recorded by the heart, the brain, the glands and centers, and projected on the screen of the aura. Thus, man is a reflector of Cosmic events and so far is not able to control the consequences of the pressure waves coming from Cosmos.

In the future, when man learns more about the subtle mechanism he possesses, and when he consciously registers and interprets impressions coming to him, he will be able to transmute and transform these impressions and use them to expand his consciousness; to improve his health and social conditions; to penetrate into the deeper layers of awareness, enabling him to manipulate the laws and energies of the Cosmos to further the purpose of Creation. A huge wave in the ocean is a great catastrophe for certain men, but it is a delight for an expert surfer.

It is the time now to record daily all of our unusual sensations. By recording them we will sharpen our impressionability, and will eventually be able to translate the meaning of these sensations and forecast our future actions. Thus we will be closer to Cosmos, and Cosmos will more clearly register Itself in us and lead us on the path to Infinity.

Man is Infinity, and the Cosmos is a great, Great Heavenly Man. Cosmos is affected by the condition of man, and man shares on his own level all that happens in Cosmos. An explosion in Cosmos may express itself as an epidemic or bring waves of emotional and mental disturbance and their physical correspondences. On the other hand, the formation of a system in Space brings joy creativity and a spirit of cooperation to the hearts of those who stand for the betterment of total Life.

In the core of each man there is a seed, the seed of the Cosmic Man a holy refuge. This book is an endeavor to unveil the mystery in that seed to present the miracle of the flowering seed; to help man witness the glory hidden within and to invite him to take the needed steps toward a life of daring joy, courage and self-mastery—upon the waves of a stormy sea.

Chapter I

SEARCH FOR THE AGELESS WISDOM

"The question of these Fire Dhyanis and their relation to man is a most profound mystery, and the entire matter is so clothed in intricate legends that students are apt to despair of ever arriving at the desired, and necessary clarity of thought. Not yet will it be possible entirely to dispel the clouds which veil the central mystery, but perhaps, by due tabulation and synthesis, and by a cautious amplification of the data already imparted, the thoughts of the wise student may become somewhat less confused."[1]

—The Tibetan

Through my studies, meditation and travels, gradually I saw that the real Teaching of the Ageless Wisdom has a supreme intention: to remind human beings that they have a divine origin, that they can be divine and have happiness, joy and bliss, if they release and live that divinity in all their relationships, recognizing it within each other and expressing it as service in their daily life. This is the essence of all true teaching. This is the goal.

In all mystery schools, in all true mythology and religions we find the image of a divine man; a man who is light, is love, is power, is the path, is the goal. He is a hero who attracts as a great magnet all our dedication, our mental focus and spiritual striving. This is the way the simple man is inflamed and drawn toward betterment, toward beauty and sacrifice. Gradually awakening within is the true hero, his essential Self.

STORIES OF THE SEARCH

By inspiring people through the image of a hero who is the embodiment of human and divine virtues, we build the foundation of human dignity and fiery aspiration toward the future. Once this foundation is laid, the man, aflame with inspiration, becomes a living beauty in all his relationships. He begins to bloom as he moves toward his essential divinity.

Training the King's Son

One of the kings of the East, knowing the need of his nation, knowing the mysteries of human nature, and knowing that he was not going to live forever, sent his three-year-old son to a far-off city, under the protection of a nurse trained for this service.

1 Bailey, Alice A., *A Treatise on Cosmic Fire*, p. 680 (published 1925).

The king believed that the future ruler of his country should be a man who knew about the life of his people. He thought that a king should know about their misery and suffering, as well as their aspirations. A man who was artificially prepared for rulership in the nursery of the palace, cut off from the daily labours of the people, could not have real understanding of the people over whom he would reign.

So his son grew up in the far-off city. He went to school and, when old enough, worked very hard to earn money for his tuition, books and other expenses. He experienced both failure and success. He saw the suffering of the people. When he was nineteen or twenty, he made some new friends with whom he visited night clubs and experienced the exciting life there. He gambled, he drank and had affairs with many girls. Slowly he lost his interest in books, in education and, finally, gave himself entirely over to pleasure.

The nurse was watching him carefully through all these years, and had kept the father informed of all his behavior, adding her increasing worry about the boy's health.

One night the young man returned very late. He had been drinking heavily. Exhausted, he sat down in the cold outside the door, not daring to awaken his nurse. The nurse, however, was watching him from the window. She noticed that he was playing with a knife. Several times he placed it near his heart, and then began toying with it again. She feared that he was psychologically preparing himself to take his own life.

Opening the door, she said gently, "You are late again."

"I know I am," he replied, rising. "I didn't want to bother you."

The nurse sensed the utter frustration, the hopelessness in the young man standing before her. There was a long pause before he spoke again.

"Good nurse," he cried, "I am tired of living. Life has no meaning. There is no drive within me. I have no goal, nothing to live for. I do not want to live!"

The faithful nurse, placing her hands upon his shoulders and looking directly into his eyes, said gently, "If you only knew who you are, you would never again be this person you have become . . ."

"Who am I?" he asked.

She burst into tears as she said, "You are the future king of our country!"

A spark of fire illuminated his eyes, now brimming with tears. He embraced her and said, "What are you talking about?"

There was a long, tearful silence. Then the nurse said, "You are the son of the king. I have watched over you these seventeen years, and my heart has ached for you. You are the future king of our country . . . your father is getting old."

At that moment, with this affirmation, the "King" within the boy awakened. He bathed himself and went alone into the forest. For a week he did not speak but remained in solitude deep in the woods. At the end of this time, he returned to the nurse and said, "I am going to my father and thank him for his wisdom in providing this great lesson for me."

It was a sunny day when the son and the father embraced on the steps of the great palace amidst music and celebration.

Years later he became king; a king who cared for the common man; a king who worked to uplift the standard of living of his people in all levels of human aspiration.

This is the human magic. If you will just remember your origin and turn your eyes to your *Future*, you will not be the same person anymore, and you will release your greatness, the hidden glory within yourself.

The Lion Cub

There is another beautiful story about a lioness who was about to bear her young. By chance, she was in a meadow where the sheep were lying on the grass. Her cub was born, but the lioness, fearful of the shepherd nearby, left her little one and went to the mountains. The shepherd soon found the young lion and took care of him, nursing him with sheep and goats' milk. Gradually the baby lion felt at home with the sheep and the shepherd. He started to eat and act as a sheep.

Months passed and one day, while he was lying on the grass with the sheep, he heard an unusual voice, a strong and awesome voice. Far, far away, from the top of a mountain, a lioness, standing on a rock, was roaring and calling her baby back home, back where he belonged. In a split second, the baby lion jumped up and ran toward the mountain, to his mother. Never again did he appear among the sheep.

This is another story of recollection of one's own origin, and the going back to that origin. Because of the importance of recollecting and returning to our Source, the Ancient Wisdom continually emphasizes the divine origin of man, and encourages man to go back "to his Father," which means to his essential Self, the hidden *glory* within man.

Search for the Jewel

To emphasize this point, Christ told the story of the rich man who was searching for a jewel. Although he was rich, he was searching for a *special* jewel. One day he heard that in a certain field there was buried a rare jewel. To find the exact location in such a large area was difficult, so he sold *everything* he had and bought the land. The word *sold* is very significant. He renounced all that he had to obtain that one precious jewel because that which he sought was his own essence. Nothing was more valuable than that jewel, his *real Self*.

When man finds his real Self, he becomes aware of the fact that in every man there is a jewel, a real Self, and this knowledge makes him love and respect every one. He is ready to sacrifice himself to help others find their own jewel and live according to the level of that awareness.

The "land" to which the parable refers is the higher mind where the jewel in the lotus is kept. It is our supreme duty to "sell" everything, to sacrifice, to labour, to renounce our lower activities, to buy the land, to make it our own, to experience it, and find the jewel. Once you "buy" that land you will have a deeper sense of justice, deeper love for your fellowman, deeper aspiration toward the cosmic values and an all-embracing compassion.

As I was traveling from country to country, from temple to temple in quest of the jewel, I met a man one hundred fourteen years old. His home was a one room hut in the middle of a forest. He devoted his time to reading and meditating. When I told him that I was searching for something real that lasted after death, something that would make me live this life more joyously in helping others to love and be joyous, he looked at me steadily with great, green eyes, and made a sign to me to rest on my knees in front of him. Placing his hands upon my head, he went into deep meditation. Then, he read from an old book a few pages which made my body feel electrified.[2] After he had finished, he told me these beautiful truths:

> "There is a mystery in man. There is a Presence beside him which is the path leading to the jewel. The shortest way to find that Presence is to watch, to observe your behavior, your emotional and mental actions, reactions and activities. You must always remind yourself that these activities do not originate in your real Self, but have two different origins. One originates in your lower vehicles mechanically. The other comes from a higher source, which is your Guardian. If you practice observation enough, you will discriminate between these two. One is mostly selfish, negative, separative, materialistic, narrow and limiting. The other is selfless, joy-giving, courageous, fearless, sacrificial, all-embracing, group-conscious, spiritual, progressive, enlightening; leading to service, dedication and gratitude.
>
> "Once you are able to discriminate between these two, the next step will be to tune yourself to the higher one, and express the impressions that you receive from that Inner Presence, which eventually will lead you to your Self, to the Jewel."

I followed his advice, and the first thing I saw in myself was a duality. Besides this duality there was a deep, misty point of awareness, which I was not able to identify, but which I knew to be there.

I found a level of consciousness in myself which was receiving special impressions from a source within, encouraging me to change the way I was living, reacting emotionally and mentally. There was also a resistance in me which was laughing at these suggestions, and making me feel at ease with my

2. This book, called *Nareg*, was written by a monk in the 10th century in Armenia.

way of daily living. Sometimes I was following the deeper guidance. Sometimes I was rejecting it and listening to the voice of my mechanical self, of my body, emotions and superficial thinking.

Following the Inner Guidance

When I was obeying the deeper guidance, my joy, my energy, my creativity were increasing, and I was feeling closer to the beauties of nature. When I was obeying the mechanical calls of my nature, my worries were increasing. I was feeling less secure, less joyous, even depressed, and my creative energy was nil.

Then the most crucial questions came to my mind. Who is he? What is he? Is that someone "me?" The more I thought about this guiding one, the clearer became my understanding of him or it, and I knew him to be different from the "me" I had always known. The choice was mine; to reject his suggestions and act mechanically, or to accept these suggestions and adapt them to my own level of consciousness and the point in time.

Many, many times it happened that when I was very thirsty and about to drink a cup of cold water, the command not to drink came from within. This was surprising to me. Sometimes during dinner I was advised to leave the table and write a letter to a friend, and to keep on fasting. Sometimes he suggested that I depart from a joyful party, go home and carry on with my studies, or go and visit a sick friend. Very often he impressed upon me the command to stop talking, or to change the subject. He also suggested that I confess my lies and other thoughtless acts to an old man, or to those whom I had wronged.

For example, once in a monastery, I took the protective cover away from an electric switch in the bathroom where our principal used to lead the students. He, himself, always turned on the light. That night, he was joking with us and, without looking, extended his hand to the wall to turn the switch. Of course he received a terrible shock, which resulted in his being pale and nervous for several hours. I was delighted, because he was often very harsh with the students.

It was midnight when an inner suggestion came to go to his room, awaken him, and tell him what I had done. Not expecting such advice, it made me hot and uncomfortable as I lay in my bed. For some time I tried to rationalize, to politely reject the suggestion and go to sleep. Then I noticed that the pressure of the advice from within lessened and I felt free to follow it or not. Just at that moment, I remembered the suggestion of my old teacher; "Obey the inner, real voice if you are sure that it speaks of courage, truth, beauty, selflessness;" Yes . . . yes . . . now, what to do. Should I disobey and lose the line of communication, or obey and suffer the humiliation brought on by my act?

At last I decided to go to my superior, my principal, and tell him how and why I had uncovered the switch. I knocked at the door three times. A faint voice told me to come in.

I entered and said, "I came to see if you need any help." This was completely rejected by the inner guidance and I felt like a coward, a hypocrite, and I knew that I was lying.

Immediately I collected myself and said, "I really came here to confess to you that it was I who took the cover from the switch."

He looked at me in great surprise, became sad, and in a very serious voice said, "Come closer."

I ran to him and embraced him, resting my head on his heart. For a few minutes we did not speak.

Then, he said, "Go and sleep."

This was a great moment for me. A great source of love and respect was released in me, and I was truly sorry that he had suffered because of me. I returned to my bed with tears in my eyes and a great joy in my heart. From that day on, he loved me and I loved him deeply. I was the one on whom he depended when he was in difficult situations and under trying conditions.

The inner guidance, day by day, increased. It was so real that I felt a presence around me every day, every moment. I found myself talking with him during the day and at night.

Often it was suggested that I take dangerous trips. On one trip I saw that a huge pine tree had fallen across a deep river. I was on my way to a friend's home to borrow a book for one of my teachers. As I walked along, I was gathering flowers and looking for the shallowest place to cross the river, when the command, or the subtle suggestion, came, "Cross the river on the fallen tree."

"No," I said, "you are joking. It would be the end of my life if I should fall." No answer came.

I sat down at the foot of a tree and began to think, "Will I be insane to try to cross the river on this great tree? Was this the suggestion of the Inner Presence, or . . . ?"

For perhaps half an hour I sat there, unable to decide. Then I said, "It takes courage, fearlessness, daring. Yes, it would be dangerous, but selfishness is being afraid of danger. At least I can try!"

When I came closer to the river, I saw that it was very swift and very deep. Again I hesitated, warning myself, "Don't be foolish. You will die!" I waited for opposition from inside, but there was not the slightest indication of opposition to this warning. This fact gave me inner courage, a feeling of self-dependence and I said, "I can do it!"

With great caution I sat down on the tree. Just at that moment a monkey-thought came to me, "Never mind, you can go back any moment you wish." I immediately rejected the thought as the voice of my physical, emotional and mental existence. I began to move along the tree in a sitting position with the help of my two hands. I focussed my eyes upon the tree and moved on, but when half-way across, I looked down at the churning waters below. It was terrifying, but it was too late to turn back. I closed my eyes long enough to establish my balance. My hands felt weak and the tree seemed to be moving under me.

I wanted to touch, to come in contact with that mysterious presence, to ask his protection and guidance . . . but he was not there! I was completely on my own! For the first time in my life I knew the meaning of courage and fearlessness—*I seemed to be one with the tree, with the river, with the whole existence*! Some hidden source of energy and joy burst within me, washing away all fear and anxiety. I began to move along the tree with an electrified feeling. Upon reaching the other side I looked back at the tree and the swirling waters of the river. I said, "Do you know what great danger you passed?" I rejected this thought at once and told myself that it had been a great joy and that there had been no danger at all.

I proceeded on to the home of my friend where three boys lived. It was very quiet, no one was in the garden, so I went up the path and knocked at the door. There was no answer. Climbing up to a window and looking into the hall, I was horrified! They were all dead!

I hurried back, crossing the river on the same tree, and gave the news to my teacher. Later, we learned that someone had killed the boys and robbed the home at the very same time that I was trying to make up my mind to cross the river by way of the fallen tree.

At another time a suggestion from within told me to enter a burning house in our neighborhood, to run upstairs, look into a certain room and return. This was a dangerous thing to do, but without hesitating, I did it. This incident was a source of joy in my heart for weeks.

Breaking Down Pride

On another occasion one of my spiritual Teachers suggested to me that I break down the pride built up by being the son of a wealthy family, by occasionally posing as a beggar for a few hours. I did not listen to him, because it would have involved the prestige of our family, something that I would have hated to do. Months went by and one day, from the depths of my being, a strong suggestion came to dress in rags, stand in front of a church and beg for money. I wondered what my beloved father would think if I were to appear near the church as a beggar. At last, however, I obeyed. It was a gray, rainy day. Dressed in old trousers and a very ragged jacket, I stood in front of a famous church, stretched out my hand and, looking down at my bare feet, started to beg.

The first few people put into my hand a few cents. Glancing up, I could see pity and compassion in their eyes. Others cursed me, saying that I was mentally ill, lazy or drugged. I managed to be indifferent to their comments until an old woman came and struck me on my shoulder.

Calling me by name, she said, "H—, my Heavens! What are you doing here? If your father knew of this—you are bringing shame to all your family!"

I closed my eyes, trying to assume indifference. I tried not to utter a word, but the lady, seeing my attitude, started to pray and cry out in a loud voice, attracting the attention of several pretty girls and some boys who knew me. This was the most tempting moment. I said to myself, "Keep your indifference. They will soon leave." At last they did go away with many humiliating remarks.

When church was over I put the money in my handkerchief, ran home and changed my clothes. No one there knew what I had been doing. I decided to go, alone, to the seashore where I could think. On my way I gave the money to a blind beggar.

Sitting by the sea, I examined the situation, conversing with myself– "I did it, although, when the old lady came, I wanted to run away. The most terrible thing was the girls. So what? I did it, but you know, my guide, whoever you are, this was not a good test; yet in a way, it was, because I learned not to be affected by the comments and attitudes of others. I know, now, what a beggar is, what people think about him and how he feels."

When I arrived home it was dark. My mother opened the door, looking at me silently.

After a moment, she said quietly, "Your father is waiting for you. Go to his room."

I did so and found him sitting in his chair, a beautiful smile on his face, reading a book. The moment I saw him, I said to myself, "There is no danger–he knows–he understands–"

I spoke to him, "Father, good evening."

Raising his eyes, he answered, "Hello! Come in."

He looked at me for fully five minutes without saying a word. Tears started to come to my eyes.

"Did I hurt you, Father?" I asked quietly.

"Sit here," he said, "take a book and try to read it as deeply as you can."

I obeyed at once, but was not able to concentrate. "What is wrong with you?" I asked myself. "Is not this another test to find whether or not you are able to overcome your emotions and forget the past? Yes, it is," I thought, and I started to read the book.

While I was deeply involved in the reading, my father came, stood at my back and said, "H—, today . . . we decided to initiate you into the brotherhood. You passed the test. You did it." He kissed me and told me to be ready to go downstairs in a few minutes. That day was one of the greatest days in my life.

The Secret Doctrine

In 1939, while studying in a monastery in Jerusalem, I received a booklet sent to me by a friend. It was a short review of a book called *The Secret Doctrine*. My interest was greatly aroused. I tried to find that book everywhere possible.

At last I discovered a secret way to escape from the monastery long enough to buy it from a bookseller. Concealing the volume as best I could, with great caution, I returned to the monastery.

It was difficult to find a secluded place to read it and a safe place to keep it. Disaster could have fallen upon my life if the teachers were to find that I was reading such a book.

Outside the monastery there was a very tall tree, probably more than a hundred feet tall. I managed to climb it, and by using a rope, I was able to pull up some small boards which I used to build a little house in the tree. The treehouse would serve not only as a reading place, but also as a meeting place for a few special friends. When it was completed, I took my new book up to the house in the tree and placed it in the safest corner. My next move was to cut all lower branches that could be of help to anyone who might try to climb up to my private refuge. I had my own method of ascent. With the help of the rope, I could climb up to the house, pulling the rope up after me. My treehouse proved to be a safe place to read the book for hours and days. The reading was slow and laborious for I knew very little English.

One of my teachers soon discovered my activities, but did not dare to climb the tree. As I read this book, the monastery teachings and the teachers seemed to become smaller and narrower. It became increasingly difficult for me to perform the unending prayers and worship required in my training at the monastery.

REVELATIONS OF *THE SECRET DOCTRINE*

I learned in *The Secret Doctrine* that our solar system and other systems have great periods of manifestation and great periods of disappearance. I learned that these two aspects of creation are called the Days and Nights of the great Mystery.[3] I discovered that there are planetary and systemic *Nights* and *Days* and that our planet has had three Days and three Nights. At the present time it is half-way through the fourth Day.

The Secret Doctrine teaches us that there are millions of solar systems in which intelligent beings are unfolding their divinity. They are attending school, so to say, to learn the mystery of creation and to gain wisdom that they may proceed on the path of Cosmic evolution. These solar systems with their globes are scattered in unlimited space. Some of them have reached an advanced stage of their evolution. Some are half-way to their destinations. Others have just begun the process of evolution.

Evolution of the Earth Chain

The living beings upon the planets of these solar systems are on different levels of the evolutionary scale. By way of analogy, we may say that some have gradu-

3. See Chap. V which describes pralaya and manvantara.

ated from high school, some from college, while others are just beginning with the ABC's of evolution. Let us study the diagram of our scheme shown in Figure 1. Schemes are great institutions of learning and becoming. The diagram pictures the seven chains of our scheme. However, the chains numbered 1 and 2 no longer exist; in the third chain only the *moon* remains with the astral and mental globes which are in the process of disintegration in higher spheres. Our chain is the fourth one, which exists as it is, with only our globe active at the present. The others are in a dormant state. The period during which a globe is fully active, supporting the main stream of life, is called a globe period. The Roman numerals indicate the planes upon which the globes function:

VII	**Physical plane**
VI	**Emotional plane**
V	**Mental plane**
IV	**4th Cosmic etheric, Intuitional or Buddhic plane**
III	**3rd Cosmic etheric or Atmic plane**
II	**2nd Cosmic etheric or Monadic plane**
I	**1st Cosmic etheric, Divine or Logoic plane**

On the physical plane we find higher and lower levels. In our chain (the fourth) we have the Earth functioning on the lowest material level, and Mars and Mercury on the higher physical. Our chain, as shown on the diagram, starts with the mental plane and through gradual materialization reaches the lowest sub-plane of the Cosmic physical plane. Beyond the mental plane are the four higher sub-planes of the Cosmic physical plane, which are unmanifested for us.

The evolution of our chain proceeds on three planes: physical-etheric, emotional, lower and higher mental planes. Our chain is the fourth order; our globe is the fourth globe of the chain; we are on the fourth planetary Round, and in the fifth Root Race. Furthermore, we are told that our Solar System is a system of the fourth order. Because of the fact that the energy Centers of the Solar Logos are located on the *Cosmic Buddhic* plane, these energy Centers are the Seven Rishis of the Seven Stars of the Great Bear.

The objective manifestation of the Solar System starts from the Buddhic plane, the fourth Cosmic etheric plane, via the fourth sub-plane of the physical plane, the fourth etheric plane. Thus, the Solar System has its location on the fourth Cosmic etheric plane.

The seven Logoi of the sacred planets, called the Seven Spirits before the Throne, are, themselves, representatives of the Seven Rishis on the Second Systemic plane, the Monadic plane. Here, as centers, they transmit the Seven Rays of the Cosmic Love Ray to centers on the Buddhic plane which are formed by the Masters and Initiates of forty-nine Ashrams. The seven Logoi also have seven corresponding centers on the fourth etheric plane. The objectification of

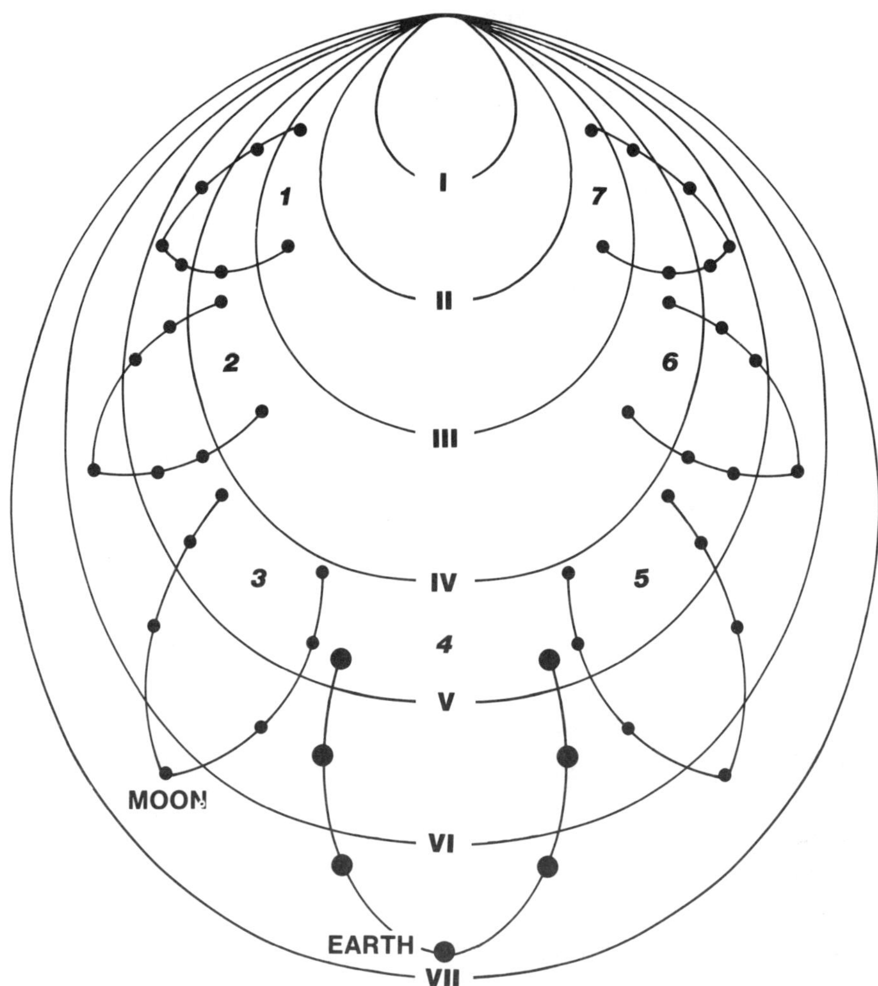

FIGURE 1. THE SEVEN CHAINS OF OUR SCHEME AND THE COSMIC PHYSICAL PLANE

these centers are the Seven Sacred planets: Vulcan, Mercury, Venus, Jupiter, Saturn, Neptune, and Uranus. They are composed of fourth etheric matter, and are objective and visible because of the degree of condensation of the matter involved. All of these Sacred planets are at their lowest degree of materialization, having six companions on higher planes.

Man can come under the spiritual influence of these Seven Sacred planets as he unfolds his etheric centers on the fourth etheric physical plane. He comes in contact also with the energy field of these Great Lives when he unfolds his Buddhic awareness. Let us remember that the Buddhic plane corresponds to the fourth etheric physical plane, and that Atmic, Monadic, and Logoic planes, which are higher Cosmic ethers, correspond to our three physical ethers. These four Cosmic ethers, Buddhic, Atmic, Monadic, and Logoic planes, in their totality, form the etheric body or the energy field of the planetary Logos. Thus, as a man unfolds through a chain of lives, the planetary Logos develops Himself in relation to Cosmos, through his seven chains.

Schemes, Globes, Rounds and Solar Systems

A scheme is the vehicle of manifestation of a planetary Logos or of a Heavenly Man. In a given cycle He increases His influence upon His bodies and tunes them in to His Central Goal. Thus, His vehicles which are formed of innumerable lives, slowly respond, integrate, align and express the "Soul" quality of the Logos and cooperate more closely in the performance of His Solar tasks.

When the planetary Logos, Who is called the First Kumara, incarnates through a chain, the wave of divine Life moves seven times around the chain of seven globes, forming seven Rounds in one chain.[4]

The period that a Life-wave remains upon each globe is called a global period, within the course of which seven Root Races develop. Thus we have seven Root Races in one global period, seven global periods in one Round, and seven Rounds in one chain period. Seven globes make one chain, seven chains form one scheme of evolution, and seven (or ten) schemes of evolution make one Solar System.

The Monad starts Its journey from the first globe of the first chain, and reaches the last sphere of the earth scheme, passing through seven Rounds on each chain.

In one scheme of evolution there are forty-nine *Rounds*. We are told that a planetary Round signifies the circling of a Monad from the first globe of a chain of globes to the last sphere of the chain, performing seven cycles on each

4. Bailey, Alice A., *A Treatise On Cosmic Fire*, p. 1175. We also have "inner rounds". The Tibetan Master says that, "The inner round is the round that is followed by those who have passed through the human stage and have *consciously* developed the faculty of etheric living and can follow etheric cycles, functioning consciously on the three higher etheric planes in all parts of the system."

globe. Each of these cycles is equivalent to seven Root Races. So we have actually forty-nine Rounds in a scheme, which is divided into three-hundred-forty-three global periods.

Let us remember that seven (or ten) schemes of evolution make one solar system, and we are told that our solar system will be created three times. The Great Life, Who functions, works and expresses Himself through this second solar system is going to create the third system as He created the first and second systems, and then He will be released from His Incarnation.

For the first solar system our Solar Logos attracted to Himself all the substance needed to construct a solar system. Through that first solar system He developed the Mind Principle, or electricity. When, after millions of years, He had achieved His goal, He withdrew His attention from the Body (solar system) and the solar system disintegrated, entering into solar *pralaya*, which lasts for one hundred years of Brahma.[5]

Following a great period of solar pralaya, He gathered the residual substance, which was permeated with the Mind Principle from the first solar system, and formed the second solar system. For this system He decided to develop the Love Principle, or the power of magnetism. This is the reason for our saying that our God is Love, and the reason that all religions emphasize love. Because of the Love Principle of our solar system, love has become the measure of man. Love has become the path of salvation and achievement.

After this solar system comes to an end, we will again have a great period of rest, and then the third solar system will be created. This time, we are told, the energy of the Will will be developed. Our Solar Logos will take His Fifth Initiation and will "complete one of His cycles".[6]

The Earth Chain

Let us study now our earth chain, the fourth chain, which is graphically depicted in Figure 2.

In *The Secret Doctrine* a chain is called a "small wheel", and our earth is the "fourth spoke". When the Life-wave makes a Round through the seven globes we have one turn of the wheel, and the wheel must "turn" seven times.

Our chain is also called "Seven wheels of Maya", because our whole chain has its being in the three lowest planes of the Cosmic physical plane.

In this diagram we have seven circles, which represent the seven Rounds in a chain. The seven spheres, numbered 1,2,3,4,5,6 and 7 represent the globes

5. See Chap. V for information about Pralaya.
6. See note under Figure 4 in Chap. XXIV.

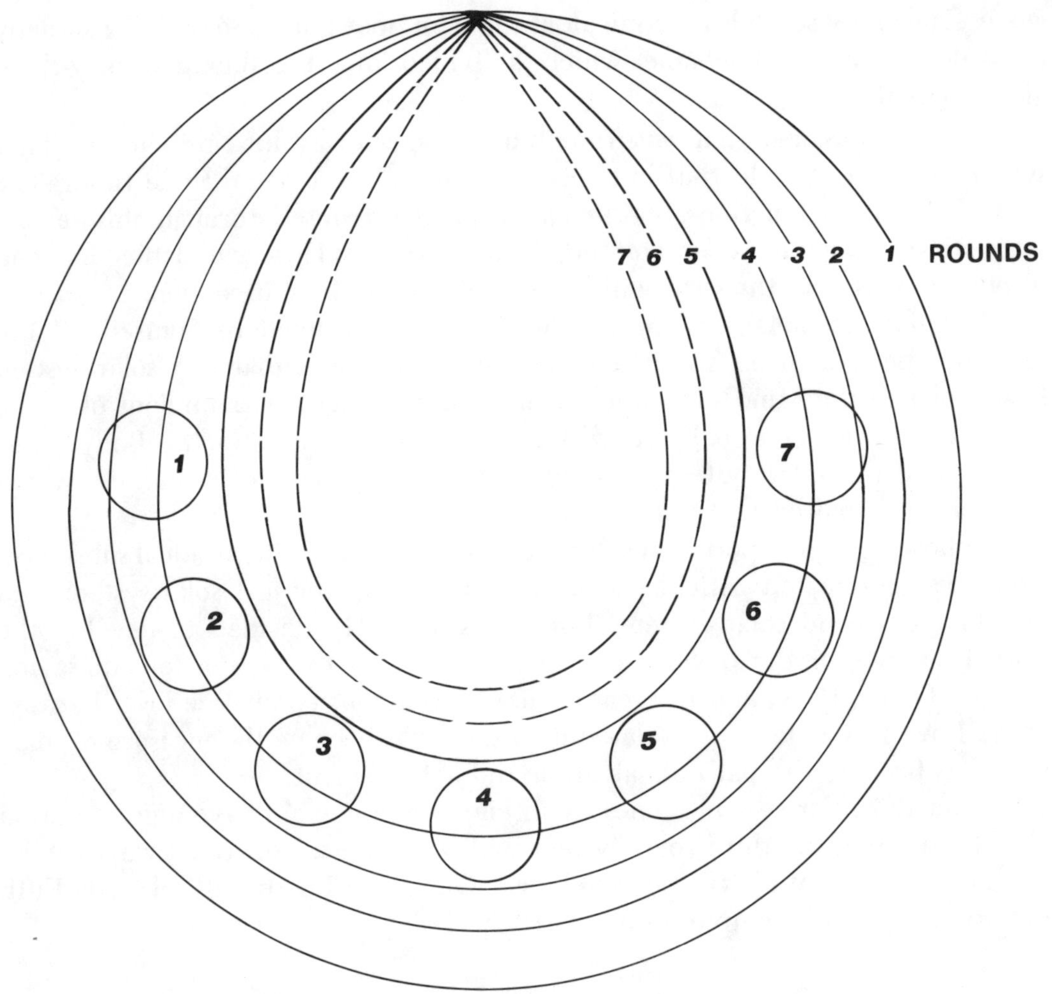

FIGURE 2. THE SEVEN ROUNDS OF THE EARTH CHAIN

of our chain. We will note that they are on the fourth cycle, the fourth Round. Globe number 3 and globe number 5 are on the etheric plane. Our earth globe is on the dense physical plane.

Planets are visible because they are the fourth globes of their corresponding chain.

The globes number 3 and number 5 correspond to Mars and Mercury as their evolution in the Solar System. Mars is behind the earth's evolution, and Mercury is more advanced than the earth. Venus is the Solar Angel of the earth. The globes number 3 and number 5 are etheric and they are not visible.

The Life-wave comes from the seventh globe of the third chain to the first globe of the fourth, or our chain. From the first globe on the mental plane the Life-wave goes to the second globe, the third globe, then to our earth and continues to the seventh globe on the mental plane. This is the first Round of our globe, a long period of evolution. Thus the Life-wave passes again and again — seven times — through seven globes before it enters into the next chain. Every time the Life-wave passes through the seven globes we have one Round. The period during which the Life-wave acts upon any one of the seven globes, is called a globe period.

The Earth chain, with its seven globes was not capable of providing habitation for entities of any kind, in the beginning.

At the start of a new chain, forms must be provided so that the in-coming lives are able to function adequately. Esoterically, "form" is a mechanism of *communication, assimilation, experience* and *protection* for the in-coming entities. These entities are not only human; some belong to the three elemental kingdoms, and some to the mineral, vegetable and animal kingdoms. All these lives must be vested, so to say, with new vehicles fit for the new conditions.

> "Occultism teaches that no form can be given to anything either by nature or by man, whose ideal type does not already exist on the subjective plane."[7]

At the beginning of our chain, we are told that a Great Being, called Manu, at the first Round of the Earth Chain brought the archetypes of all future forms. These archetypes were and are "electro-models", models built by electrical waves, which slowly materialize themselves and provide the blueprints around which the forms of all nature are built or are in the process of being built.

Our archetype incarnates through matter, century after century, until the form reflects perfectly the whole nature of the archetype. This accounts for the fact that nature, whether it be a flower or the body of a man, goes through slow but progressive development toward more beauty.

When the department of the Manu decides to remove a form from nature, it removes its archetype and the form slowly degenerates and fades away. On the other hand, if they want to vivify a form, they charge the archetypes.

Human Development

These archetypes were brought down by Manu from a higher sphere. With the permission of the Solar Lords, they were handed over to certain Lords from the Moon, called Barhishads. These Beings were in charge of the work of setting the activities of the first chain in motion. In *The Secret Doctrine* the act of fashioning the form for the human race is referred to as follows:

> "The great Chohans (Lords), called the (*Lords*) of the Moon, of the airy bodies. 'Bring forth Men, (*they were told*), men of your nature. Give them (*i.e., The Jivas or Monads*) their forms within. She (*Mother Earth or Nature*) will build coverings without (*external bodies*).' "[8]

Thus was created "the model vehicle," the etheric body, of the first man. As cycle after cycle passed, this model vehicle attracted atoms of matter and

7. Blavatsky, H. P., *The Secret Doctrine*, Orig. Ed., Vol. I, p. 282, footnote.
8. Blavatsky, H. P., *The Secret Doctrine*, Orig. Ed., Vol. II, p. 75.

our dense physical body was built. Hence, the Monad, the essential Spark, had as Its first dwelling the "model vehicle" and then Its dense physical body. Because of this, we are told in the Ancient Wisdom, the physical body is the shadow of the model body. H.P.B. refers to it as "the inert vehicle or form, on which the body is moulded."[9]

The occult philosophy ". . . teaches that the first human stock was projected by higher and semi-divine Beings out of their own essences."[10]

The human Monad, was brooding over this model body, but It had no mind, and the relationship between Its gradually condensing vehicle and the Monad was not yet built.

This task of building a relationship between the Monad and Its vehicles was undertaken by other advanced Beings who were called Solar Pitris. *The Secret Doctrine* calls them by more than thirty-four names. Terms frequently used in this book are, Solar Angels, Guardian Lights or Lords of Flame.

In each of the seven globes of the first Round, these Great Beings, from globe seven of the Moon chain, gave forms to these archetypes, by solidifying them according to the density of the plane on which the different globes were situated in our first Round.

In the Ancient Wisdom we are told that when new entities are in the process of coming down to a new chain, the least advanced entities come first and inhabit the very primitive forms. Advanced ones follow later as the forms develop and become suitable for them.

When the cycle of the moon chain was in the process of ending, the Great Ones in the chain made every possible arrangement to transport the many kinds of creatures into the new chain. The Moon animal-men came first to our earth chain, and during 100,000 to 200,000 years many other forms of life were brought in.

Those who came first were living on a globe within the mental plane, and we are told that they did not continue their evolution from the point where they had left off on the Moon chain, but recapitulated all of its stages many times. First they entered into the first elemental kingdom. From there they passed into the second and third elemental kingdoms, then into the mineral, vegetable and animal kingdoms, eventually reaching the human kingdom once again, at the end of the first Round, on the seventh globe. After that they entered the first globe in the second Round as a very primitive humanity.

Returning to Figure 2,

- On the arc of *descent*, it is the substance of globes 1, 2 and 3 that controls man.
- On the fourth globe the conflict starts between the substance of the globe and the Indweller of the form.

9. *Ibid.*, p. 593.
10. *Ibid.*, p. 87.

– On the arc of *ascent*, it is the Indweller that controls and creates through the substance of globes 5, 6 and 7.

We will note on the previous diagram in Figure 1 that in the *first chain*:

1. The first and seventh globes were formed of *Atmic* element.
2. The second and sixth globes were formed of *Buddhic* element.
3. The third and fifth globes were formed of *higher-mental* element.
4. The fourth globe was formed of *lower-mental* element.[11]

Similarly, the minerals found in each globe were Atmic minerals, Buddhic minerals, and higher and lower mental minerals. This means that the vehicles of the Monad were built, successively, of Atmic, Buddhic, and higher and lower mental minerals. Those Monads of the mineral kingdom, who graduated from the first chain, entered into the second chain as the vegetable kingdom, but the vegetables were of Buddhic, astral and higher and lower mental substance. The bodies of the Monads had become more dense than on the previous chain.

The Monads of the vegetable kingdom who graduated from the second chain, entered into the third chain as animals. The Monads then had animal bodies, but the bodies of these animals were composed of higher and lower mental, astral and etheric matter. Those animals that graduated from the seventh globe of the third chain, entered into the first globe of our chain (the fourth chain) as prototypes of the human kingdom. Their development on our chain proceeded as follows:

1. On the first globe their forms were built with lower mental matter, fiery matter.
2. On the second globe they built astral forms.
3. On the third globe they had forms of lower mental, astral and etheric matter.
4. On the fourth globe, the earth, their bodies were more dense and eventually became hard physical bodies.
5. On the next globe, the fifth globe, we will have etheric bodies.
6. On the sixth globe we will have astral bodies.
7. On the seventh globe our bodies will be of higher and lower mental substance.

The Secret Doctrine teaches that "Humanity develops fully only in the Fourth—our present Round. Up to this fourth Life-Cycle, it is referred to as 'humanity' only for lack of a more appropriate term. . . . Man, or rather that which becomes man, passes through all the forms and kingdoms during the first Round and through all the human shapes during the following Rounds. Arrived on our Earth at the commencement of the Fourth in the present series of life cycles and races, MAN is the first form that appears thereon, being preceded only by the mineral and vegetable kingdoms . . ."[12]

11. The Tibetan Master says: "The fifth globe, E, . . . usually belongs to the astral plane, and the sixth and seventh, F and G, . . . to the Rupa and Arupa levels of the mental plane, . . ." Bailey, Alice A., *A Treatise on Cosmic Fire*, p. 382.

12. Blavatsky, H. P., *The Secret Doctrine*, Orig. Ed. Vol. I, p. 159.

Man made his entrance into the fourth globe in a fiery-ethereal form. Gradually he developed an airy body, later a watery body, and finally a material body. As the globe, itself, passed through such states, in the first, second, third and fourth Rounds, so did man's form.

On the fourth planetary Round, all the previous states on previous globes of our chain were repeated for the first, second, third and fourth races, on racial scales. The first race of the fourth Round "oozed out" of the bodies of the Lords of the Moon, called Pitris. The bodies of this first race were immaterial, transparent, ethereal, and spiritual, but the Mind Principle was dormant in them. For this reason they were called "mindless," and because of this, there was no connecting conscious link between the bodies and the Monad. They possessed only one sense, the sense of *hearing*. This race is called the "Self-born Race." Their bodies could "stand, walk, run, recline, or fly," and "Neither fire nor water could destroy them."[13] The race vanished into the second Root Race. Their fiery bodies became the etheric bodies of the second Root Race.

The second Root Race, which emanated from the First Root Race, was propagated by means of building, as the amoeba, by the process of cellular division. The bodies were boneless, largely astral-etheric, and possessed a faint spark of mind. They were phantom-like semi-monsters. Their speech consisted of chant-like sounds, composed of vowels alone. Two senses were developed—*hearing* and *touch*. They were able to respond to the impact of water, air and fire. This second Root Race, called the Sweat-born Race was golden-yellow in color.

The third Root Race, known as the Lemurian Race, or Egg-born Race, is described in *The Secret Doctrine*:

> " While the early sub-races of the Third Humanity [Third Race] procreated their species by a kind of exudation of moisture or vital fluid, the drops of which coalescing formed an oviform ball—or shall we say egg— that served as an extraneous vehicle for the generation therein of a foetus and child, the mode of procreation by the later sub-races changed, in its results at all events. The little ones of the earlier sub-races were entirely sexless—shapeless even for all one knows; but those of the later sub-races were born androgynous."[14]
>
> "The 'sons of Passive Yoga' [the Third Race] . . . issued from the second Manushyas (Human Race), and became oviparous. The emanations that came out of their bodies during the seasons of procreation were ovulary; the small spheroidal nuclei developing into a large soft, egg-like vehicle, gradually hardened, when, after a period of gestation, it broke and the young human animal issued from it unaided, as the fowls do in our Race."[15]

---

13. Blavatasky, H.P, *The Secret Doctrine,* Vol. II, pp. 18–20.
14. *Ibid.*, p. 140.
15. *Ibid.*, p. 175.

The Third Race, the Lemurian Race, had ape-like bodies, composed mostly of gases, liquids and solids. They were androgynous, having both sexes in one body. As they became more and more dense, they developed bones as the earth developed its rocks toward the middle of the Lemurian period. Their language was mono-syllabic, and the senses developed were those of *hearing, touch* and *sight.* "This race could live with equal ease in water, air or fire, for it had an unlimited control over the elements."[16]

Again, it was in the third sub-race of the Third Root Race that organs of vision were developed. In addition to the two eyes, a third, single eye was developed in the middle of the forehead. This single eye was capable of seeing etheric and astral forms.

Story of Individualization

During the middle period of the Third Root Race, a most remarkable happening took place. This great event was the act of *individualization. The Secret Doctrine* says that:

> ". . . Having passed through all the kingdoms of nature in the previous *three* rounds, his physical form . . . was ready to receive the divine pilgrim at the first dawn of human life, i.e.—18,000,000 years ago. It is only at the mid-point of the third Root Race that man was endowed with *manas* [mind]. Once united, the *two* and then the *three* made one; for though the lower animals, from the amoeba to man, received their Monads in which all higher qualities are potential, all have to remain dormant till each reaches its human form, before which stage Manas [mind] has no development in them . . ."[17]

This story is given in detail in the following quotation:

> "The Sons of Wisdom, The Sons of Night, ready for rebirth, came down. They saw the vile forms of the First Third. 'We can choose', said the Lords, 'We have wisdom.' Some entered the Chhayas. Some projected a Spark. Some deferred till the Fourth. From their own Rupa they filled the Kama. Those who entered became Arhats. Those who received but a Spark, remained destitute of knowledge; the Spark burned low. The Third remained mindless. Their Jivas were not ready. These were set apart among the Seven. They became narrow-headed. The Third were ready. 'In these shall we dwell,' said the Lords of the Flame and of the Dark Wisdom."[18]

16. *Ibid.*, p. 230.
17. *Ibid.*, p. 256.
18. *Ibid.*, p. 170.

This was most fascinating to me. I continued to read and read, feeling deeply that in these ancient writings was the key to the human mystery, and to the identity of my Inner Guide. I continued my studies in *The Secret Doctrine* wherever I went in Asia. Gradually the whole picture of the human psyche became clearer and clearer. I began to grasp the meaning of the passage which had so captured my interest when I first began reading *The Secret Doctrine*:

The Sons of Wisdom, . . . The Sons of Wisdom were very advanced beings, Angels who were emerging from their Night and coming into the Day of a new creation. It was on the fourth chain and at the fourth globe that these Celestial Hosts came to our planet. They came during the period of the Third Race, ready to start a new cycle of experience and expression.

[*They*] *came down*. . . . This means that these Beings came from their state of development to the lower spheres of creation, to the physical earth.

They saw the vile forms of the First Third. . . . Vile forms were human beings with huge, animal-like bodies, possessing no intellect. They were devoid of intelligence. The "first third" refers to the first half of the Third Root Race which was a senseless, unintelligent race.

'We can choose', said the Lords, . . . This means that these Beings were Lords of mind, discrimination, and choice.

Some entered the Chhayas. . . . Chhayas means shadow, the copy, or the etheric body of human beings which is the prototype of the physical body. Some of the Lords of Flame entered into this electromagnetic atmosphere of man. Others, instead of entering into the atmosphere of man, projected a spark of intelligent substance into man's elementary mental cloud.[19]

Some deferred till the Fourth. . . . Some of the Lords neither entered nor projected a spark, but went away to wait until the Fourth Root Race came into being.

From their own rupa they filled [intensified] *the Kama*. . . . Those Lords of Flame who entered into the atmosphere of man, stimulated the astral or desire body of humanity. They filled it with their essence, with *will power*, which changed in the vehicles of primitive man and became *desire*. . .

Those who received but a spark remained destitute of knowledge; . . . It took ages and ages to inflame the spark of mind, and to make it a real tool for the acquisition of knowledge. The knowledge referred to here is higher knowledge, abstract knowledge, and could be assimilated only as the spark of intelligence developed.

The spark burned low. . . . The spark of intellect was in a very slow process of development and unfoldment.

The third remained mindless. . . . The "third" refers to those human-animal

19. Saraydarian, H., *The Magnet of Life*, pp. 32–33.

forms that received neither the spark nor the Lords of Flame within themselves, because they were not ready.

Their Jivas were not ready. . . . Jiva is the Monad, the divine Spark within the human form, the Real Man. This becomes clear when we understand that man is the Monad; not the form, not the vehicle, not even the Lord of Flame who entered into his sphere.

These were set apart among the Seven. . . . The "Seven" refers to the primitive human species and to the Seven Root Races. The mindless ones, whose Jivas were not ready, played no part in the destiny of the Seven Root Races. They were "set apart", cast aside.

They became narrow-headed . . . They were dumb. They bred monsters going on all fours. These remained destitute of knowledge.

The third were ready. . . . The Monads of the Third group were awakened enough to be able to receive the Lords of Flame.

'In these shall we dwell,' said the Lords of Flame and of the dark wisdom. They entered into the higher planes of man to lead the divine Monad, the Jiva, from darkness to light, from the unreal to the real, from death to conscious immortality, from chaos to beauty. This happening in many occult books is called the *act of Individualization.*

The Monad

Many times I felt that beyond my physical, emotional, and mental impressions, actions and responses, there was a deeper source of reality. I sensed that it was something other than my Solar Angel. It was "me," but it seemed impossible to touch that reality and say, "Me." At rare moments in an intuitive flash, I used to *be* "Him," but the next moment I was merely a reflection in the waves of material substance.

We are told that there was only Space, an ocean of living fire, a radiating Sun. This living fire projected millions of sparks which moved toward and passed through the involutionary arc, becoming matter in seven cosmic steps. In *The Secret Doctrine* we read:

> "For the Monad, or Jiva, per se, cannot be called even Spirit; it is a Ray, a Breath of the Absolute, or the ABSOLUTENESS rather; and the Absolute Homogeneity, having no relations with the conditioned and relative finiteness, is unconscious on our plane. Therefore, besides the material which will be needed for its future human form, the Monad requires (a) a spiritual model, or prototype for that material to shape itself into; and (b) an intelligent consciousness, to guide its evolution and progress, neither of which is possessed by the homogeneous Monad, or by senseless though living matter. The Adam of dust requires the Soul of Life to be breathed into him. . . . Therefore, when the hour strikes for purusha [spirit] to mount on Prakriti's [substance] shoulders for the formation of the Perfect Man . . . the Celestial Ancestors

> (Entities from preceding worlds . . .) step in on this our plane, and incarnate in the physical or animal man, as the Pitris had stepped in before them for the formation of the latter. . . . The pitris shoot out from their ethereal bodies still more ethereal and shadowy similitudes of themselves, or what we should now call 'doubles' . . . in their own likeness. This furnishes the Monad with its first dwelling, and blind matter with a model around and upon which to build henceforth."[20]

According to *The Secret Doctrine*, the first two-and-one-half races did not have real human form. They were fiery, cool and radiant, *ethereal*, in the first round; ". . . luminous and more dense and heavy during the second round; watery during the third" and dense at the fourth round.

The Lunar pitris and Solar Angels cooperated to equip man with higher principles and with lower vehicles. The Solar Angels formed the causal center, to serve as anchorage for the Monadic life. They also formed and extended the thread of consciousness anchoring it in the brain. Some of the Angels then entered and indwelled in man.

The lunar bodies or the lower vehicles were constructed by the Lunar pitris. They first built the lower mental body, next the astral body, and then the etheric body. Later the etheric body attracted atoms of matter and formed the physical body.

Thus, around the fulcrum of the Monad, the Solar Angels built the higher wing of balance and the Lunar pitris built the lower wing. The two were tied together with the life and consciousness threads.

In the first Round the human form was fiery. In the second Round the human form was airy. It was watery on the third and on the fourth Round the human form materialized as did our own earth or globe. This means that the Monad reached Its densest state of materialization.

Development through Root Races

On each global period, Seven Root Races developed. The first race and the second race did not have proper names. The third race was called the Lemurian Race. The fourth Race was the Atlantean Race. The present one, the fifth, is called the Aryan Race.

In the *first* race man was mindless. He was living near the north pole in eternal summer. His color was yellow-white. In the *second* race man was sexless and boneless, possessing a very dim spark of mind inherited from the previous solar system. His speech consisted of chant-like sounds. His color was yellow. In the *third* race the Monad had an androgynous body. Both sexes were in one body. The bodies became more dense. This race was living on the Lemurian continent which was destroyed by volcanoes and sank into the ocean. Their color was red-brown.

---

20. Blavatsky, H. P., *The Secret Doctrine*, Vol. I, pp. 267–268.

At the middle of the third race, Sanat Kumara took incarnation on higher etheric planes. According to *The Secret Doctrine* and the Teaching of the Tibetan Sage, one hundred and five Kumaras, including our Kumara, came to our planet. For ages long, when the earth and its kingdoms were still in formation, they rendered needed service, working as great divine engineers between the earth and the Solar System, and among the unfolding kingdoms of nature. Through the ages most of them have gradually left our planet until we now have only seven Kumaras. They correspond to the Seven Rays.

Three of these Kumaras are esoteric and act as the three major centers of the Planetary Logos; the head, the heart and the throat centers. They head the ruling, teaching and organizing departments of the seven Cosmic Physical Planes. The remaining four, having etheric bodies, are exoteric. They have close relationships with the planetary centers, with Shamballa, the Hierarchy and humanity. Our Kumara acts as the representative for our Planetary Logos, while the other six Kumaras transmit energy from six planetary schemes to our earth.[21]

At that time, at the middle of the third race, so-called man was a mindless human form in which the life principle was the Spark. His evolution was very slow and for ages and ages he was not able to enter into the path of self-determination and self-actualization. The Tibetan Master says:

> "Those who are demanding to be saved have cried aloud. Their voices penetrate into the formless world and there evoke response. Those who in distant aeons have pledged themselves to save and serve respond. Their cry, too, rings forth and, ringing, penetrates into the dark and distant places within the worlds of form.
>
> "And thus a vortex is established and kept alive by that constant dual sound. And then a touch is made and for a space during time, the two are one—the Saving Souls and the Units to be served.
>
> "Slowly the vision of the Saving One becomes a light which guides the Crying Ones into the place of light."[22]

---

21. Three of these Kumaras, called buddhas of activity, change cyclically, but our Kumara remains. It is interesting to note that with these seven Kumaras there are four Karmic Lords, making the total number twelve, if we include the Central Life, our Planetary Logos. Thus we have twelve Zodiacal signs, twelve planetary Lives, the Twelve Disciples and the Lotus of twelve petals.

There is confusion in the minds of students of the Ageless Wisdom concerning the difference between the Planetary Logos and Sanat Kumara. We are told that Sanat Kumara is the physical incarnation of our Planetary Logos. He is the Lower Self; the Planetary Logos being the Higher Self.

In esoteric books the *Planetary Logos* is called the Planetary Spirit, the Great Sacrifice, the Heavenly Man, the Silent Watcher, The Initiator.

Sanat Kumara is referred to as the Lord of the World, The One Initiator, The Mind-born Son of Brahma, The King, The Youth of Eternal Springs, The Fountainhead of the Will, The Ancient of the Days, The Lord of Sacrifice.

22. Bailey, Alice A., *Esoteric Astrology*, p. 326.

Sanat Kumara brought with him numberless Beings, who were called by various names; for example, Agnishvattas, Fire Devas, Lords of Flame, Solar Angels, Manasa Putras, Celestial Exiles, Fire Dhyanis, Sons of Wisdom, Holy Ascetics, Holy Virgin-born, and many others. These great Beings or Angels came to our planet to help humanity enter upon the path of conscious evolution. They came in groups. The first group watched humanity, and decided that it was not yet ready to receive help. Ages later the second group came and planted the spark of intelligence in man. These beings, called the Promethean group, brought the celestial fire to humanity. They implanted the spark of manas (mind) in man, and for the first time, man started to have mental responses. Without this fire it would have been almost impossible to lead man on the path of evolution. It was the first time in his history that man began to give attention to his environment, to his body and to the changing phenomena of the rivers, the lakes and the oceans, the clouds, the winds and the rains. He began to seek ways of survival, not just for the moment but for his future survival.

Man was beginning to use the spark of mind, but this was not enough; so the third group of Solar Angels or Agnishvattas entered into the man to form a bridge between the three lower planes: the physical-etheric plane, the astral plane, and the lower mental plane—and the three higher planes: higher mind, the buddhic plane, and the atmic plane. We are told that there were sixty thousand million of these Angels. Thus, the physical, astral and mental levels were connected with the higher levels of the Solar Angels. The Solar Angel has as its vestures the Spiritual Triad; atma-buddhi-manas.

Man has only physical, astral and lower mental substances. Thus, the Solar Angel became a bridge between man and higher principles, giving him the opportunity to climb the ladder of evolution and to function first as a soul and then as an awakened Monad.

In common usage we understand the word personality to mean an influential, socially appealing man, or the integrated sum total of physical, emotional and mental vehicles. The true esoteric meaning of personality is much different. Real personality is the totality of these three bodies, highly cultivated and integrated by a unit of life which is nothing else but the unfolding or awakening Spark, the man himself, *the unfolding human soul.* The Tibetan Master says: ". . . personality, when fully developed is the appearance of God on earth."[23]

In addition to this unfolding human soul or ego, we have the Solar Angel on higher mental levels. After the Spark achieves the stage of Personality He should move forward until He experiences at-one-ment, a mystic marriage with the Solar Angel. This is the stage in which the light of the Solar Angel embraces the unfolding Monad, dispersing accumulated hindrances around Him and stimulating radiation of the Spark, the core of the Monad. This mystic marriage is

23. Bailey, Alice A., *A Treatise on The Seven Rays,* Vol. II, p. 267.

called the process of Soul-infusion. After soul-infusion man is on his way to another stage.

For the first time man feels that he is not the body, not the emotions, not the mind, but a still higher entity; an entity not limited by his three vehicles or by time and space. This realization slowly deepens and he learns that to be a Soul means to be free from the limitations of all his vehicles and to be aware of a plan in the universe, a plan with a great purpose behind it.

The Solar Angel is still present until the fourth Initiation which is a stage of great expansion of awareness. When the unfolding human soul enters into the fourth Initiation he has built the Rainbow bridge between the mental unit and the mental permanent atom.[24] With the help of the Solar Angel he has built the higher bridge between the mental unit and the Spiritual Triad which is actually the domain or vehicle of the Solar Angel. At the fourth Initiation when the chalice or the causal body is destroyed, the Solar Angel departs. He often leaves His own buddhic-atmic vestures to man who uses them until his vestures become ready at the fifth Initiation. Man is now a Soul. The physical, emotional and mental bodies or the "personality vehicle" now presents a mechanism through which the Human Soul, functioning in the Spiritual Triad, expresses Himself in these three lower worlds and uses them as fields of service. Here man is a duality. He will be a unity when he enters his monadic consciousness.

For many ages these teachings were mysteries. They were told only to the Initiates in secret temples. But this is the age of revelation. Very soon all these mysteries will be taught in colleges and universities all over the world.

After individualization, to help further the progress of humanity, great Beings incarnated among human beings, and became kings and priests. We are told that, ". . . under the guidance of their *divine* Rulers, [the Lemurians] built large cities, cultivated Arts and Sciences, and knew Astronomy, Architecture and Mathematics to Perfection."[25]

Members of the Lemurian Race were mostly black or dark brown, but their color gradually changed to blue-black, to blue gray, and later, to gray-white. At the end of the seventh sub-race, they lost their single eye. A great catastrophe ended the Lemurian civilization, but those who were initiated into the Secret of Wisdom hid themselves in safe places, and thus became the link between the Third and Fourth Root Races.

The Fourth Root Race, the Atlantean, developed the senses of *hearing, touch, sight* and *taste.* They created great civilizations which were ended by submersion in the depths of the ocean.[26] The Fifth Root Race, the present race, which

---

24. Saraydarian, H., *The Science of Becoming Oneself*, Chap. XVIII.

25. Blavatsky, H.P., *The Secret Doctrine*, Vol. II, pp. 330–331.

26. The Tibetan Master speaks of the Fourth Root Race: ". . . Many of the present advanced humanity individualized on the moon chain and only took physical bodies on the earth chain during the fourth root race, thus escaping incarnation during the first three rounds, and the first two races of the fourth round." Bailey, Alice A., *A Treatise on Cosmic Fire*, p. 364.

is called the Aryan Race,[27] has developed *hearing, touch, sight, taste*, and *smell.* In the next two races, the Sixth and Seventh, two more senses will be developed, and then our chain will enter into rest, into great pralaya.

Current Humanity

In esoteric teachings we are told that our earth humanity is composed of five groups of developing human souls:

- Lemurian Souls who form our present earth humanity and who were animals on the moon chain.
- Souls who came in on Atlantis.
- Souls who were human on the moon chain and so entered our earth chain as human beings.
- Souls who came from pralaya between the first and second solar systems.
- Souls who were very advanced and were waiting for the proper conditions to incarnate.

This means that developing humanity as a whole is on many and varied levels, and that as a consequence of there being five kinds of souls, each group has a different approach to reality and to the problems of humanity. The link between all should be loving understanding.

When we speak of individualization, the fact of the coming of the Solar Angels, and when we speak of building a bridge between the form and the essence of man, we are referring to the humanity which graduated as the animal kingdom from the moon chain, entering into our earth chain as beings-to-be-human, and later to be individualized at the fourth round in the Lemurian Race.[28]

We must repeat that the process of individualization on our chain was different from the process of individualization on the moon chain. On the moon chain the latent presence of the fiery spark of mind built the bridge between the two poles of being, matter and spirit. In the case of earth humanity, however, the gap was bridged by the in-coming Solar Angels. We are told that individualization upon the moon chain (which is the chain preceding our chain) took place in the fifth race of the third Round. Individualization of our earth humanity took place in the third Race of the fourth Round, the Round through which we are presently passing. Those human beings who came to our chain in the Atlantean period had already individualized in a previous chain.

Thus, from globe to globe, from Race to Race, from chain to chain, and from scheme to scheme, the Real You, the Divine Flame, the Spark of the Central Spiritual Sun, will unfold, bloom, and proceed to Its Cosmic Destiny.

---

27. The Aryan Race is the Fifth Root Race. The sub-races of the Aryan Race are: (1) Hindu, (2) Aryan-Semitic, (3) Iranian-Armenian, (4) Keltic, (5) Teutonic and (6) Aquarian, just having its beginning in various parts of the earth.

28. When we refer to the souls who came from the moon chain, we are referring to those beings, who being human, came to our chain to continue their evolution.

When we refer to the Lemurian Race, or earth humanity, we are referring to those moon animals who entered into our chain as human beings and formed our earth humanity.

Chapter II

THE TEMPLE DRAMA

"Each Initiation into the Mysteries contained the question—'Is thy ear open?' Such opening signified first of all the ability to maintain vigilance." [1]

—M.M.

I was very young when my father took me to a secret meeting. We rode together on horseback under the bright light of a full moon. It was a very still and beautiful night. I could see the branches of the trees bending low as we brushed past them in the moonlight. The stones were shining in the path under the horse's feet.

After riding for an hour we arrived at the meeting place, a deep, natural cave with capacity for no less than five hundred people. Many people were sitting cross-legged in silence on oriental rugs. The atmosphere was heavy with the scent of sandalwood and pine. The soft, soothing music of a flute was penetrating into my heart as some kind of energy.

When the members were all assembled the doors were closed. A huge man with a heavy beard appeared upon the stage and spoke in a clear, strong voice, "Today we are going to search for the Treasure, the Treasure within all of us. We shall find the way to the Treasure." After a few moments of silence, beautiful, rhythmic music floated through the air. We could hear the soft, steady beat of drums and the plaintive tones of the flute.

Suddenly a man leaped on to the stage and began a beautiful dance, moving in perfect harmony with the music. Then, to my amazement, the dance began to degenerate. The dancer changed his movements until he was completely out of harmony. He reached a point where the rhythm of his dance was in direct contrast to the rhythm of the music. A few moments later three men rushed on to the stage and attacked the dancer. The first man struck him with a sword and the dancer fell to the floor as though dead. All lights were extinguished and for several moments there was complete darkness. Then, a candle began to glow on the stage and by its light, we could see the half-naked figure of the dancer lying upon a long, low table. A man of radiant, angelic beauty entered. In rhythmic step he moved to the table. With his dagger he opened the chest of the man lying there and ran away into the darkness. Then one of the three men who had attacked the dancer came forward, put his hand into the chest and brought forth the heart, a glowing fluorescent heart. Raising it above his head he chanted a few words. Fiery music burst forth and he began to sing an ancient mantram. His deep, powerful voice flowed through the hall like a great, surging river rushing down to the sea.

1. Agni Yoga Society, *Fiery World,* Vol. I, par. 225.

The music stopped abruptly and he chanted a few more words. The heart began to open like a lily. I saw that the first tier of petals was slowly opening. The second tier opened and as I watched intently the unfolding of the third tier of petals, a blue light flashed forth from the very center of the flower. Myriads of flying sparks filled the darkness illuminating the hall and revealing the presence of the angel who had wielded the dagger. I was beholding a sight of rare beauty, inexplicable beauty. As we sat spellbound by his radiant splendor the angel disappeared into darkness. The man still holding the flower, now in full bloom, placed it back into the breast of the man on the table. Again, there was a period of total darkness and absolute silence. I was aware that these intervals of silence were periods of deep meditation.

As the meditation came to a close we could hear again the soft strains of music. A single beam of light shone upon the man lying on the table. Slowly he arose. Clad in a beautiful robe of radiant white and brilliant blue he stood in the center of the stage under the bright beam of light. He looked about in wonder and ecstasy as he said,

"I was dead in body, in heart, in mind,
but I killed my dead body.
The Angel opened the gates.
I took my heart from within and
by the hands of my mind,
dedicated it to Cosmos, to the Future.

And it opened,
radiating the glory of love.
I am alive! I am awake!
Salutations to the Inner Glory of man!
The seed of the Sun is free!"

Heavy darkness fell upon the room during a long period of meditation. I remember closing my eyes and trying to recall the drama again and again; each time in greater amazement and each time thrilled to the center of my being. At the close of the meditation a member of the audience led the crowd in a short, simple chant which expressed in words and melody, gratitude to all creation and to the Light beyond understanding.

We were again on horseback returning home under the clear, bright light of the full moon. I noticed that my father was still in meditation as we rode over the stony, white path. For a long time I dared not speak, but when we had traveled for some distance I said, "Father, I know what they were doing. I know the message." "What?", he asked. I did not answer, but fell into deep silence and meditation. We arrived home in silence. Never again did we speak of the drama.

Years passed . . . difficult and painful years which brought about great changes within myself. I began to realize more fully the depth of meaning behind that beautiful temple drama, still vivid in my memory. It portrayed the release of the inner glory of man and presented in dramatic manner the technique to be used in achieving that glory. The dancer who first appeared upon the stage was the divine Monad in tune with Its Source, but as It symbolically descended into matter, Its rhythm and beauty were lost, killed, or put to sleep in the body. The three men who entered next represented the physical, emotional and mental bodies. These bodies "attacked" and killed the Monad. This meant that through the glamours, illusions and inertia of these bodies, the Real Man had fallen asleep spiritually.

The Angel was the Lord of Flame. He opened the gates or established communication between Himself and the awakening Spark. This was accomplished through centuries and centuries of meditation by the Solar Angel. The heart was touched. The real heart is the causal body, the chalice or the lotus, upon the third plane of mental substance. The flower of the chalice had opened tier by tier in full glory, and the divine light, love and power radiated from its petals. As its radiance increased and reached its greatest heights, the Solar Angel, the Lord of Flame, left, and the chalice was destroyed. The Solar Angel had completed His task. He was no longer needed; for man, the Monad, was fully awakened. He had arisen and gone to his "Father," his true Self. Man had become Himself.

This drama was a technique used in mystery temples to explain the relationship between the Real Man and his Solar Angel and between the Solar Angel and the vehicles of expression.

One may ask, "If the Solar Angel is the guide, then what has a Master of the Wisdom to do with that guide?"

The Master helps with the bridging and fusing process between the higher-self, the Solar Angel, and the lower-self, the unfolding human soul. Since the Master lives in both the human and the soul spheres, He can relate man to his Angel by direct impression, hints or instructions.

After a man is led to his Solar Angel, the Solar Angel in turn, relates him to the Hierarchy in general, and to his own Master in particular. We are told that a Master takes a man into his Ashram or into His sphere of instruction, after obtaining the permission of his Solar Angel. Thus the Master puts the man into conscious relationship with his Soul, and the Soul leads him into conscious relationship with his own Master.

After the Fourth Initiation a higher degree Initiate takes the responsibility of directing his steps into greater light and labour.

The developing, unfolding human soul is the Monad plus the level of development with which he is identified. What is the Solar Angel really doing? He is trying to awaken the sleeping Monad. He is calling man back to himself. He is the lioness *reminding* the baby lion to feel his own reality, his own essence and to be himself. He is encouraging man to enter into the path of his Kingship as did the son of the king when he "remembered" who he was. The Solar Angel never forces Its will on the personality except when something is interfering with the *karma*[2] of man. The Solar Angel stands in man as a point of light, love and power, ready to be invoked and to evoke, or respond. Man thus enlists the help of his Solar Angel according to his aspiration, demand, karma and conditions under which he lives. It stands in man as a shining standard of achievement and mastery, and as a great magnet toward which all the aspirations of man are eventually attracted.

In some literature of olden days the Solar Angel is referred to as the Big Brother who progresses in his own line of evolution through deep meditation and service rendered to the Hierarchy. He is the Presence who watches the unfolding human soul, *the hope of glory* of the individual whom He ensouled ages ago. He is the Presence, the Inner Guide, standing ready to assist as man grows and becomes able to stand on his own feet; able to face his own problems and to solve these problems with his own two hands. Thus is man prepared to enter into the path of mastership. The lives of our physical bodies are as days to the Solar Angel. He watches the progress of the human soul age by age until man reaches a high stage of development.

Our obstacles are opportunities for mastership and our visions and labours are windows through which the Solar Angel can shine forth into our darkness. He stands as the ideal image toward which we strive. He is not a dead image, but an image which inspires, uplifts, leads and blesses in proportion to our unfoldment toward His beauty. He stands as the Sun. He does not pull us up to help us grow, but rather He conditions our growth and we depend upon our unfolding petals to drink the light, life and power from His greatness. Man, or the developing human soul, first recognizes the Solar Angel as the source of intelligence, then as the source of love and much, much later as a center of power. Through these three aspects the Solar Angel inspires the human soul and leads him toward his Real Self. Through the major part of his manifestation the human soul, or the awakening Monad, identifies himself with the three lower vehicles and with every changing state in those vehicles. These points of identification which are in constant change are called "I's." This is the trap into which he has fallen. It may be compared to the labyrinth of the ancients, a maze through which the wandering man or Monad must find his way or perish.

The difference between the Solar Angel and the human soul is very simple. The Solar Angel is the gardener, "the initiate of all degrees." The Monad is the acorn, the original Spark. The unfolding human soul is the oak tree growing from the acorn under the care of the gardener. It is the expanding Spark. When the tree reaches a stage at which it does not need care; when its roots are well anchored and its branches healthy and strong, the gardener slowly withdraws his attention and leaves the tree alone. When the Monad, the Spark, has expanded, when the human soul is fully developed, the Solar Angel withdraws His attention and leaves the man alone.

2. See Chap. XVIII.

The human soul is not the Angel until one day, after millions of years, he becomes a very high degree Initiate and decides to incarnate in an animal-man to lead him from darkness to light. So we may say that the term, Solar Angel, is the name of an office. Actually, He is a Monad Himself, on the path of His Cosmic development and unfoldment. The human soul is a state of awareness achieved through the help of the Solar Angel. It is a passing stage on the liberating path of the Monad. It is a stage in the growth of the oak tree well tended by the gardener.

After the lotus we have another vehicle which is called the Spiritual Triad. The Spiritual Triad is formed of three energies emanating from manasic, buddhic and atmic permanent atoms. This vehicle is the reflection of the Monad on these higher levels. The Ego, which is the Solar Angel with Its vehicles, is called the reflection of the Monad in the sense that the Solar Angel works largely in the Spiritual Triad. It belongs to Him until that time when the developing human soul has achieved continuity of consciousness in the Spiritual Triad.

The developing human soul is also called the reflection of the Monad. This is the "real" reflection. In the beginning the Monad fell deep into the waves of matter and became a mere reflection of Himself. As He strives to return to Himself, to be Himself again, He gains experience through His life expression. This experience becomes an integral part of the Monad. As awareness expands, the developing human soul becomes less the reflection and more the Monad, Himself.

The Tibetan Master says, "The human soul (in contradistinction to the Soul as it functions in its own kingdom, free from limitations of human life) is imprisoned by and subject to the control of the lower energies for the major part of its experience."[3] He adds,

> ". . . and he (the disciple) begins to realize himself as the Soul. Then, later, comes the awful 'moment in time', when pendant in Space, he discovers that he is not the Soul. What then is he? A point of divine dynamic will, focussed in the Soul, and arriving at awareness of Being through the use of form. He is Will, the ruler of time and the organizer in time, of Space."[4]
>
> "Purpose will reveal itself; the Whole will stand revealed, and then the soul loaded with riches and fruits of labour long will vanish as the mist and only God, the living One, be left."[5]
>
> ". . . personality and ego disappear and only the Monad and its form upon the physical plane remain."[6]

Here personality ceases being representative of the unfolding human soul, or the Monad, because the unfolding human soul becomes Himself, the Monad,

3. Bailey, Alice A., *A Treatise on the Seven Rays*, Vol. II, p. 69.
4. Bailey, Alice A., *Rays and Initiations*, p. 107.
5. *Ibid.*, p. 117.
6. *Ibid.*, p. 480.

and the personality merely serves as a vehicle of expression for the Monad. "Just as the personality is lost sight of in the light of the soul, the solar Angel, so the soul itself disappears and its power and radiance fade out when the Presence, which it has hitherto veiled, appears and dominates the scene at the end of the greater world cycle." [7]

> "Basically, it is not desire which prompts return but will and knowledge of the plan. It is not the need for achieving an ultimate perfection which goads the Ego on to experience in form, for the Ego is already perfect. The main incentive is sacrifice and service to those lesser lives that are dependent upon the higher inspiration (which the spiritual soul [Solar Angel] can give) and the determination that they too may attain planetary status equivalent to that of the sacrificing soul." [8]

The Lords of Flame or the Solar Angels were liberated "intelligent essences." They were Nirvanis from the preceding Maha-Manvantarana. (See *The Secret Doctrine,* Vol. II, p. 83.) "They are the fire-dhyanis, and emanate from the Heart of the Sun." [9] "(. . . they are called Manasaputra, born of 'Mahat' or Brahma) had to pass through earthly human experiences to become *all-wise* and be able to start on the returning ascending cycle." [10] They . . . "are entities from higher and earlier worlds and planets, whose *Karma* had not been exhausted when their world went into pralaya."[11] They are also called Egos and,

> "The Ego, (being to the man on the physical plane what the Logos is to His system) is likewise the animating will, the destroyer of forms, the producer of pralaya, and the One Who withdraws the inner spiritual man out of his threefold body; he draws them to himself the centre of his little system. The Ego is extra-cosmic as far as the human being on the physical plane is concerned, and in the realisation of this fact may come elucidation of the true cosmic problem involving the Logos and 'the spirits in prison'." [12]
>
> ". . . *The Agnishvattas* [Solar Angels] *construct the petals out of Their Own substance, which is substance energised by the principle of 'I-ness,' or ahamkara.*" [13]
>
> "Individualisation is literally the coming together . . . of the two factors of Spirit and matter by means of a third factor, the intelligent will, purpose and action of an Entity." [14]
>
> ". . . and the day dawns when the life which expresses itself through the medium of the Ego, the Thinker, the Solar Lord or Manasadeva, seeks to

---

7. Bailey, Alice A., *Esoteric Astrology,* p. 105.
8. *Ibid.,* p. 324.
9. Blavatsky, H. P., *The Secret Doctrine,* Vol. II, p. 96.
10. *Ibid.,* p. 176, Orig. Ed., p. 167.
11. Blavatsky, H. P., *The Secret Doctrine,* Vol. III, p. 517.
12. Bailey, Alice A., *A Treatise on Cosmic Fire,* p. 149.
13. *Ibid.,* p. 712.
14. *Ibid.,* p. 345.

loose itself from even this limitation and return to the source from which it originally emanated."[15]

The Solar Angel is the custodian of the great Plan for our planet and for our solar system. He is in tune and in communication with the Cosmic Beings and is a member of the Hierarchy in subtle levels. Cyclically he passes some portions of the plan to the "shadow," to the developing human soul. These communications with the shadow bring inspiration, higher urges and impulses, as well as divine aspirations. The Solar Angel first makes contact through *the life thread.* This is the reason that His communications are not formulated thoughtforms or words, but come through as inspiration, impulse, impression or touch. Later his communication becomes more direct and better formulated as the disciple or unfolding human soul builds *the bridge, the consciousness thread,* between the mental unit and the mental permanent atom.

In some cases or on some occasions the Solar Angel withdraws and sheds no light upon the problems of man. His purpose in so doing is to give man the opportunity to help himself; to strive harder in solving his own problems without depending upon his Solar Angel for guidance. At times when this withdrawal occurs, a deep depression descends upon the pilgrim and if the withdrawal is for a very long period, he passes through an experience of loneliness which is known as the dark night of the human soul. He feels that he has been deserted and left alone between heaven and earth. This state is only illusion, for the Solar Angel is the eternal Silent Watcher. Very often, instead of leading you as a child is led, he inspires you to bring forth your courage, hope, daring and to exercise detachment. He watches silently as he inspires you to master your problems, that you may enter into the path of mastership.

As communication between the reflection and the Solar Angel goes deeper, and as the monadic or divine current pours down to lower levels of existence, a whirlpool of energy is gradually created on the higher mental plane. This vortex of energy resembles a cup formed of nine flower-like petals. It is the chalice or lotus so often referred to in occult literature. Enclosed by three more petals, in the very center of the chalice or lotus, is a jewel, a Spark of fire. This jewel is the Monad, the Real Man; all else is reflection. As ages pass and man obeys his Inner Lord, the chalice becomes more radioactive and man radiates streams of love energy, light energy, and will energy.[16]

Eventually, all the personality vehicles, physical, emotional and mental, enter into a process of transfiguration and man becomes a shining light. From that moment on he is in communication with a greater Center of Love, the Hierarchy of the Masters. Lives pass and the glory of the Inner Lord burns the chalice. The inner fire, the Monad, is released. Man becomes Himself. The

---

15. Bailey, Alice A., *Initiation Human and Solar,* p. 136.
16. Saraydarian, H., *The Science of Becoming Oneself,* Chap. XII.

reflection returns to its Source. At this point man enters into the path of Higher Evolution.

Often in esoteric literature, we find reference to the soul of the planet or the soul of rocks, vegetables and animals. This use of the word *soul* is not incorrect because all that exists is created by the contact of spirit and matter. According to the Ancient Wisdom, the soul comes into being when these two poles meet. Spirit and matter relate and all of Creation, or any part of it, begins to develop through the power of the spirit hidden in the form. This new, unfolding sentiency or consciousness, is the soul of matter and the soul of other subtle kingdoms. In the human kingdom it eventually forms a center by itself, and the hidden jewel, the Monad, begins to express itself as man progresses through Initiations.

One of Christ's disciples addressed the people as, "My little children, with whom I travail in birth again until Christ be formed in you." [17] Here the word *Christ* refers to the unfolding human soul which is slowly developing and liberating itself from the inertia, glamours, and illusions of the body and is progressing toward the goal of becoming Himself. The same disciple, being aware of the meaning behind this mystery, also said, ". . . the creation itself shall be delivered from the bondage of corruption into the glorious liberty of the children of God . . . for we know that the whole creation groaneth and travaileth in pain until now." [18] This is true. The whole of creation has been working for millions and millions of years to help in the development of Monads as they proceed upward from level to level, until they reach the stature of Sons of God.

In esoteric tradition the Monad is the Father, the Spark. The Soul is the Son, the Path. Matter is the mother, the form. In biblical terminology these Three are the Holy Trinity, the Father, Son and Holy Spirit.

Sometimes people are mystified by the fact that the offspring of animals are so self-sufficient at birth, while the new-born human infant is completely helpless. There is a logical explanation for this difference. The human soul incarnates in a more advanced creature whose intellect is more or less developed to some degree. This being so, he needs a more advanced mechanism enabling him to meet his needs and to control his environment. Animals are not as developed as human beings and do not have Solar Angels. They need only a simple mechanism of expression. The brain and nervous system of the new-born animal is sufficient unto this need, while the human being with his more complex brain and nervous system, must undergo a period of training and learning before he achieves a degree of independence.

We may ask, "How can we communicate with our Solar Angels and kno that they are answering or guiding us without our falling into the traps of ev forces, post-hypnotic suggestions, or other complexes in our nature?" The answe is that we must begin by preparing an atmosphere through which communicatio

17. Galatians, 4:19.
18. Romans, 8:21–22.

from higher sources may flow. This can be accomplished by trying to put into practice the following suggestions:

1. Live a harmless life.
2. Express love, beauty and truth in daily living.
3. Meditate regularly on the deeper meanings of love, beauty, truth, gratitude, service, labor, sacrifice, sincerity, harmlessness, or use the Seven Ray Technique.[19] In so doing you will create the right atmosphere for communication if you persevere and are sincere in your attempts.
4. Each day practice some self-examination without personality attachment.
5. Try to heal any wounds that you have inflicted upon others.
6. Study spiritual literature from *Hierarchical sources* daily.
7. Visualize yourself standing in the light of your Angel every day at the sunset hour.
8. Refuse to obey any inner suggestion dropped to your conscious mind, until examination shows that it relates to positive action toward good. If the suggestion is coming from a high source it will be true, beautiful and harmless; it will express gratitude, sincerity, love, sacrifice, courage and fearlessness; it will serve to bring upliftment and joy; it will emphasize unity and responsibility; it will call upon you to strive harder to achieve.

   Any suggestion which relates to these several points is coming from the Solar Angel. All suggestions which do not relate are from other sources and should not be followed.

In conjunction with the suggestions concerning meditation, self-examination, and spiritual reading you may feel the need to involve yourself in *periodic fasting* or to set aside periods when you will *keep silence* for an hour, a day or a week. You may reach a level which calls upon you to exercise detachment and observation.[20]

The records of past centuries show that many advanced beings had visions of their Solar Angels, but that they thought they were beholding angels, Masters, the Christ or God Himself. For example, in the West, Pythagoras, Plato, Plotinus, Samblichus, and Proelus had this experience at their advanced Initiations in Egypt. Porphyry states that Plotinus met or united with "God" six times. Saint Luso "saw the angel in her heart and she was fair to look upon." Saint Teresa thought that her vision was the Christ, "judging by the brightness." Saint Francis of Assisi and Saint Catherine of Siena also reported similar meetings with the Inner Dweller. Jacob Boehme's book, *Aurora,* presents many instances of such happenings. In the *New Testament* we read that Peter had an Angel who often appeared to his brethren. Goethe reported that he once met with his Soul face to face.

Aristotle, in his writings, suggested that the vision of God is the ultimate goal of man. Of course, no man can see God; it was the Solar Angel to whom

19. See Chap. VII for technique of meditation on seven rays.
20. Saraydarian, H., *The Science of Becoming Oneself,* Chap. XIX.

he was referring. In Sufi literature reference is made to the Solar Angel as the Beloved One:

> "They have sung of him as infinite and unattainable; but I in my meditations have seen him without sight."[21]

Al-Junaid of Baghdad wrote:

> "Now I have known, O Lord,
> What lies within my heart
> In Secret, from the world apart,
> My tongue hath talked with my adored."[22]

Rumi says,

> "O heart, as you go to that Sweetheart
> You must lose your heart;
> Heedless go to the audience-chamber of Union.
> When you have reached His door,
> Hidden from every creature,
> Leave yourself outside
> And then go in."[23]

When we are referring to the indwelling Solar Angel, the first Master of the man, we are not ignoring the existence of other devas, other Angels or Messengers. We know that throughout the ages these Great Beings have helped man on the path of evolution, cyclically or when group or great national need has required their help.

The mystery of the Indweller was clearly given to Anna Kingsford, the great mystic. In her book, *Clothed With the Sun,* she presents some interesting information about the Solar Angel. She calls it, "genius, or daimon" (a ministering spirit). She continues,

> "My genius looks like Dante and like him is .always in red."[24]
>
> "The genius of a man is his satellite. Man is a planet. God—the God of the man—is his sun, and the moon of his planet is ISIS, its Initiator, or genius."[25]
>
> " 'Yea,' says the angel genius to his client, 'I illuminate thee, but I instruct thee not. I warn thee, but I fight not. I attend, but I lead not. Thy treasure is within thyself. My light showeth where it lieth'."[26]

---

21. *Kabir's Poems,* p. 21.
22. A. J. Arberry, *Sufism,* p. 59.
23. Rice, O. P., *Cyprian the Persian, Sufis,* p. 61.
24. Kingsford, Anna B., *Clothed With the Sun,* p. 55.
25. *Ibid.,* pp. 59, 60.
26. *Ibid.,* p. 62.

Chapter III

MONADIC EVOLUTION

"I died from the mineral and became a plant,
I died from the plant and reappeared in an animal;
I died from the animal and became a man.
Wherefore then should I fear, when did I grow less by dying?
Next time I shall die from the man,
That I may grow the wings of an angel.
From the angel, too, I must seek advance;
Once more shall I wing my way
Above the angels, becoming that which entereth not the imagination
Verily unto HIM do we return."[1]

One day, while sitting on a mountain, enjoying the vast ocean below, and breathing in the fragrance of giant redwood trees, I saw beside me a little sprout coming up out of the ground with a heavy piece of earth on its back. It seemed to me that it was making a great effort to come up to the light to see the sun. I asked myself,

"Does this tender sprout know that two human eyes are looking at it?"

I wanted so much to make it feel that I was really sharing its labour and greatly appreciating its effort. As I watched, another thought came to me,

"Was I, myself, a plant, a flower like this one, millions of years ago? Did some human eyes watch me, think about my destiny and of the great effort I was putting forth to emerge from the dark earth to the light of the sun? How many millions of years have passed since then," I wondered, "and what great labour and suffering did I endure before I was able to enter the human kingdom?"

"Now that I am a human being, sitting on this mountain and thinking about my little brother, this tiny sprout, is there a greater One who is watching me with like sympathy, and thinking about my destiny on the endless path? Will I be able, one day, to overcome the heavy layers of glamour, illusion and ignorance, and start blooming on a divine plane? Will I, someday, be able to see "the face of the true Spiritual Sun, hidden in a disk of golden light?"

The path seemed too long and the space too dark. Then, the joy of Infinity filled my heart as I suddenly realized that the whole existence is moving toward a great consummation. The seedling was there to show me (the Monad, the Spiritual Seed) that I must strive toward far-off worlds.

1. Jalal ed-Din Rumi.

ENDLESS PROGRESS

There is a belief that after a man becomes a Soul, a living, awakened Soul, and releases the Solar Angel, his progress comes to an end, and he enjoys eternal peace and bliss as a Soul. This is not the case. The fact is that, after he becomes a Soul, greater horizons open before him. His next step is to start functioning as a Triad, a Spiritual Triad, expressing pure reason, love and power; then the man starts to become himself, a *Monad.*

The Tibetan Master, speaking of the endlessness of progress, says that after the Sixth Initiation, seven paths open ahead of the Initiate, and He must choose one of them. These paths are:

"1. The Path of Earth Service.
2. The Path of Magnetic Work.
3. The Path of Training for Planetary Logoi.
4. The Path to Sirius.
5. The Ray Path.
6. The Path on which our Logos is found.
7. The Path of Absolute Sonship."[2]

It is important to remember that these paths do not end on a summit of achievement, but that they serve as bridges, leading to further Cosmic unfoldment. The Master, again speaking of these paths, says:

"Path 1. The Path of Earth Service leads to the cosmic astral plane.
Path 2. The Path of Magnetic Work leads to the cosmic astral plane.
Path 3. The Path for Training for Planetary Logoi leads to the higher levels of the cosmic mental plane.
Path 4. The Path to Sirius leads to the cosmic astral plane.
Path 5. The Ray Path leads to the cosmic mental plane.
Path 6. The Path the Logos Himself is on leads to the cosmic buddhic plane.
Path 7. The Path of Absolute Sonship leads to the cosmic mental plane."[3]

Let us understand that on Cosmic scales, the Cosmic Physical, Cosmic Astral, and Cosmic Mental planes are considered as thresholds. Imagine, if you will, forty-nine layers of substance between matter and space. Then, imagine a beam of light passing through these forty-nine layers, and striking the lowest plane. There can be seen a focus of light, which age by age, travels up to the Cosmic Physical plane, and gradually proceeds upon the remaining forty-two planes, in greater radiation and beauty. The first plane on the Cosmic Physical plane, the forty-third plane, is the highest level of our Cosmic Physical plane.

We are told that a Monadic cycle on these seven planes of the Cosmic Physical plane is one hundred years of Brahma, which means 311,040,000,000,000 mortal years, or the duration of a solar system. Following this, the Monad will

2. Bailey, Alice A. *The Rays and the Initiations*, p. 396.
3. *Ibid*, p. 399.

start another step on the Cosmic scale, through the Cosmic Astral plane (steps forty-two through thirty-six); and so on until It reaches step number one, the highest Level of created Cosmos. What will happen beyond that, no human mind can contemplate.

The main point to grasp here, is the fact that the Monad is a Ray, but that it *seems* to be individualized as It strikes any particular plane and creates a focus there. The *root* of the Monad extends into the *Space* beyond the manifested Cosmic planes, but the Monad is anchored on the Monadic plane of the Cosmic Physical plane. From there, It extends Itself downward into the physical, emotional and mental mechanisms, creating the illusion of "I." The developing human soul within these three vehicles, learns through experience. Gradually it is guided back to its anchorage and directed toward the ultimate Home. Thus, throughout ages, the Monad journeys through rounds, chains and schemes, eventually unfolding Its true Essence toward the Mother Space.[4] Blavatsky says in *The Secret Doctrine:*

> "The Monad is, . . . first of all, shot down by the Law of Evolution into the lowest form of matter—the mineral. After a sevenfold gyration encased in the stone, or that which will become mineral and stone in the Fourth Round, it creeps out of it, say, as a lichen. Passing thence, through all the forms of vegetable matter, into what is termed animal matter, it has now reached the point at which it has become the germ, so to speak, of the animal, that will become the physical man. All this, up to the Third Round, is formless, as matter, and senseless, as consciousness."[5]

> "The Occult doctrine teaches that while the Monad is cycling on downward into matter . . . the lower Dyan Chohans [Solar Angels] are evolving, *pari passu* with it, on a higher and more spiritual plane, descending also relatively into matter, on their own plane of consciousness, when, after having reached a certain point, they will meet the incarnating senseless Monad, encased in the lowest matter, and blending the two potencies, Spirit and Matter, the union will produce that terrestrial symbol of the 'Heavenly Man' in space—PERFECT MAN."[6]

Thus, from plane to plane, the ascent of the Monad continues with increasing consciousness, awareness and greater beingness, which are degrees of experience gained throughout Its journey on the forty-nine planes.

We are told that the appearance of the Solar Angels was a special event, because in the Moon chain, individualization took place in a different way. They did not have Solar Angels to individualize. In our case, individualization occurred at that moment when, with the help of the Solar Angel, the Monad felt Itself to be a conscious being, for the first time, on the Physical plane, and entered

4. Saraydarian, H., *The Science of Becoming Oneself*, Chap. XIV.
5. Blavatsky, H. P., *The Secret Doctrine*, Vol. I, pp. 266–267.
6. *Ibid.*, p. 267.

into the human kingdom. Individualization is that moment in which, with the help of the Solar Angel, a bridge of light is thrown between the form and the Spark; thus the path of evolution is opened ahead of Him, and He, the Monad, is made conscious of His separation from the animal and other kingdoms.

As we know, the Solar Angel helps the Monad until the Fourth Initiation. At that time the Chalice is destroyed and the Guiding Soul, the Solar Angel, is released. Now the Monad must travel the Path on Its own.[7] Always, however, on the path of Evolution there is to be found One Who stands between the existing condition of the Monad and the Future.

Some people, particularly those who delve into the study of metaphysics, think of all Monads as ephemeral drops which travel on, only to be lost in the ocean. This is not true. The fact is that the Life is becoming a Cosmic Three, or let us say, a Cosmic Symphony in which each Spark has its own place in the whole plan. The Unity of which we are speaking is not the annihilation of individuality, but a harmonizing of individualities with the Cosmic Three; harmonizing them as notes in the Cosmic Symphony. The Life is in the process of composing this great symphony and He needs the many different notes to produce harmonious chords. No symphony is ever created by simply mixing all notes together into one. The Tibetan Master emphasizes this point in the following:

> "Yet, though we are merged with the whole, we do not lose our identity, but forever remain separated units of consciousness, though one with all that lives or is." [8]

The *Self* cannot be explained, thought of, imagined or visualized. It can only be *experienced* in direct *beingness*. If you try to define the Self, you are defining the process of your development and not the Self. The Self is experienced through realization, *sādhana*. Other people are able to observe whether you are going toward the All-self, or to lower states of expression. As you gain more control over your not-self, you come closer to your Real Self. This is the only measure that you have to use for a long period of time; until, suddenly, you open to the realization of Self.

Because of our habitual ways of thinking, we often use a misleading vocabulary. For example, we say:

— To communicate with the Monad . . .
— When a man stands in the light of thc Monad . . .
— Man unites with the Monad at the Fifth Initiation . . .

In such expressions, the illusion of duality is suggested or emphasized. Actually, the Monad is the Man. Man is standing in his own light and is aware of himself in proportion to the degree of his awakeness. Unification of man with the Monad

7. Saraydarian, H., *The Science of Becoming Oneself*, Chap. XII.
8. Bailey, Alice A., *A Treatise on Cosmic Fire*, p. 572.

means that man turns his awareness a little more into his depth through lesser or greater Helpers. It is like the unfolding and flowering process of a seed. In the East the lotus is a sacred flower. It is interesting to note that in the lotus seed, one can see the pattern of a full-blooming lotus blossom. The process of evolution, of unfoldment, of becoming oneself, is not unlike the growing process of the lotus seed. First, there is the seed, then the seedling, the growing, the unfolding, the blooming and flowering. The seed becomes itself in total actualization.

INITIATIONS

The unfolding and blooming process of the Monad is carried on through nine Initiations, or through nine stages of expansion in freedom, in greater awakening and in becoming His true Self. In esoteric writings, these nine steps toward Infinity are called:

The Birth
The Baptism
The Transfiguration
The Crucifixion
The Revelation
The Decision
The Resurrection
The Transition
The Refusal

The last two Initiations are so far from our consciousness that the Masters speak very few words or say nothing at all about them.

On the Cosmic Physical plane man is influenced by one of the Seven Rays. We are told that he is influenced by a different Ray at each Initiation. The following tabulation will indicate the Initiations and the Rays influencing man at these Initiations:

First Initiation	**Seventh Ray**
Second Initiation	**Sixth Ray**
Third Initiation	**Fifth Ray**
Fourth Initiation	**Fourth Ray**
Fifth Initiation	**First Ray**
Sixth Initiation	**Third Ray**
Seventh Initiation	**Second Ray**

Please note that the Second Ray is the Synthesis of all Rays in this Solar System, the Love System. This being so, an Initiate of the Seventh Degree has power on *all* Rays. This is the way in which the Rainbow is built with all the colors of the Seven Rays. Furthermore, we are told that:

> "At the Seventh Initiation his vision penetrates beyond the Solar ring-pass-not, and he sees that which he has long realized as a basic theoretical fact, that

our solar Logos is involved in the plans and purposes of a still greater Existence, and that the solar system is but one of many centres of force through which a cosmic Entity vastly greater than our own solar Logos is expressing Himself."[9]

It is at the Fourth Initiation that the Initiate is completely released from the fourth sub-plane of the mental plane. He stands on the two lower planes of the Buddhic plane, face to face with *his own essence*—with *himself* as reflected in a mirror—"and contacts the love aspect of the Monad." He makes the first contact with the Planetary Logos.

At the Fifth Initiation, the mirror disappears and the unification in the Monad takes place. It is in this Initiation that he contacts the Will aspect of the Monad and functions on the Atmic plane or on the third ether.

At the Sixth Initiation He contacts that great Life Who is called the Solar Logos, and there dawns within His being, the *oneness of all existence.* He functions on the monadic plane, or the second cosmic ether.

At the Seventh Initiation, the resurrected Initiate has the right to "come and go in the courts of Shamballa," and He escapes from the Solar ring-pass-not, from the four Cosmic ethers. He dominates the whole Cosmic Physical Plane and functions on the Cosmic Astral Plane.

At the Eighth and Ninth Initiations, He enters into more glory—glory beyond human understanding.

As man progresses, his inner Magnet becomes stronger. Human magnetism is produced when the unfolding soul starts shining as a flame, as a divine flame on monadic levels, and its light expresses itself through the Buddhic or through purified Astral spheres. This is the secret of the magnetic pull of Great Ones who move multitudes, nations and continents, stimulating them to move toward more light, and toward Right Human Relations.

When we study esoteric literature, the lore of the Ageless Wisdom, we find that the human Monad, the Real Man, the Self, not only must pass the seven major Initiations on our planet, but that He must also, eventually, tread the Solar Path and then, the Cosmic Path. To give a "flash picture" of the relationships among these great Paths, we present Figure 3.

COSMIC									1	2	3	4	5	6	7	8	9	**COSMIC**
SOLAR					1	2	3	4	5	6	7	8	9					**SOLAR**
PLANETARY	1	2	3	4	5	6	7	8	9									**PLANETARY**

FIGURE 3. INITIATIONS AND OBJECTIVES ON THE FOURTH CHAIN

9. Bailey, Alice A., *Initiation, Human and Solar*, p. 123.

The diagram clearly shows that the Fifth Initiation on our globe corresponds to the First Solar Initiation. The Ninth Planetary Initiation corresponds to the Fifth Degree Solar Initiation and to the First Degree Initiation in the Cosmic sphere. For better understanding we may say that:

1. The First Cosmic Initiation is the goal of a human being. This means that he must take nine Planetary Initiations and become a Fifth Degree Solar Initiate before he is able to enter into the First Degree Cosmic Initiation.
2. The Second Cosmic Initiation is the goal of the Planetary Logos. This means that He must take the Sixth Solar Initiation to be able to enter into the Second Cosmic Initiation.
3. The goal of the Solar Logos is the Third Cosmic Initiation.

Our Planetary Logos has to take the Fourth Solar Initiation in this Fourth Chain. This Initiation corresponds to the Crucifixion Initiation which is one of suffering and renouncement. You may see the effect on our chain and, particularly, on our globe. On the fifth chain, he may take the Fifth Solar Initiation, becoming a Cosmic Initiate of the First Degree. On the sixth chain, He will reach His goal by taking the Second Cosmic Initiation. On the seventh chain, He may reach Cosmic Transfiguration.

These Initiations have to do with the passing from one plane to another. For example, our Solar Logos is on the Cosmic Mental plane, but His goal is the Cosmic Buddhic plane, which will be reached when He takes the Fourth Cosmic Initiation. Our Planetary Logos is on the Cosmic Astral plane, and His goal is the next higher plane, the Cosmic Mental plane. He will achieve this goal when He enters into the Second Cosmic Initiation, leading Him to the Cosmic lower-mental plane.

ONWARD FROM THE HUMAN STAGE

Thus the human Monad progresses through the atom and eventually passes through all the lower kingdoms until He reaches the human stage. The next step for Him will be Mastership. He will not remain there, but will enter into degrees of unfoldment which are equal to a Planetary Logos, and later, to a Solar Logos. He will not remain there either, but must proceed into the Divine Darkness where no human light can penetrate, as yet.

Our Planetary Logos was a man who became a Master. He took Planetary and Solar Initiations and, we are told, is now working on the Cosmic Astral plane. There, He is already controlling the fourth sub-plane of the Cosmic Astral plane, and is working on the next higher sub-plane. Similarly, our Solar Logos is working on the Cosmic Mental plane in an effort to move on to the Cosmic Buddhic plane. All of this indicates to us how much we have yet to accomplish before we can reach these ever-progressing Lives.

We are told that our Cosmic physical plane is composed of dense, liquid, gaseous, and fourth, third, second and first Cosmic etheric sub-planes. The physical body of our Planetary Logos is built with the substance of the mental plane of the Cosmic physical plane. His centers are located in the Fourth Cosmic Ether, which is the buddhic plane of the Cosmic physical plane. Thus the buddhic, atmic, monadic, and divine planes correspond to our fourth, third, second, and first lower ethers. The objective body of the Solar Logos is built on the first Cosmic etheric plane, or the plane of Adi, our Divine plane.

When we refer to our vehicles of expression, we are referring to the aggregate of cells and living atoms, but when we refer to the centers of the Planetary or Solar Logoi, we are referring to the aggregate of Initiates, Masters, or Planetary and Solar Lives and Devas.

Divine awareness is the highest state of awareness that a Monad can achieve on the Cosmic Physical Plane, but this achievement comes only at the Seventh Initiation, after which He enters into the Cosmic Astral Plane. As the Monad passes from one plane to another of the seven Cosmic physical planes, He must, in the same manner, pass from one to another of all seven Cosmic planes to reach His Home in greater glory, as a King, as All-knower, All-powerful.

The Monad has seven spirillae of the most subtle Cosmic substance around Him. On each Cosmic plane, one of the spirillae unfolds, drops down and disappears. These seven spirillae correspond to seven Monadic senses, seven primordial rays, seven schemes, seven globes, and seven Root Races. Each works on its own plane to bring about the unfoldment of the Monad. This is the reason that all Souls, Nirvanis, Planetary and Solar Logoi, Great Existences and Lives beyond our Solar system are progressing toward greater unfoldment on the higher Cosmic planes. Where will their journey end and what conditions await them there? How could a human being even guess at the answers?

All progress, unfoldment and blooming have their preordained times, planned as is a great airport where each plane has its proper time schedule for departure and landing. Any delay or non-scheduled landing causes serious difficulties or complications in the whole system of operation.

So it is with us. We have eternities ahead of us, but we cannot lose one minute on the path of progress, without creating a complex situation in our timetable and various reactions from our three bodies. Too rapid progress creates tremendous pressure upon our system. Progressing too slowly creates tremendous friction. The result of this pressure and friction is expressed in our system as malfunction, disease and psychosomatic turbulence.

DRAMATIC ACTION

When a man, a nation, a humanity or a globe is retarded on the path of progress, the Greater Command takes dramatic action to clean the consequences of pressures and frictions and restore progress of life on the planet or system.

In 1922, the Tibetan Master speaking about the destruction of the Races, stated that the Fifth Race, the Aryan, or the present one, may end itself by fire. This fire will be the result of the combination of two fires. One is the electricity which we are using; the other will be the fire called Solar Fire. When these two fires are combined with evil intentions or with ignorance, then we will have the most dangerous conditions on the earth. He quotes the Bible . . . "the Heavens will melt with fervent heat." (II Peter 3:10) and continues:

> "This will be seen in a still greater degree in the next Round, and will cause that destruction by fire of the forms of the men who have failed, which will liberate the lives on a stupendous scale, and thus temporarily 'purify' the Earth from elements which would tend to hinder the evolutionary process. As the cycles pass away, the balancing of these fiery currents will be gradually brought about, and will result in a planetary condition of harmony, and of esoteric equality, which will provide ideal environment for harmonious man." [10]

The failure of the moon referred to in occult books, evoked the Solar Fire and turned that planet into a globe of ashes.

In one of His books, M.M. says:

> "The condition of the Earth requires an extraordinary physician. The planet is sick and if efforts to push it forward do not succeed, then it may be better to remove it temporarily from the chain—it may become as the moon." [11]

10. Bailey, Alice A., *A Treatise on Cosmic Fire*, p. 524.
11. Agni Yoga Society, *Community*, par. 30.

Chapter IV

THE AURA AND THE ETHERIC BODY

"The benevolent thinker is surrounded by a rainbow, and through his light brings healings."[1]

—M.M.

There is a colorful and scintillating egg-shaped sphere around our body, called in the Ancient Wisdom, the Aura. It is a sphere which not only surrounds our physical body, but which also penetrates into the body, permeating each cell and each atom.

The aura is a combination of mental, astral, etheric and pranic substances plus the radiation emanating from the Presence within, called Solar radiation. These elements form the aura of an average man.

- The etheric body has the same shape as the physical body. It not only extends out from the body three to twelve inches, but it also penetrates into and all through the physical body as a whole. It can be distinguished from the other bodies by its key color which is violet—a greenish violet.
- The emotional body radiation is silvery blue in color, and is in constant motion and change.
- The mental body's key color is yellow tinged with orange.
- The radiation of the Presence is mostly midnight blue flecked with golden sparks.

These are key colors, but many, many different shades of the same color or altogether different colors appear in the aura as the result of auric response to outer and inner stimuli.

THE AURA

Many different colors are coming from the centers as they shed their light into the aura. These colors may be orange, green, gold, blue, silvery blue, rose, yellow, purple, white, violet or indigo. They appear in the aura when the corresponding center is used or stimulated. Sometimes, if more than one center is used or stimulated, several colors radiate into the aura, persisting or fading according to the stimulation and response. They produce either harmony of great beauty or chaos. Harmony charges the aura; chaos saps energy.

We also have in the atmosphere around us, a "health aura". The etheric spleen is the organ which receives the fires of space, or prana, and distributes

1. Agni Yoga Society, *Aum*, par. 123.

them throughout the body via the network of the etheric body, physical spleen and its auxiliary center between the shoulder blades. This causes a certain vibration on the surface of the aura which is called the health aura. It is of a golden color, and those who see subjectively can determine the health of a person by observing its density, continuity, and purity of color.

Our auras emanate very subtle sounds which may be harmonious or chaotic. The Sacred Sound is beneficial in bringing harmony into the aura as a whole.

There are also emanations of fragrance and often low quality odors.[2] Fragrance attracts desirable energies, forces and even devas, while odor repels them and attracts entities of very low order.

The percentage of Solar elements, or substances, in the various bodies, or vehicles, differs from person to person according to the individual's development and stage of spiritual evolution. As man progresses on the Path, his Solar radiation increases and slowly creates a symphony, a rhythmic harmony within the aura, through the color and scintillation of auric waves. Eventually a man stands in the center of a wheel with twelve radiations of sparkling colors. As he moves forward in spiritual growth, he not only clears his aura of glamour, illusion and many other kinds of obstructions, but he also adds to the beauty of its symphony by bringing in new energies and new substances. Eventually he adds other subtle energies from the intuitional, atmic, monadic, and divine planes. With these energies in his aura, he is clothed in a garment of rare beauty—a garment fit for the *Feast*. The Feast is the symbolic expression of divine communication.[3]

Our aura reflects not only our physical, emotional and mental shocks, feelings and thoughts, but it also reflects the emotions and thoughts of others. For example, if you are sitting by a depressed person, his emanations will reflect themselves in your aura and create different effects in it. If your aura is organized and healthy, it may act as a refining agent for that person's aura; it may insulate and protect itself or reject the depressive waves and prevent them from entering into its sphere. If, however, the emanation of the other person is of high quality, your aura absorbs and assimilates it, using it as nourishment in the form of love and blessings. These are high quality "vitamins" for the aura.

Thought has an immediate effect upon the aura. Thoughts based on self-denial, sacrificial service and unity; thoughts originating from great insight or revelation; thoughts of admiration and ecstasy produce great changes within and on the surface of the aura, bringing new living energy into it. This energy, originally evoked from the plane of Nirvana, or the buddhic (intuitional) plane, spreads throughout the aura. We may call it the substance of *bliss*.

When the aura is charged with such energy, it radiates joy, peace, beauty, trust, and powerful electromagnetism which heals and uplifts. This bliss substance,

---

2. Low quality odors are due to decaying thoughtforms and glamours in the aura.
3. Matthew 22:11–14.

or energy, can be passed on to inanimate objects, plants and trees, or human beings. In man it accumulates as crystals of bliss upon the brain and nerve channels, and invigorates the whole nervous system with living energy. Since ancient times we have known that Great Ones used the technique of blessing, and that people have always been eager to receive the blessings of their parents or Teachers.

The main reservoirs of the substance of bliss are the Chalice, the heart centers and the Solar aura. In contrast to this energy, we have the substance of *imperil,* which is created when man is irritated through negative, emotional, criminal and selfish thoughts. As this substance accumulates in the nerve channels, it eventually causes great fatigue and poisons the whole system. A highly clairvoyant person can see the changes produced in the aura through these two contrasting substances.

Morya Sahib, the great Sage, speaking about bliss and imperil, says that the rose is beneficial for Bliss, and that pure thoughts factually dissolve the imperil, cleaning out the nerve channels.

When a great disciple or Initiate touches your aura, it shines forth with glowing colors and radiation. This cleanses away many obstructions and much congestion, providing the voltage is not too strong for you. If the voltage is too strong, it damages your aura by burning away the receptive atoms, which then form a protective barrier between your aura and the strong charge. Thus we can see that it is necessary to prepare oneself physically, emotionally, mentally and spiritually before coming in contact with advanced disciples and Initiates.

In the aura are seventy-seven palpitating centers of light of different colors in flower-like formations, having many petals of radiation. Some of them are in the etheric substance, ten to twelve inches out from the body. Some are in the astral substance and some in the mental substance.

In the aura of a developed or advanced man, there are colors of rare beauty around his chest and above his head. They are called *chalices*. The lower one is the chalice of Love and the higher one is the chalice of Life. The higher chalice radiates nine petals which penetrate into the three vehicles of personality, etheric, astral and mental. They integrate, align and fuse them with a network of energies, the center of which gathers all electromagnetic and creative currents within the aura. Later, when the chalice starts to respond to Cosmic currents, this network of energy in the aura acts as a creative agent for Cosmic beauties.

When a disciple works, serves and sacrifices himself, forming around his aura is a layer of energy of deep orange or ruby red. It is called *the shield.* This shield is the emanation of his Master's higher energies which build a protective net around the disciple's aura. After the shield is built, the man is protected from involutionary and dark entities, from the destructive arrows of agents of evil on the physical and astral planes. It creates an insulation through which destructive vibrations cannot penetrate into the aura. This shield is a combination of the man's Solar aura and the radiation of his Master. Sometimes the Master even makes for His chosen one a temporary robe of protection which he may wear in times of necessity.

The aura is highly sensitive to sound, and we are told that the healing art will use color and sound more and more to create better health in the etheric, astral and mental bodies, the conditions of which reflect on the physical body.

Great sages tell us that a lofty thought, a pure thought, has a great healing quality. They emphasize the fact that feeling and expressing gratitude is an effective way to bring about purification of our aura and within our organism. When our aura is pure enough and there is intense aspiration and striving, it evokes the fire of space. Gratitude is a powerful energy which charges the whole aura, and leads man into great creative action and heroic living. Under such conditions, man's motions or actions must be slow and solemn, because any abrupt movement disturbs the rhythmic and scintillating motion of the aura.

It is interesting that a *look* can produce many changes in the composition of the aura. The changes occur not only within the aura of the man at whom you are looking, but also in your own aura. Eyes emanate a vast amount of energy if the man is advanced on the Path. The right eye radiates the energy of intuition, which creates within you an urge to sacrifice and serve, while the left eye radiates the energy of mind, which creates within you an urge to organize and harmonize. Besides these effects, the density and colors of the auras of both parties undergo many changes. It is important that our "looks" radiate blessings, love, peace, gratitude, admiration and power.

The same is true of our spoken words. They create great changes in the aura of the listener and in the aura of the speaker. If they are charged with wrong motive and negativity, they distort the harmony of the aura and literally cause burning in different parts of it. We can understand why Christ once said that, that which comes out of your mouth harms you more than that which goes into your mouth.

Advanced disciples choose the members of their groups with extreme care and caution, because any new-comer may cause changes within the group aura. If a group aura is of high quality and is unified, it acts as a magnet to the energies of space, and to those thought waves which come from great Souls. These energy currents can be used to create new beauties and new discoveries. If this magic mirror is distorted by disturbances in it, it cannot function, and this causes many difficulties to the physical bodies of group members who automatically try to absorb the shocks.

It is most important that there be harmony among group members. They should be filled with love and positive feelings toward one another. Criticism is one of the most powerful means of disturbing the group aura, making it ineffective for a long period of time, if the group is not protected by the shield of the Master. The great Sage Morya Sahib says that, "Selfhood, crudity, self-pity, conceit will produce nothing except a repulsion, as of some gaseous substance."[4] These qualities of darkness must be avoided by any well-intentioned group.

4. Agni Yoga Society, *Fiery World*, Vol. III, par. 54.

The magnetism of the aura is unique. When a man creates harmony and rhythm in his aura, spiritual radiation increases and his centers function as electron tubes, attracting greater waves of beauty, ideas, energy, love, peace and impressions from other minds and from space. Soon such a man stands as a powerhouse of beauty, and draws unto him those who have similar vibrations and motives to serve humanity and to stand as a fountain of spiritual blessings. This kind of magnetism occurs when members and the group as a whole strive toward a higher life through esoteric meditation and sacrificial service. The magnetic quality is created only within those who meditate and serve in harmony and cooperation.

We often poison our aura and make it a "hot-bed for the germination of diseases" through our distrust and hypocrisy. Such a condition, says Morya Sahib, "creates repulsion in the auras with black and gray spots".

The developing human soul is a seed of spirit in the chalice. As he grows in controlling his vehicles and in disidentifying himself from plane to plane, he infuses the aura with great beauty. You can see thrilling harmony among the geometric energy formations, scintillating colors, and the rhythm of pulsating centers, of varying duration and intensity of radiation.

As the man approaches the third initiation, pure white predominates over all other colors within the aura, and the Solar Angel, the Guardian of the ages, increases His fiery energies and creates the condition called soul-infusion. Man now is vested with the robe of glory and is ready to enter into the temple of the Most High and dine with the Lord.

THE ETHERIC BODY

People are sometimes confused about the difference between the etheric body and the aura. The etheric body is the blueprint of the physical body. It is formed of four kinds of substances which are called four ethers. Each of these ethers has a different function.

- The lowest, the fourth ether, is called *chemical ether*. It carries a certain kind of energy which helps the body assimilate food and grow. It is controlled by base of spine, generative organs, solar plexus and spleen.
- The third ether, called *life ether*, produces energies for propagation. It is controlled by the throat center.
- The second ether is *light ether*. It carries heat and energy to the muscles and the nervous system. It is controlled by the heart center.
- The first ether is called *reflecting ether*. It helps in formulating thoughtforms. In it are stored all of our memories. It is controlled by the head center.

These ethers are basically from the substance of four cosmic ethers, combined with the finer physical substance and worked with by lunar pitris to form the prototype of the physical body. As man progresses on the Path, a transmutation process takes place in the ethers, and the fourth ether is slowly replaced by the substance of the fourth Cosmic Ether, called intuitional or buddhic plane.

The third ether is gradually changed to atmic, the second to monadic and the first to divine substance. The man then lives on the physical plane, but functions within all of these higher planes and has total continuity of consciousness. To help you see the whole picture of the relationship of the ethers with the centers, let us repeat that the fourth ether is controlled by four centers which are:

Base of spine
Generative organs
Solar plexus
Spleen

Each of these centers is related to other centers on higher ethers. For example:

1. Base of spine of the fourth ether is directly related to the head center on the first ether.
2. Generative organs of the fourth ether are directly related to the throat center on the third ether.
3. Solar plexus of the fourth ether is directly related to the heart center on the second ether.
4. Spleen has a direct line of communication with the physical and astral atoms, and with the astral and mental counterparts of the spleen.

The etheric brain is largely composed of the first ether. The etheric adrenals, generative organs, solar plexus and spleen are made up of the fourth ether. The thyroid gland functions in and carries energy from the third ether. The thymus gland receives its energy from the second ether via the heart center. The pineal gland receives its energy from the first ether via the head center. These seven centers in the etheric body are related to the astral and mental centers and to the Lotus. For example:

– Base of spine is related to the head center on the first etheric plane, to base of spine on the fourth astral plane, to the head center on the first astral plane, to base of spine on the fourth mental plane, and to the sacrifice petals of the Lotus. It makes contact with the *atmic permanent atom* via these petals, and terminates in the threefold Monad.
– The generative organs, within the fourth ether, are related to the throat center on the third etheric plane, to the generative organs on the fourth astral plane, to the throat center on the third astral plane, to the generative organs on the fourth mental plane. They reach the *manasic permanent* atom via the knowledge petals.
– The solar plexus, on the fourth etheric plane is related to the heart center on the second etheric plane, to the solar plexus on the fourth astral plane, to the heart center on the second astral plane, to the solar plexus on the fourth mental plane, to the love petals of the Lotus, and terminates in the *buddhic permanent atom.*
– The spleen is related to the physical and astral permanent atoms, to the mental unit on the fourth mental plane, to the throat center on the third etheric, to

the spleen on the fourth astral plane, to the spleen on the fourth mental plane, and terminates in the innermost petals of the Lotus.
– Three higher permanent atoms, manasic, buddhic, and atmic are related to the Monad by direct lines.

The human mechanism is a very complicated electrical phenomenon. All of these relationships are carried on through electrical fires. Man has his existence not only on the physical plane with his dense physical body, but his existence extends onto the etheric, astral and mental fields, and beyond these into four higher electrical spheres which in the Ancient Wisdom are called Cosmic Ethers.

The Secret Doctrine says that man is the microcosm and the whole existence is the macrocosm. Man is the "image" of the cosmic whole, and man was created in the "image" of the Creator. What great joy awaits those who can see these great beauties of existence! These subtle relationships indicate that no experience or happening on any center is limited to that center, but is registered and responded to on all points of relationship. Any physical, emotional, or mental plane happening is reflected on each of these planes and projected on the screens of the higher mind and beyond. Thus, man is an open drama to those who watch him from higher spheres.

All of the ethers are highly influenced by our thoughts and emotions. Great thoughts of Infinity, thoughts charged with good will, with love and gratitude carry to the ethers a high voltage healing energy which improves their condition by bringing in greater harmony and greater sensitivity. Pure thoughts and loving, positive emotions carry Soul energy down to the etheric vehicle through the centers and the etheric brain. Thus the health of our body depends chiefly upon our thoughts, emotions, and even upon our motives.

In the future it will be possible to register the condition of these centers and the condition of the bodies to which they are related. Thus, a perfect diagnosis will be possible for the overall condition of a man.

If the knowledge petals are not growing fast enough, or are growing too slowly and causing trouble in the generative organs, the physician will not prescribe pills or suggest surgery, but will prescribe those methods and ways of living which will facilitate the unfolding or balancing of the petals, and thus heal the lower conditions.

When all these systems and relationships are in order, we will have health, joy, creativity, clear mind, penetrating intelligence and continuity of consciousness on all planes of the human being. In the New Age, man will be observed not only as a physical phenomenon, but also as an etheric, astral, mental and spiritual phenomenon. Steps will even be taken to tune man in with the cosmic whole to increase his creativity and radioactive glory.

In the aura of man (not in the etheric body), stronger lines of electricity travel between the base of the spine and the head. These two currents create square, triangular or circular contacts of energy or force. An undeveloped man has mostly square patterns of circulation between the seventy-seven slightly palpitating centers within the etheric, astral, and mental bodies, while the developed man has largely triangular patterns of circulation above the diaphragm.

An advanced disciple or Initiate has mostly circular patterns of contact, the greater circle being formed between the base of the spine and the head center. This fiery ring circles in four motions. One strand of the ring climbs from the base of the spine and reaching the head center, descends to the base of the spine. This circular action goes on continuously. Another strand moves in the opposite direction, and thus the two currents are continuously flowing into each other as they circle. The third strand circles around the body within the aura, forming a fiery veil. This same strand rotates and revolves around the axis between the head and the base of the spine. Within these fiery wheels can be seen other wheels revolving around different axes, in third and fourth dimension, releasing sparks rhythmically as they intersect, forming as a whole, many geometric figures. These figures may be a five-pointed star, a chalice or spirals and combinations of these figures. We must remember that man is an atom, in comparison to Cosmos!

In esoteric books there are hints given about the four lower centers and the three higher centers of the Solar System. These lower centers are planets within the Solar etheric body. Reference is also made to the Solar Lotus and the Spiritual Triad of the Solar Logos. The human constitution is an exact replica of the Solar constitution. "As above, so below."

Chapter V

PRALAYA MANVANTARA

"Cosmogony should evoke thoughts which exalt. While the god of an unawakened people is conceived as sitting on the rim of an insignificant ball, the superior spirit peers into the Infinite, vesting himself in the joy of unbounded knowledge. Do not demean the Infinite." [1]

—M.M.

When I was studying and meditating about the path upon which we as personalities, Souls, or Monads, are treading toward the Absolute, I thought it important that we have a glimpse of the great expanse of time in "one hundred years of Brahma" with its *Nights* and *Days*.

In esoteric literature these Nights are called pralaya. Pralaya is a Sanskrit word formed of two words: *pra* and *laya. Pra* means away; *laya*, from the root *li*, means to dissolve. The Days are called manvantara; *manu* and *antara*. Antara means between (two manus).

Esoteric books tell us that there are forty-nine Manus; seven Manus for each globe and seven globes to a chain. They are the "patrons or guardians of the race cycles in a manvantara, or a Day of Brahma," the lapse of time between one manu and the next.

In *The Secret Doctrine* we read that the sun, moon and planets all have their growth, changes, development and gradual evolution in their life period. They are born as infants, become children, adolescents and adults; they grow and finally die. Thus the *pralaya* and *manvantara*, or the *Nights* and *Days* of the existing *forms*, are subjective and objective states of all that manifests in the Cosmos.

We have different manvantaras and pralayas. For example, a human being enters into pralaya or rest when the life energy is withdrawn from the physical permanent atom found in the causal body, and the physical body disintegrates. The man then enters into rest, but there is a higher pralaya into which he enters when he passes into the fifth Initiation.

In the case of the Planetary Logos, the life energy is withdrawn from His physical permanent atom, found on the second plane of the Monadic plane, and the physical planet disappears, entering into pralaya. This is planetary pralaya.

1. Agni Yoga Society, *Agni Yoga*, par. 88.

In regard to the Solar Logos, the life energy is withdrawn from His physical permanent atom, which is found in the plane called Adi, the first Cosmic ether, or on the divine plane, and the Solar System starts to disintegrate, producing Solar pralaya.

When the life energy is withdrawn from the permanent atom the form disintegrates, but the life continues on higher planes. The Tibetan Master says, "pralaya is simply subjectivity, and is not 'that which is not,' but simply that which is esoteric." It is the obscuration of form, the extinction of form, but not extinction of the "prototypes."

In considering the planetary Nights and Days, we are taught that there is a global pralaya between each globe and the next one to follow. There is a greater pralaya between each chain, and mahapralaya between two Solar Systems. Furthermore, we are taught that the time between two globes is one Day of Brahma (Night has equal duration) or 4,320,000,000 mortal years. The time between two chains is one Year of Brahma or 3,110,040,000,000 mortal years.

In esoteric writings, the dissolution of a planetary chain is called planetary nirvana. The dissolution of a solar system is called paranirvana, which is a great cycle, or a maha-kalpa.

After these great Nights, the Day starts with all its creations. This is the period of activity which in Sanskrit is called *Manvantara*—the period, or the cycle of manifestation, of expression, or the Day of Brahma, the outbreathing of Brahma.

We have individual manvantara, planetary and solar manvantara. As the Day follows Night, manvantara follows pralaya. At the dawn of a manvantara the Solar Logos incarnates and the Solar System comes into being. The same thing happens within shorter cycles for a Planetary Logos when He resumes labour after a great rest.

Maha-manvantara meaning great manvantara, refers to the active period of seven successive chains, called a scheme of evolution. The period of activity or manifestation of a single chain is simply called manvantara—the Day of Creation. We may speak of a man's cycle of activity on the physical plane, as a human manvantara.

> "The appearance and disappearance of the Universe are pictured as an outbreathing and inbreathing of the 'Great Breath,' which is eternal and which, being Motion, is one of the three symbols of the Absolute—Abstract Space and Duration being the other two. When the Great Breath is projected, it is called the Divine Breath, and is regarded as the breathing of the Unknowable Deity—the One Existence—which breathes out a thought, as it were, which becomes the Kosmos. So also is it that when the Divine Breath is inspired the Universe disappears into the bosom of the Great Mother, who then sleeps, 'wrapped in her Ever-Invisible Robes.' "[2]

2. Blavatsky, H. P., The Secret Doctrine, Vol. I, p. 74.

Chapter VI

THE RAYS AND THE HUMAN SOUL

"The seven rays are therefore embodiments of seven types of force which demonstrate to us the seven qualities of Deity. These seven qualities have consequently a sevenfold effect upon the matter and forms to be found in all parts of the universe . . ."[1]

—The Tibetan

The Creation, as a whole, is the condensation of energy. We have the manifested, tangible creation and, behind that, the forces and energies that sustain, control and direct the course of this manifested whole.

We have a cosmic mechanism in the infinite space, the parts of which are the galaxies, constellations, solar systems, comets, planets and so on. We have the great design behind this mechanism and the intelligent Power that creates, controls and directs it.

The Ancient Wisdom teaches that from the unknown Darkness of Infinite Space a Ray emanated, and as it traveled in Space, it changed into three Rays. Furthermore, these three Rays changed into seven and then into forty-nine as they descended into substance and matter.

THE SEVEN RAYS

The Seven Rays are composed of numberless Sparks coming down from the unknown Central Furnace and eventually reaching lowest materialization. For aeons and aeons each Spark has been traveling and will continue to travel back Home to re-enter into the Causeless Cause. According to the Ancient Wisdom, all angels, super-human beings and Gods are varying degrees of unfoldment of these Divine Sparks.

There is a very shocking statement in *The Secret Doctrine*. It says:

> "The Doctrine teaches that, in order to become a divine, fully conscious God—aye, even the highest—the Spiritual Primeval Intelligences must pass through the human stage. And when we say human, this does not apply merely to our terrestrial humanity, but to the mortals that inhabit any world, i.e., to those Intelligences that have reached the appropriate equilibrium between matter and spirit, as *we* have now, ever since the middle point of the Fourth Root Race of the Fourth Round was passed.

1. Bailey, Alice A., *A Treatise on the Seven Rays*, Vol. 1, p. 19.

"Each entity must have won for itself the right of becoming divine, through self-experience."[2]

These Sparks belong, essentially, to the original three Rays of aspect. They are numbered as First Ray Monads, Second Ray Monads and Third Ray Monads, but they can express themselves on any of the Rays of attribute on lower levels, and as their unfoldment proceeds, they enter into their true original Ray of Aspect.

Our solar system is a small part of the Cosmos, and we are told that seven Great Beings cyclically influence our solar system and hence our planet. These seven Great Beings are the Seven Rays which act in our solar system through the command of the Great Ray Life behind our visible sun.

In ancient times they were called Seven Streams or Rivers, Seven Paths, Seven Beams of Light, Seven Notes from the Cosmic Harp, Seven Wise Ones, Seven Rishis, or the Seven Horses that carry the Sun.

These Seven Rays condition the life of our solar system and therefore, our planet; various combinations of these rays create the many psychological types of men, planets and solar systems. In modern understanding they are streams of energy. They are substantial. They produce effects on human beings. They condition civilizations and cultures.

We are told that man is a combination of five rays. This means that the physical body, the emotional and mental natures, his personality and his spiritual nature act under the influence of the different rays. It is this difference in ray influence which creates different character, different types, different tendencies and drives, and different psychological moods in man.

The Science of the Rays in the near future will take the place of today's psychology, and people will be understood, dealt with, educated and placed in their appropriate labours according to their rays. Special meditation and healing techniques will be used for faster and better results.

We are told that these energies act in cyclic movement, as does everything in nature—they appear, they influence, and eventually they turn their focus to other directions.

In esoteric language they are:

1. First Ray—the Ray of Power and Politics
2. Second Ray—the Ray of Education and Psychology
3. Third Ray—the Ray of Philosophy
4. Fourth Ray—the Ray of Beauty and Harmony
5. Fifth Ray—the Ray of Science or Concrete Knowledge
6. Sixth Ray—the Ray of Religion and Worship
7. Seventh Ray—the Ray of Ceremonial Order and Finance.

These rays influence planets, kingdoms, nations, groups and individuals through the various energy stations or centers within these bodies. In a human

2. Blavatsky, H. P., *The Secret Doctrine*, Vol. I, p. 132.

being, these centers are called the seventy-seven whirlpools of energy and seven endocrine glands. The rays are responsible for different functions within these centers and glands, creating in them different responses to their environment. These functions and responses are conditioned by the achievement, or the level of human consciousness and beingness. The higher the level of man, the better his centers and glands will respond to these ray influences. A distorted mind and distorted centers and glands respond to the rays in an aberrant way and create complications in their corresponding organs and mechanisms.

All the rays are divine and their purpose is to further the process of evolution and work out the divine plan on earth, in the solar system and beyond. They are the seven Cosmic Keys, galvanized by Cosmic Love. Knowing them and using them for our evolution will bestow upon us health, happiness, enlightenment and joy.

THE PERSONALITY RAY

In many esoteric books the word *personality* is used in very subtle ways. When the small case letter, *p*, is used, *personality* refers to the three lower bodies as a unit. When the word is capitalized, *Personality*, it denotes the evolving human soul, the fragment, the fallen Spark in the process of returning to its Source. This fragment identifies with the rays of the physical, astral and mental bodies as it progresses and gains control over these three vehicles. When it has achieved integration of the three lower bodies, the Personality ray, apart from the physical, emotional, mental rays, comes into effect. *The Personality ray is the ray of the evolving human soul.*

In esoteric circles there is great confusion concerning the ray of the Personality. The Personality is the sum total of the three lower bodies aligned and integrated on a high level of development. Each body has its own ray or its own type of energy. Many students mistakenly believe that the strongest ray of the three bodies is the Personality ray. For example, if the physical body is first ray and that ray is acting more forcefully than the other component rays, it may seem that the Personality ray is first ray. Others think that it is the synthesis of the three rays of the lower vehicles. The Tibetan Master says, "The energies of the personality which is of such a potency (being a fusion of three ray energies) that it has evoked a ray which dominates the personality and is called the personality ray."[3] The word *evoked* is very significant. As the personality is formed, synthesizing the three rays of its parts, physical, emotional and mental, the *real entity* in the personality blooms and evokes a ray. This ray may be one of the rays of attribute of the Monad, or it may be a ray of aspect of the Monad reflecting itself in the newly blossoming soul. The Tibetan Master very subtly states that, "the ray of the evolving human soul is always a sub-ray of the egoic ray."[4]

---

3. Bailey, Alice A., *The Rays and the Initiations*, p. 563.
4. Bailey, Alice A., *A Treatise on the Seven Rays*, Vol. II, p. 358.

This means that the ray of the evolving human soul is a branch on the trunk of the egoic, or the spiritual ray, and thus is conditioned by the power of the egoic ray. So, too, are our seven systemic rays sub-rays of the great Cosmic Love Ray, and all their functions must be synthesized into the Cosmic Love Ray.

As an example, if a man's Soul ray is *Will-power* or first ray, and the Personality ray is *Love* or second ray, the Personality may be deeply colored or strongly influenced by the first ray of the Soul. Love will be expressed by power and the power will function through the great inclusiveness quality of the love ray, on the personality levels.

This will continue up to the fourth Initiation. During this time of greater fusion between the Personality and Soul the two rays will gradually function as two sides of one reality, until the time comes when the Soul will depart from the Chalice, and the unfolding human soul will function as a *Soul*, changing its sub-ray to the parent ray. Here is the subtle point. This ray which was the ray of the Solar Angel, is in its turn a sub-ray of the Monadic Ray, which was the ray of the unfolding human soul. For example, let us say that a man has:

– A first ray Monad
– A second ray Soul
– A fifth, third or seventh ray personality

During his evolution and on the path of discipleship and Initiation, this fifth, third or seventh ray of the unfolding human soul will change into the *second ray*, the ray of the Solar Angel, the Soul. Then on the path of advanced Initiation this second ray will become the servant of the first ray, and eventually will change into its true parent ray, the first ray (through the third ray).

To learn what the Personality ray is we must clearly understand that the Real Man, the Spark, the Monad, is as a diffused light in the three lower bodies. As the three bodies begin to become organized, individually and collectively, the diffused light condenses and slowly becomes a center by itself. This center is the lower self. So we may say that the lower self is spread throughout the three bodies. In most individuals the lower self is under the control of one of its three bodies, serving its ends and purposes. Gradually, as the bodies develop and as the stream of light from the Solar Angel penetrates into them, the diffused light of the Monad begins to recollect itself and form a center. This center is the character of man. By character we mean special or exceptional character, for it highly influences the three bodies. As this center develops, the personality becomes more outstanding and more dominating. The developing of the center, the building of character, is the result of the Monad at work in the three bodies. The ray of the Monad is beginning to express itself through the form of personality. Eventually, when the personality is developed, it will be the real shadow; the vehicle of the Spiritual Triad; later it will become the vehicle of the Monad.

We have some interesting information in several esoteric books about the rays. We are told that a man has six permanent atoms, and that each permanent atom has seven spirillae. On the path of evolution each spirilla becomes active and radiatory under the impact of the three major rays of the individual man. The Personality ray affects the 1st, 2nd, 3rd and 4th spirillae of the permanent atoms, causing them to become active. The Soul Ray affects the 5th and 6th spirillae of the permanent atoms, and the Monadic Ray affects the 7th spirilla, the highest. Thus as the *seeds*, or permanent atoms, unfold and become active, the substance of the corresponding sub-planes of each plane changes, becomes refined, and responds to a greater light. Eventually it is transmuted to the higher counterparts on higher planes. Thus the processes of transmutation, transformation and transfiguration take place.[5]

It is appropriate also to mention here that the major rays of man (Monadic, Soul and Personality rays) have a great effect upon the physical, astral and mental living atoms and cells. They cause the polarization of man to shift from the personality vehicles to the Spiritual Triad. Through this process the Personality ray eventually changes its polarization from the physical to the mental permanent atom. The Soul Ray changes its polarization from the astral permanent atom to the Buddhic permanent atom, and the Monadic Ray changes its polarization from the mental permanent atom to the Atmic permanent atom.

The Personality ray changes in cycles of long duration. This fact indicates that the evolving soul is influenced by changes in the bodies. The Monadic ray can be First, Second or Third Ray, but in expression, as the Personality ray, it may follow these cyclic patterns:

FIRST RAY — FIFTH RAY — SEVENTH RAY
SECOND RAY — FOURTH RAY — SIXTH RAY
THIRD RAY — FIFTH RAY — SEVENTH RAY

If, for example, the Personality ray is Ray 1, it changes to Ray 5, then to Ray 7 and back to Ray 1. If it is Ray 2, it changes to Ray 4, then to Ray 6 and back to Ray 2, after identifying with the Soul ray.

We learn that there are three major types of Monads, not seven. The ray of the Monad is always one of the three Rays of Aspect. The three types of Monads are Sparks from the Central Spiritual Sun, expressed through three Logoi; Third Logos, Second Logos and First Logos. Those Monads who emanated from the Third Logos are Monads of Intellect or Third Ray. Those who emanated from the Second Logos, are Monads of Love or Second Ray and those Monads who emanated from the First Logos are Monads of Will and Power or First Ray.

As we have said, human beings have five rays:

---

5. See Bailey, Alice A., *A Treatise on Cosmic Fire*, pp. 70–71.
Also, Saraydarian, H., *The Science of Becoming Oneself*, Chap. XII.

1. Physical ray
2. Emotional ray
3. Mental ray
4. Personality ray
5. Soul ray

The real ray of a person is his Personality ray. The Soul ray can have a tremendous effect on the Personality ray. On many occasions it will fuse with the Personality ray until this ray flourishes completely and man enters into the Fourth Initiation. At the Fourth Initiation man becomes a Soul, or the diffused monadic light recollects itself and forms a center by itself on the intuitional level. It begins to radiate as the owner or ruler of the form called man. He is now a Soul and because of this achievement, the Solar Angel has departed and the causal body has been destroyed. We assume that the ray of this Soul will be the same as the major ray of the Personality in the last incarnation before the Fourth Initiation was taken. This assumption would bear out the fact that the Soul rays of advanced Initiates are essentially the same as their monadic rays. If, however, a man is not a free soul, if his Solar Angel is still present, the ray of his soul may differ from his monadic ray. We must understand that Monads are timeless and that three types of Monads are coexistent, but only one is predominant in a world cycle. For every world period one monadic ray type is the controlling power for that world cycle. The Tibetan Master says:

> "When the Personality finds for itself (after lives of stress and search) its spiritual note with the right key and subtone, what is the result? It accords with its monadic note, it vibrates to the same measure, it pulsates with the same colour, the line of least resistance is at last found, and the indwelling life is liberated and returns to its own plane. But this work of discovery is very slow and the man has to pick out the chord with infinite care and pains. First, he finds out the third of the Personality and sounds that forth, the result being an ordered and harmonious life in the three worlds. Then he finds the dominate fifth of the Ego, the keynote of the chord, and sounds that in unison with the Personality note. The result is that a vacuum is formed (if I may so express it) and the liberated man with his informing soul—the threefold spirit plus mind and experience—the Three completed by the Quarternary and the Fifth—escapes upward to the Monad. It is the law of attraction demonstrating through sound. Like to like and kind to kind, driven thereto by unity of sound, of colour and of rhythm."[6]

The departure of the Solar Angel marks a great step forward in man's journey on the Path of Return. When the evolving human soul enters into that vast expansion of consciousness called the Fourth Initiation, the Solar Angel leaves the man. The evolving human Soul has already built the web of the Triad and

6. Bailey, Alice A., *Letters on Occult Meditation*, p. 56.

is able to function in the awareness of the Spiritual Triad. Man begins to know his own Kingship, and the powerful energy of his own Essence releases itself more potently, radiating outward through the Spiritual Triad. When the Solar Angel leaves the human being at the Fourth Initiation, the Temple of Solomon, the lotus or chalice, is completely burned away.[7] We are told that at this Initiation, the innermost petals of the twelve-petaled lotus slowly open and the fire of the spirit sealed within the Monad is released. The fire burns all petals and flows down, uninhibited, to the threefold lower unit, galvanizing it into a mechanism capable of performing as an instrument of the Spiritual Triad without the Solar Angel acting as an intermediary between the Triad and the lower mechanism. This is the fiery baptism to which Christ refers in the Bible.

Actually there are three kinds of baptism for the human being: the baptism of water, the baptism of the Holy Spirit, which is at the third Initiation when the evolving human soul is fused with the Solar Angel, and the third baptism, the baptism of fire at the Fourth Initiation when the Solar Angel leaves the man to stand alone in full awareness of the Spiritual Triad.

After the Fourth Initiation, man enters into the fifth; he has become a *Soul.* He can function within the great mechanism of the Spiritual Triad, releasing more power, more goodness, and more beauty from his own Essence, the Monad; using it to further the divine plan and to achieve the divine purpose on earth. At this stage "he goes no more out" by the force of Karma. If he wills to "come out" into physical incarnation, he may do so, but he has reached that stage of development which enables him to reincarnate on the physical level without losing his continuity of consciousness, without losing his real identity. At this stage we say that the human soul is in full bloom and he has achieved conscious immortality.

---

7. Saraydarian, H., *Science of Becoming Oneself*, Chap. XII; also Saraydarian, H., *The Magnet of Life*, Chap. XI, p. 86.

Chapter VII

TECHNIQUE OF MEDITATION ON SEVEN RAYS

"All leaders in every field were and are men of meditation! Meditation sometimes lasts a minute, sometimes an hour, sometimes days, until the mind reaches its goal."[1]

One of the richest and safest ways to come in contact with the Soul and use the treasures of the chalice for our creative living and service, is to study and know the Ray to which our Soul belongs. This knowledge is very important because it creates a closer rapport between Soul and personality and presents possibilities for greater infusion. To facilitate this infusion, and to secure greater guidance from the Indwelling Presence, we can meditate according to the Ray of our Soul.

Such meditation will give us a tremendous advantage in creating a direct line of communication to the Soul, invoking Its help in all our activities upon the physical, emotional and mental planes, as well as in our individual and group situations.

This is not an easy task. Before we can handle this kind of meditation, we must have preparatory years of meditation, as given in the books, *The Science of Meditation* and *The Science of Becoming Oneself*, by the present writer. All that was given in these volumes can be of greater usefulness in light of instructional material presented in this chapter, and other enlightening teaching given throughout the book.

The intelligent student of the endless path must know where he stands on the path of evolution, and using his spiritual discrimination, choose those exercises or forms of meditation which he needs at that particular time, always knowing that the foundation must be based on solid rock, and must be built slowly and carefully with his own "feet and hands."

The method which is presented for your consideration at this time is an advanced method, but it is not very different from other meditations. Being an advanced method, however, it must be handled with extreme care and watchfulness.

There are seven types of energy which condition all activities and expressions of our nature and the kingdoms. Our Soul belongs to one of these energy streams. It may belong to one of the higher three rays, the Rays of Aspect, or to the lower four, the Rays of Attribute. Generally the Soul Ray is a Ray of Aspect,

1. Saraydarian, H., *The Fiery Carriage and Drugs*, p. 73.

but the Soul chooses Rays of Attribute for certain cycles and for specific work in relation to Its obligations.

To know the Ray of our Soul is not easy when we are lost in the agitated sea of our physical, emotional and mental life. Once we step into greater dedication, service and sacrifice for our fellow man, we catch glimpses of the splendour of the Soul Ray, which inspires in us moments of great joy, sacrifice, danger, renunciation, life intention and heroic action. In these rare moments, we sense the nature of the Ray of our Soul, until that time when our personality fuses into the Soul light, and we eventually become a living Soul, harmonized with the Ray of the Soul.

We must remember that at certain times we can change our ray meditation from one ray technique to another, when we see the need for bringing balance into our nature. In all these techniques please refer to the proper form of meditation given in *The Science of Meditation.*[2]

Let us remember that the Soul on its own level is in deep meditation and is trying to impress the man with the divine plan, and to impart to him the need for endless striving on the path. Our aim in these meditations will be to synchronize ourselves with the Soul's meditation.

With this ray method, it will be helpful if you understand that these meditations are a combination of prayer, meditation and invocation. A few words about these three methods will be useful in our ray method approach.

At a certain stage of human history a time came when man felt an urge to surpass himself, to stretch himself and touch beyond. This was the unconscious answer of the human being to the conscious call coming from his Soul. As man tried to meet this call he became aware of surrounding obstacles and hindrances, the pain and the suffering, and he began consciously to ask help from an unknown Presence who was near him, but far from his touch.

On the path of his struggle he developed a technique of communication which was called prayer. Prayer was performed with an intense desire and aspiration to contact the Presence and ask Its help. It seems that man was first aware of his Soul, his first Guide and Teacher. Later he felt that a greater Presence existed in the universe which could be contacted.

Throughout centuries man developed three outstanding techniques to contact the Presence within and without. The first was prayer with all its manifold expressions. The next was meditation, and the third was invocation. Actually, all three of these are parts of the technique of contact.

Man felt from the beginning that he was an exile, and gradually sensed the magnetic pull of his home. This home was not a location, but a state of awareness and beingness. This home could not be reached by elevating his position, but by transformation of his nature and by victory over the obstacles causing a gap that separated him from that home.

2. Saraydarian, H., *The Science of Meditation*, pp. 92–154.

PRAYER, MEDITATION AND INVOCATION

Prayer is man's first endeavor to stretch himself, and to try to touch the unknown, to meet his physical, emotional and mental needs, and to surpass his own beingness by becoming a greater organism through which he is able to communicate more deeply as he progresses toward Infinity.

The Inner Presence and the presence in nature may be called the *Law of Cause and Effect*. This Law is an energy field extending throughout the Cosmic planes, and any action upon this energy field creates a corresponding reaction relative to the level and intensity of the action. Thus a wish, a desire, an aspiration, a thought can be an act of prayer, a form of action which creates the corresponding reaction from the energy field, from the Law of Cause and Effect.

Prayer is not only a verbal asking; it is also an emotional demanding and a mental searching. For example, when Einstein was trying to penetrate mentally into the Laws of nature, he was performing an act of prayer because he was asking something from the unknown and causing that unknown to be at least partially revealed. "Ask and you will receive . . . Knock and it will be opened," said the Great Christ.

As man continued to use this method of contact through prayer, he developed some power of observation and saw that prayer was more effective when it was accompanied by thought energy or related to the thinking process. He started to think about the true nature of his needs, his desires, aspirations, urges and drives, and developed a system of using the mind, which eventually evolved into thinking and meditation.

Meditation is a form of prayer carried on, on the mental plane, for enlightenment and transfiguration. It is a mental action upon the energy field, the Law, to bring about the corresponding reaction from it. During meditation your aspiration for enlightenment, for transfiguration is highly intense. You are trying to merge with the light of your Soul to receive answers to your needs; to gain wisdom, insight, inspiration and greater impressions from the Inner Presence, adapting treasures gained to the need of the time.

The next step on the path of communication is invocation. Invocation is carried out upon the foundation laid by prayer and meditation. Actually, invocation is a combination of these two, plus the using of will power over the Laws and energies of nature.

After a man knows how to use the technique of prayer and meditation, he tries to build a kind of formula through which he can penetrate deeper into the Law of Cause and Effect and bring forth creative results from his communication. Invocation is a formula of words which, when properly sounded under the power of will energy, lifts the veil, opening the way for you to enter into the unknown and receive according to your needs and demands.

Invocation has a preparatory stage which is called affirmation. Through affirmation man creates the right atmosphere and conditions in which to use the invocation more effectively. This is important because everytime you ask and receive without being prepared to contain energies received; without being ready to assimilate and express these energies, you damage or destroy your mechanism and become an obstacle upon the path of evolution.

Thus as you pray, meditate or invoke, use these three approaches as means of contact with the Beyond. Use them in such a way that when you pray you also meditate and invoke; when you meditate your meditation is infused with the spirit of prayer and invocation; when you invoke, your invocation is charged with the spirit of prayer and meditation. In the following chapters all three forms of contact are used to enable you to experience deeper communication with your Soul and beyond.

RAY MEDITATION TECHNIQUES

For each ray meditation we have selected words for seed thoughts. Meditating on these seed thoughts will be of great help in releasing latent energies within and opening new horizons. Also, as you ponder and meditate upon these seed thoughts, you cultivate corresponding virtues in your nature, and as these virtues are cultivated, organic and constitutional changes take place in your physical and subtle bodies; changes which will facilitate communication with your Soul.

We must also consider the personality ray and the way in which it can be brought into harmony with the Soul ray through meditation; first to create a balance and then a vehicle for the Soul to use to express Itself.

This can be accomplished as follows: After you know your Soul and Personality rays, use your Soul's ray meditation technique. Study, work and serve in your Personality ray field. For example, if your Soul is second ray and your Personality is first ray, choose second ray meditation, and carry on with your studies on the first ray meditation. In other words, use the list of words given in the First Ray Meditation as guides for your studies, activities and service.

First Ray Technique

This is the Ray of Power, the Ray of the ruler, leader and synthesizer. Steps for First Ray Meditation:

1. Relax your body.
2. Do the kneeling exercise (if you wish).
3. Align your three lower bodies.
4. Say the following:

May the energy of my divine Self inspire me,
And the Light of the Soul direct;
May I be led from darkness to Light,
From the unreal to the Real,
From death to Immortality,
From chaos to Beauty.

5. Sound seven OMs.[3]
6. Meditate on the seed thought.
7. Record the results of your meditation.
8. Say the following:

More radiant than the Sun,
Purer than the snow,
Subtler than the ether,
Is the Self,
The Spirit within my heart,
I am that Self,
That Self am I.

9. Then visualize yourself standing in the Sun; see your physical body, your emotional and mental vehicles infused with a golden-orange light. Then see yourself as a transfigured personality, standing on a high mountain.
10. Say the Great Invocation:

From the point of Light within the Mind of God
Let Light stream forth into the minds of men.
Let Light descend on Earth.

From the point of Love within the Heart of God
Let love stream forth into the hearts of men.
May Christ return to Earth.

From the centre where the Will of God is known
Let purpose guide the little wills of men—
The purpose which the Masters know and serve.

From the center which we call the race of men
Let the Plan of Love and Light work out.
And may it seal the door where evil dwells.

Let Light and Love and Power restore the Plan on Earth.

11. Sound three OMs silently, saluting Master M.
12. Do not move for three minutes, and do not speak for ten or fifteen minutes.

One of the important things in your meditation will be the seed thought, which must be changed every month for a year; every other month in the second year; and every sixth month in the following years. You may also repeat your seed thought at different times.

---

3. Please read *The Science of Meditation*, pp. 107–119, 148–149 and "The Sacred Word and the Soul," Chap. XXIV in this book.

The following seed thoughts may be used for this meditation:[4]

1. Will to initiate
2. Will to unify
3. Will to evolve
4. Will to harmonize or relate
5. Will to act
6. Will to cause
7. Will to express
8. Striving
9. Promptness
10. Rulership, leadership
11. Law
12. Synthesis
13. Sacrifice
14. Renunciation
15. Steadfastness
16. Endurance
17. Strength
18. Self-control
19. Magnanimity
20. Energy, power
21. Fire
22. Purification
23. Beingness
24. Is
25. Heroism
26. Humility
27. Truthfulness

You may use the meditation form given in *The Science of Becoming Oneself* alternately with this meditation (see pages 152–156).

If at any time you see that the first ray energy is becoming uncontrollable, change your meditation to the second ray meditation for a few months, then return to your proper first ray meditation.

Students of politics will make outstanding progress by meditating upon the seed thoughts given above.

Second Ray Technique

This is the Ray of Love-Wisdom. Steps for Second Ray Meditation:

1. Relax your body.
2. Do the kneeling exercise (if you wish).
3. Align your three bodies.
4. Say the following:

May the Holy Ones whose pupils we aspire to become,
Show us the Light we seek;
Give us the strong aid of Their compassion and Their wisdom.
There is a peace that passeth understanding;
It abides in the hearts of those who live in the eternal.
There is a power that makes all things new;
It lives and moves in those who know the Self as One.
May that peace brood over us, that power uplift us,
Till we stand where the One Initiator is invoked,
Till we see His Star shine forth.

After saying this invocation, slowly and with great attention, try to visualize a deep rose-colored lotus twelve inches away from your back at the middle

4. Saraydarian, H., *Bhagavad Gita*, Chap. XVIII, verse 43.

of the shoulder blades. Try to visualize the lotus radiating a rosy or blue light, flooding your personality and the place where you are sitting. This will take only one minute.

5. Sound three OMs.
6. Meditate on the seed thought.
7. Record the results of your meditation.
8. Say the following:

I am a point of light within a greater Light.
I am a strand of loving energy within the stream of Love divine.
I am a point of sacrificial Fire, focussed within the fiery Will of God.
And thus I stand.

I am a way by which men may achieve.
I am a source of strength, enabling them to stand.
I am a beam of light, shining upon their way.
And thus I stand.

And standing thus, revolve
And tread this way the ways of men,
And know the ways of God.
And thus I stand.

9. Visualize a fiery rose-colored ball with a violet triangle in its center and a second fiery ball, blue in color, in the middle of the triangle.
10. Say the Great Invocation.
11. Sound the OM three times, offering salutations to the Christ and blessing the world.
12. Do not move for three minutes and do not speak for ten or fifteen minutes.

The following seed thoughts may be used for the Second Ray Meditation:

1. Compassion
2. Understanding
3. Affinity
4. Communication
5. Serenity
6. Patience
7. Endurance
8. Faithfulness
9. Intuition
10. Unselfishness
11. Blessing
12. Education
13. Healing
14. Beatitude
15. Interdependence
16. Unfoldment
17. Right human relations
18. Charity
19. Inclusion
20. Enlightenment
21. Affiliation
22. Thought, thinking
23. Tolerance
24. Expansion
25. Righteousness
26. Expansion of Consciousness
27. Magnetism

You may alternate this mediation with the Antahkarana meditation, given in *The Science of Becoming Oneself*, pages 183–220.

Here, again, we must repeat the fact that the line of least resistance can create one-sidedness. To avoid this danger, occasionally change your ray meditation, and thus balance your nature.

Students and teachers of Education will experience great unfoldment in doing the above meditation.

Third Ray Technique

This ray is the ray of activity and adaptability. It is the ray of philosophers and abstract thinkers. Steps for Third Ray Meditation:

1. Relax your body.
2. Do the kneeling exercise (if you wish).
3. Align your three bodies and hold them for a moment in a yellow radiance pouring down from above your head.
4. Say the following:

   I am a server in the world of man,
   Of that Brotherhood of Light,
   Whose Life and Light sustain all in life
   In this manifested Universe.
   May my light so shine in harmony with Their Light,
   Ere long the "Day be with us"
   When those that wait shall be liberated
   Into Light and Life of Peace.
   To this I relinquish
   All sense of limitation,
   Taking my place in the ranks of Light bearers,
   Who live only to bless and serve.

   As you sound this invocation, imagine that you are standing in the throat lotus, ten inches behind your neck.
5. Sound five OMs.
6. Meditate on the seed thought.
7. Record the results of your meditation.
8. Say the following:

   I am one with the Light which shines
   Through my Soul, my group brothers and my Master.
   This Light which is rooted in the healing love of the One Soul
   Radiates upon me and permeates every part of my body,
   Healing, soothing, strengthening and dissipating
   All that hinders good health and service.

9. Visualize a flaming, rosy sun in a yellow sky.
10. Say the Great Invocation.

11. Sound the OM three times, offering salutations to the Master R., and blessing the world.
12. Do not move for three minutes, and do not speak for ten or fifteen minutes.

The following seed thoughts may be used for the Third Ray Meditation:

1. Light
2. Enlightenment
3. Intuition
4. Reason
5. Intellect
6. Organization
7. Money
8. Tolerance
9. Devotion
10. Energy
11. Common sense
12. Adaptability
13. Affiliation
14. Sincerity
15. Synthesis
16. Joy
17. Accuracy
18. Knowledge
19. Utilization
20. Discrimination
21. Service
22. Electricity
23. Goal-fitting
24. Flaming rosy Sun
25. Aquarian Age
26. Balance
27. Sight or Vision

Students of philosophy will greatly improve their mental insight, and the understanding of abstract concepts by using the above meditation technique.

Fourth Ray Technique

The fourth ray is the Ray of Harmony through conflict. It is also called the Ray of Beauty. Steps for Fourth Ray Meditation:

1. Relax your body.
2. Do the kneeling exercise (if you wish).
3. Align your three bodies, holding them in an orange light.
4. Say the following:

   O Lord of Beauty,
   Let me stand in your temple of color supernal,
   and within the symphonies divine.
   May I achieve harmony with the Heart of the Cosmic rhythm,
   And radiate, the uplifting, expanding Beauty of that Heart
   In all my actions and aspirations.

5. Sound three OMs, visualizing orange and yellow concentric circles scintillating with movement in space.
6. Meditate on the seed thought.
7. Record the results of your meditation. They may be music, a blueprint of a painting or sculpture, a dance, etc.
8. Say the following:

I stand within the harmonizing strain and stress,
And bring into fusion
The East and West, the North and South,
The form and the mind;
And radiate Beauty to build the Path
Of the Coming One.

9. Visualize a cross with a yellow rose at the center and a bird standing upon the vertical arm of the cross.
10. Say the Great Invocation and at the end, offer salutations to Master Serapis and the unnamed Egyptian Master.
11. Sound the OM three times.
12. Do not move for three minutes, and do not speak for ten or fifteen minutes.

The following seed thoughts may be used for the Fourth Ray Meditation:

1. Beauty
2. Harmony
3. Rhythm
4. Proportion
5. Light and shadow
6. Creativity
7. Agreement
8. Manifestation
9. Taste
10. Serenity
11. Confidence
12. Purity
13. Balance
14. Perception
15. Inner Vision
16. Relation
17. Ecstasy
18. Labour
19. Triangle
20. Intuition
21. Art
22. Music (listen to Music mentally)
23. Inspiration
24. Prototype
25. Solar Angel
26. A Painting or a Statue (see the work of art mentally)
27. Synthesis

Students of art will greatly profit by doing the above meditation. All of these words must be meditated upon in the light of Harmony, Creativity and Beauty.

Fifth Ray Technique

The fifth ray is the Ray of Concrete Knowledge or Science. Steps for Fifth Ray Meditation:

1. Relax your body.
2. Do the kneeling exercise (if you wish).
3. Align your three bodies, holding them in an indigo light.
4. Say the following:

Let the triple aspect of the mind merge within me,
Let the higher, let the divine link
And the concrete thus merge within me.

And make me a pure channel
For the Light of the Soul,
For the Energy of the Triad.

And may Love reveal the Mind Divine
And the Mind Divine reveal the pure Love.

And May I be led from darkness to Light,
Dispersing the knowledge at the right time,
In the right proportion for the glory
Of the One.

5. Sound three AUMs. Please note that these are AUMs.
6. Meditate on the seed thought.
7. Record the results of your meditation. They may be a scientific formula, a new insight into one of the scientific fields, a new revelation or a new realization.
8. Say the following:

May my mind reflect the Divine Knowledge,
A Knowledge related to the whole.
May my chalice hold the energy of that Knowledge,
And may I radiate it into darkness,
And create Light.

9. Visualize a male and a female form in green and indigo robes, standing back to back. The male wears a shining, silvery helmet upon his head, and the female holds a chalice in both hands.
10. Say the Great Invocation, and at the close, offer salutations to Master Hilarion.
11. Sound the OM three times, starting it in your imagination within your ajna center between the eyebrows, and ten inches away from your head.
12. Do not move for three minutes, and do not speak for ten or fifteen minutes.

The following seed thoughts may be used for the Fifth Ray Meditation:

1. Form
2. Knowledge
3. Intellect
4. Consciousness
5. Thoughtforms
6. Problems
7. Energy
8. Crystallization
9. Reverence
10. Connection
11. Sympathy
12. Door
13. Accuracy
14. Justice
15. Perseverance
16. Common sense
17. Independence
18. Research
19. Fact
20. Order
21. Punctuality
22. Detachment
23. Electricity
24. Mind
25. Surgery
26. Abstract
27. Correlation

All of these words must be meditated upon in their true meaning in relation to person, and to Cosmos. Students of science will make great progress through these meditations.

Sixth Ray Technique

The sixth ray is the Ray of Devotion, the Ray of Sacrifice and Idealism. Steps for Sixth Ray Meditation:

1. Relax your body.
2. Do the kneeling exercise (if you wish).
3. Align your three bodies, and hold them in a violet or a silvery blue light.
4. Say the following:

   May the Light that is my Soul
   Dispel all glamour.
   May the power of Love that is my Soul,
   Release me from attachment.
   May I be given strength to serve,
   That those I love
   May tread the lighted way.

   As you sound this mantram, imagine that you are standing in the heart lotus, at a point twelve inches away from your back between the shoulder blades.
5. Sound the OM seven times.
6. Meditate on the seed thought.
7. Record the results of your meditation.
8. Say the following:

   May the sense of responsibility be developed in me
   That I may rightly serve the Plan.

   May the purity of vision which sometimes I have felt,
   Enable me to tread the Path of service.

   May I stand free
   And may I set free those I meet and love
   That they, too, may rightly serve.

   May the Divine Self inspire me
   And the Light of the Soul direct.
   May I walk in that Light.
   May that Light shine upon my way.
   May I pour forth that Light on others.

9. Visualize a pitcher on the head of a man dressed in silvery blue.
10. Say the Great Invocation.

11. Sound the OM three times, offering salutations to Chohan Jesus and bless the world.
12. Do not move for three minutes, and do not speak for ten or fifteen minutes.

The following seed thoughts may be used for the Sixth Ray meditation:[5]

1. Sacrifice
2. Devotion
3. Love
4. Tenderness
5. Intuition
6. Loyalty
7. Reverence
8. Gratitude
9. Gentleness
10. Strength
11. Purity
12. Austerity
13. Tolerance
14. Serenity
15. Balance
16. Inclusiveness
17. Desirelessness
18. Warrior
19. Crucifixion
20. Forgiveness
21. Trust
22. Suffering
23. Detachment
24. Consecration
25. Path
26. Master
27. Self-discipline

Those who truly want to serve in the field of religion, or in the field of any humanitarian service, will make great progress by meditating on the above seed thoughts.

Seventh Ray Technique

The seventh ray is the Ray of Ceremonial Law, Order or Magic. It is also the Ray of Economics or Finance. Steps for the Seventh Ray Technique:

1. Relax your physical body.
2. Do the kneeling exercise (if you wish).
3. Align your three lower bodies fusing them into the Light of your Soul which is radiating indigo or violet rays.
4. Say the following:

   I am the Soul, the Word incarnate.
   Through Life and Word and Deed I speak to men.
   That radiance pure am I.
   With the Light within
   I tread the Lighted Way.
   I hold aloft the Light
   That others, too, may walk and see.

5. Sound the AUM three times.
6. Meditate on the seed thought.

5. Saraydarian, H., *Bhagavad Gita*, Chap. VIII, verse 42.

7. Record the results of your meditation.
8. Say the following:

I am a point of light within a greater Light.
I am a strand of loving energy within the stream of Love divine.
I am a point of sacrifical Fire, focussed within the fiery Will of God.
And thus I stand.

I am a way by which men may achieve.
I am a source of strength, enabling them to stand.
I am a beam of light, shining upon their way.
And thus I stand.

And standing thus, revolve
And tread this way the ways of men,
And know the ways of God.
And thus I stand.

9. Visualize a mountain covered with violet colored flowers, rising into an indigo sky. See a goat upon the mountain.
10. Say the Great Invocation
11. Sound the OM three times, holding your consciousness above the head. As you sound the OM, send an indigo light to the ajna center, then to the heart center, and from there to the throat center, seeing the three centers as a triangle. Offer salutations to Master R. and bless the world.
12. Do not move for three minutes, and do not speak for ten or fifteen minutes.

The following seed thoughts may be used for the Seventh Ray Meditation:

1. Ceremony
2. Magic
3. Ritual
4. Color
5. Sound
6. Glory
7. Organism
8. Order
9. Rhythm
10. Shrine
11. Money
12. Plan
13. Sacred Fire
14. Initiation
15. Alchemy
16. Economy
17. Mystery
18. Beauty
19. Energy distribution
20. Sharing
21. Five-pointed Star
22. All-seeing Eye
23. Manipulation of the Wand
24. Candidate
25. Hierophant
26. Door
27. Temple of Solomon

Those who feel they must serve in the field of economics and finance, and strangely enough, in the field of Free Masonry or ceremonial order, will make great progress meditating upon the seed thoughts given for this ray.

General Note

The time period for these meditations can range from fifteen to thirty minutes, but please remember that the time duration and seed thoughts are only guides.

You may choose your own seed thoughts according to your ray and you may set your time limit according to your ability, after careful consideration.

For further study on the Seven Rays, we recommend the books dictated by the Tibetan Master to Alice A. Bailey on this same subject:

The five volumes of *The Seven Rays*
A Treatise on Cosmic Fire
A Treatise on White Magic
Letters on Occult Meditation

Chapter VIII

MEDITATION ON THE PLAN

"There is a great Purpose behind this creation. Those who are able to contemplate upon that Purpose are building a LINE OF APPROACH to that great Purpose. This LINE OF APPROACH is called the PLAN for our planet, which can be recognized and lived as a path of least resistance toward the future. . . ."[1]

—Aquarian Educational Group

One certain way to establish communication with the Soul is to find what the Soul's plan is for us, individually.

We are told that the Soul is well informed concerning the Hierarchical Plan and that one of His tasks is to further that Plan through the individual whom He serves as a Silent Watcher and Guardian.

The individual plan of each person is a part of that great Hierarchical Plan, which in turn is an appropriation in time and space for the purpose of the Soul of the planet. To find the individual Plan means to find the path of least resistance in *conscious* evolution; to find the fountain of creativity, talent and genius within our being; to find the final Wielder of the plan and experience soul-infusion.[2]

This kind of meditation leads one to the realization of the brotherhood of humanity; develops a sense of responsibility; builds the courage to penetrate into the Plan of the Hierarchy and to become a servant of the Plan. Those who know the Hierarchical Plan are called co-workers. The great brotherly love which exists among them, encourages them to give sacrificial help to one another as they work together to further the Plan.

This meditation may be used once a week within your own meditation form. At that point where you begin to meditate on your usual seed thought (step 6), meditate instead on the subject of *your Soul's plan for you*. There are five progressive steps:

1. SILENCE is the process of cutting the conversation line between your personality vehicles and their corresponding spheres of expression through an increasing rate of radiation.[3]
2. LISTENING is the magnetic tension in which there is no conditioning thought.

---

1. Aquarian Educational Group, *The Creed of the Aquarian Educational Group*, par. 19.
2. Saraydarian, H., *The Science of Meditation*, Chap. XXX.
3. Saraydarian, H., *The Science of Becoming Oneself*, Chap. XIX.

3. Registration is the contact with a phase, or that part of the Plan related to you. It may be registered on the higher mental plane as pure impression, a great beauty, a challenge, a sense of responsibility, or it may register as only a slight hint.
4. Formulation is the process of adaptation of the sensed plan. It is that point where real meditation starts. It is the stage of personal relationship with the plan of the Soul. The success of a man's life depends upon the right formulation and adaptation of the plan as he senses it.
5. Expression is the putting into action of the formulated plan, relating it to your daily activities and expressing it practically in your daily relationships.

Using these five points will not exceed ten minutes. At the end of one year you may increase the time to twenty minutes. When you have completed that part of your meditation in which you have used the five steps, simply continue your own special form on the Ray line of your choice.

Chapter IX

RECHARGING AND HEALING MEDITATION

"Have you ever thought, my brother, that just as there is a discipline of pain and of sorrow, there may also be a discipline of joy and of achievement? This is a thought worthy of attention."[1]

—The Tibetan

With any of the preceding meditations you may use the following meditation to recharge your personality, to purify it of glamours and other hindrances, and to create a healing process in your body.

1. Relax your physical body.
2. Do the kneeling exercise (if you wish).
3. Align your three lower bodies.
4. Say the following Invocation:

   Lead me, O Lord,
   From darkness to Light,
   From the unreal to the Real,
   From death to Immortality,
   From chaos to Beauty.

5. Visualize one of the following:

   – An eagle of white light.
   – A sphere of pure blue light.
   – A five-pointed star in a glow of pure orange light twelve inches above your head.

6. Raise your consciousness into the light and fuse with it, remaining silent, mentally and emotionally. This will take five minutes or less.
7. You will start feeling the light penetrating your mental body and cleansing it of many kinds of limitations. Meditate upon what the limitations are and upon the fact that the light is clearing them from the mental body.
8. Feel the light penetrating into your astral sphere and purifying it of many emotional problems. At this point you need not think or meditate, just visualize the process of purification as it is taking place in the body.

---

1. Bailey, Alice A., *Discipleship in the New Age,* Vol. II, p. 671.

9. Feel the light penetrating into your etheric body and electrifying it, creating great harmony between the etheric body and the nervous and blood systems, recharging your whole body.
10. When you have done the above, immediately begin to visualize again; see the light of your Soul flooding all of your personality and radiating out into the room, into your office, to wherever you may be going.
11. Keep a minute of silence without imagination and thought.
12. Say the Great Invocation.

Warning

Do not exceed fifteen minutes in doing this meditation. If, later, you feel some unpleasant sensations, discontinue the meditation for a few days. The incoming energies may create friction with the crystallized ridges in your subtle bodies and cause some unpleasant or uneasy feelings. This does not happen when your bodies are in pure condition as they relate to each other, and when you are not creating thoughts and emotions in opposition to the radiating light, love and power of your Soul.

Chapter X

INTUITIONAL AWARENESS

"Tell those who find the trials cruel that their goal-fitness lies in whether the tempering of spirit progresses or retrogresses. . . . labor is ready for all desiring to progress."[1]

—M.M.

Man does not achieve without labour, without working on himself. The present mental capacity of man is the result of his endless labour.

The destiny of man is ever progressing development and unfoldment. Nature provides all possibilities; man must use these possibilities through labour and striving. Those who do not progress or surpass their former level of beingness, create hindrances and obstacles on the path of others who are striving toward expansion of awareness, and greater realizations.

The next step to be taken by humanity as a whole is to develop its faculty of intuition, and use it as a mechanism for closer contact with the One Reality.

In the past, the cultivation of the intuition was the major task of the Egyptian, Chaldean, Indian and Persian Initiates. They were the Ones Who, through expanding Their Teaching to Central America, South America and Europe, brought about great cultures and civilizations.

It is time now that advanced members of humanity start developing the faculty of intuition to bring about greater cultures and greater civilizations. It is only through the opening of the faculty of intuition that the traps, set by the mind in our modern civilization, can be by-passed; that the survival of humanity and the life of the planet as a whole can be guaranteed.

How can we develop intuitive awareness? The answer is simple; through the use of creative imagination and meditation on symbols, parables and music. This procedure requires great patience and labour.

As the student of the Wisdom starts this labour, he must collect many symbols from as many different sources as possible, and arrange them in whatever order he wishes. He may use actual, ready-made symbols or drawings of symbols.[2] When he has collected a considerable number, he must set a special time for his labour of *looking at them*, to see how they are formed, or drawn. This is not meditation proper; it is an act of *observation*.

---

1. Agni Yoga Society, *Agni Yoga*, par. 634.
2. A number of symbols and hints can be found in *The Science of Meditation* by H. Saraydarian, pp. 167–185.

After six months he must put all symbols aside and start collecting as many parables as possible from various sources—ancient and modern. This accomplished, he must follow the same procedure for the parables as he did for the symbols. He will place them in the desired order and *read them daily*, to familiarize himself with the exoteric side, the story side of the parables. He will continue with the reading for a period of one year without missing a single day.

The next labour concerns music. The student must make a collection of fine music and after arranging the recordings in order, he will *listen to them daily* for twenty or twenty-five minutes. The important point in listening will be to follow as closely as possible the variations in notes, pauses and rhythms. This will go on for another six months. At the end of these three periods, the real meditation will start.

This meditation will be done first on a parable, next on a symbol, and then on music. All these objects may be used at the same sitting, or they may be alternated; using a symbol one day, a parable the next, and music on the following day. If done separately, twenty-five minutes will be the *maximum* period for meditation.

Start with a Parable:

1. Sit in your special place of meditation.
2. Read the parable.
3. Recount it to yourself, silently, with eyes closed.
4. Read it again to be sure that you did not forget any part of it; if you are not sure of this, recount it again and again until you are sure you are thoroughly familiar with the content.
5. Then think along these lines: Does it have any other meaning? Can I apply it in my practical life? Does it open a door of new understanding for me? Can I understand things better through this parable? What is the purpose of this parable? Why was it written? Is my thinking influenced by this parable? Do I see any change in my attitude toward others, and toward life as a whole? Does it make me more sensitive to subtle impressions, hints and suggestions? Do I feel joy increasing within me? Do I feel an increasing energy in my physical body, in my positive emotions and thoughts? Does it reveal something hidden in my nature; a relationship, an event? Does it present a psychological law; a way to grow and unfold?

You may create many other questions if you wish, but the important thing is to give logical answers to these questions. The time limit for individual questions is up to you. You need not handle more than two questions at a time.

After you have dealt with the questions for a period of ten minutes, turn to your symbol and observe it for a few seconds. Close your eyes and try to imagine or visualize it. When you are able to imagine or visualize your symbol with reasonable success, close your eyes and start your meditation.

Think:

1. What does this symbol mean to me?
2. Can I see an abstract concept through this symbol?
3. Does it synthesize many concepts or ideas?
4. Does it open a path toward unity, or at-one-ment?
5. Can I use it as a formula to solve a problem?
6. Does it act as a magnetic station in my mind to attract new thoughts, ideas and visions?
7. What does it teach me?
8. Does it have a physical, an emotional or a mental meaning?
9. Does it turn a key to individual planetary, solar or cosmic mysteries?
10. Does it carry energy?
11. Does this energy change its expression as I change the color and the proportion of the parts of the symbol?
12. Can I see the mathematics behind it?

From this long list you may use only one question a day, or several, if you wish. Recording your findings in a note book will help you to see whether you are going deeper and deeper as you meditate.

The next step is to play your chosen music and try to find relationships among the parable, the symbol and the music. As you proceed in doing this, try to answer the following questions:

– How can I create a symbol which will tell the story of my parable?
– What story can I create to unveil the mystery of my symbol?
– What kind of music can I play to express the meaning of my parable and symbol?
– Can I recall any parable, symbol and music that fit together well?

In my book, *The Science of Meditation*, I gave some exercises on symbols. These exercises will help tremendously if the steps are followed as given on pages 173–181. The exercises must be performed separately from the meditation, at some other time of day. This particular meditation may be done as one unit, using all three objects at the same time, or it may be done separately, using the three objects in proper sequence. The mechanics of this form of meditation are such that they link the objective and subjective mind, the concrete and abstract mind, and relate them to the plane of intuition, to the plane of esoteric ideas and meanings. Once you establish a certain relationship between your twofold mind and the plane of intuition, you become an ever flowing fountain of inspiration and creativity; you expand your field of service not only on the concrete mental plane, but also in the subjective planes, through your thoughts, visions, and intuitive understanding.

Very often people cannot differentiate between intuition and many emotional and mental impressions. Intuition, says the Tibetan Sage, is synthetic understanding; a comprehensive grip of the principle of universality, and loss of the sense of separateness. It embodies Universal Love, and an identification with all beings. Intuition is light itself and enables one to contact the light center in all forms. Realization follows intuition. True self-actualization starts with intuition, because it is only through intuition that reality is seen and realized within oneself.

Intuition then reveals three great qualities, illumination, understanding and love; a love that "negates all that builds barriers, makes criticism and produces separation". "The Intuition concerns unity and is the capacity of the Self to contact other selves, and is not a faculty whereby the not-self is contacted." "An Intuition is an idea clothed in etheric substance, and the moment a man becomes responsive to those ideas, he can begin to master the technique of etheric control." ". . . It is the sense of synthesis, the ability to think in wholes, and to touch the world of causes." The destiny of the human soul is not only to master his physical, emotional and mental instruments, but also to penetrate into another kind of substance, the intuitional substance, to create a new mechanism of communication with the Cosmos and with the higher stations of the Cosmos.

After the human soul transcends his mental instrument, the great horizon of the Spiritual Triad opens before him. This means that the abstract mind, the world of Intuition and the world of Will are within his reach, within the range of his attainment. He has transcended the personal and is entering now into the universal and Cosmic.[3] This kind of meditation has been tested by the author with high school and college students with striking results. Their behavior, their attitude toward life, their ability to learn and to master were radically improved. Such teaching gives meaning to their lives, organizes their energies and opens the path for them to touch their transpersonal selves from which pours all joy and beauty.

---

3. Read *The Science of Becoming Oneself* by H. Saraydarian, pp. 138–141.

Chapter XI

VISUALIZING THE MASTER

"If you can visualize the image of the Teacher in your consciousness with the most complete detail, you can transform your consciousness into His, and thus act seemingly through His power."[1]

—M.M.

Visualizing the Master is an advanced technique which can be used after a man realizes that he is a Soul-infused personality with pure motives, and his life is directed toward service for humanity. Any impurity in the mental, emotional and even in the physical body, can create complications when greater energies are contacted through meditation, and especially through visualizing the Master.

The Tibetan Master wrote about this teaching on September 21, 1920, in *Letters on Occult Meditation* in which he says:

> "As you know, the student has often been told to visualize himself and the Master—about the size of a quarter inch—within the circumference of the etheric heart. He is told to picture, toward the close of his meditation, the heart etheric, and therein build minute forms of the Master to Whom he is drawn and of himself. This he proceeds to do with due and elaborate care, with the aid of the imagination and loving effort, working daily on his figures until they become to him very real, and their building and forming becomes almost an automatic part of his meditation form. Then comes a day . . . when he becomes conscious *within his brain* that these figures are not the little puppets he thinks, but that he is within the figure representing himself, and that he stands literally and in all verity before the Master. This occurs at rare intervals at first, and the consciousness of the fact is held but for a few brief seconds; as progress is made, and every department of his nature and of his service develops, with greater frequency will come the experience, with longer periods will it be marked, until there comes a time when the pupil can link up as easily in this manner with his Master as earlier he formed his figures."[2]

The same teaching regarding this technique was given by M.M. in 1931 in *Hierarchy*:

---

1. Agni Yoga Society, *Hierarchy*, par. 90.
2. Bailey, Alice A., *Letters on Occult Meditation*, pp. 289–290.

> "... for this one must visualize the Image of the Teacher with utmost precision, even to the minutest detail, so that the Image should not falter, nor suffer distortion, nor change its outline, as frequently happens. But, if following the exercise of concentration, one succeeds in invoking a constant Image of the Teacher, through this one may gain benefit for oneself, for one's nearest ones and for the works." [3]

The Master also speaks about the technique of visualization:

> "When your consciousness prompts you to the necessity of possessing the constant Image of the Lord, retire to a quiet place and direct your sight upon the selected Image. But remember, one must decide irrevocably, because in case of treason the constant Image will be as a constant reproach. After an intense study of the Image, close your eyes and transmit it to the third eye. Thus exercising, you will attain a vivid Image and you will feel a special intensified tremor of the heart. Soon the Image of the Lord will remain inseparably with you. You can test yourself before the sun and you will still see the Lord before you, sometimes without color but afterwards vividly and even in action. Your prayer will lose the need of words and only tremor of the heart will suffuse your understanding. Thus one may reach in life much of the useful, but consciousness must correspond to it." [4]

For further information concerning the technique of visualization and the third eye, please read Chapter XXIII in *The Science of Meditation.*[5]

MEDITATION FORM FOR VISUALIZING THE MASTER

To use this technique of visualizing the Master in meditation, the following form should be used for at least a few years. When you have achieved success in the visualization, you may work out your own technique and your own manner of approach to your Master.

1. Relax your body.
2. Focus your consciousness in the higher mental plane.
3. Visualize the etheric heart center, twelve inches away from your body in line with the area between the shoulder blades, but slightly closer to your left shoulder.
4. Visualize the heart as a twelve-petaled rose or lotus. From its center radiates an electric blue light, slowly filling your threefold personality vehicles, purifying them and raising their vibrations.
5. Begin building the Image of your Master. Viewing a picture of Him several times a day will make the constructing of the Image easier. Try to remember

---

3. Agni Yoga Society, *Hierarchy*, par. 90.
4. *Ibid.*, par. 89.
5. Saraydarian, H., *The Science of Meditation*, Chap. XXIII.

His features as accurately as possible. By doing this during the day or before the mediation, it will gradually be easier to visualize His Image.

6. Once the Image starts to form, relax yourself more and more, taking deeper and deeper breaths, but keeping your concentration on the Image. Sometimes it may form and then disappear, or it may change and become a different image. Do not feel irritated, but with serenity and joy bring back your concentration and build again. Joy and serenity are important in this process. They are the creators of the right conditions in which this work is possible without danger or damage.
7. When the Image of your Lord is built, build one of yourself and then raise the two images together to the heart center in your head. Try to see them through your third eye instead of through your two etheric eyes. This will be of great help in focussing the images and making them appear translucent. At this point the Master's Image may take action and you may see Him blessing you or teaching you about deeper beauties on the Path. When such communication is achieved, we say that the Silver Thread between the Master and the pupil is established and the pupil is now ready to be a World Server, standing for one humanity. The appearance of the Image may last a very short time at first, but the energy and inspiration will last for months or years.
8. After the Image fades away, or even if it remains before your eyes, start your meditation, for meditation is the closest communication with your Master.
9. Meditate on a certain seed thought for fifteen minutes, in the light of your Master. In so doing you may greatly enlighten your mind and become a pure channel for wisdom, joy and beauty.
10. At the close of your meditation say the *Gayatri*[6] and sound seven OMs. Then relax for ten minutes and go about your daily duties in peace.

The following seed thoughts are suggested (step 9):

1. Love
2. Gratitude
3. Joy
4. Bliss
5. Serenity
6. Patience
7. Endurance
8. Humility
9. Service
10. Tolerance
11. Compassion
12. Wisdom
13. Blessings
14. Sacrifice

6. The Gayatri in Sanskrit:

"OM—Bhur, bhuva, Svah!
Tat savitur varenyam
Bhargo devasya dhimahi,
Dhiyo yonat prachodayat."

The literal translation reads:

OM—all that are on Earth
mid-World and Heaven
Let us think
about the Light adorable,
of the divine Sun of Life
which may Enlighten our souls.

15. Courage
16. Daring
17. Striving
18. Solemnity
19. Purity
20. Oneness
21. Hierarchy
22. Christ
23. Brotherhood
24. Understanding
25. Contact

Each seed thought should be used for seven meditations before choosing a new one. When all of the above list has been taken into meditation, begin over again in the same manner.

WARNINGS CONCERNING THIS MEDITATION

In presenting an advanced technique such as this one involving visualization of the Master, some warnings must be given:

1. The exercise must be stopped immediately if pain is felt in the heart, the head or the eyes; if one experiences palpitation of the heart, indigestion or shivering. Such conditions indicate that enough purity to stand under the pressure released by the visualization has not yet been achieved. Give yourself a little more time. "Put your house more in order," and when the symptoms have passed, begin again, wisely and slowly.
2. During this period of special visualization, the disciple must avoid sexual relations, meat, alcohol, any kind of hallucinatory drugs, or smoking; he should live in a quiet and pure place where the air is clean and the psychic atmosphere is pure.
3. If the disciple feels the need to speak to another about the results of his meditation or visualization, it should be only to a very trusted person. Otherwise he should remain silent concerning the experience.
4. The disciple must be aware of the fact that he can do great harm to himself and others if he indulges in idle speech, harmful thoughts and negative emotions after such a meditation. He can protect himself only with love, serenity, tolerance, joy and gratitude. If these qualities are lacking, he is in danger physically and mentally.
5. It must be strongly emphasized that such a meditation must not be done out of curiosity or selfishness, but out of sincere aspiration to serve humanity and only after due preparation in purity, knowledge and realization.
6. This meditation should not be performed daily, but once a month at full moon time. Forcing your nature by pulling strong energies down upon yourself before you are ready to handle them, may bring dire consequences. The technique can be very safe for those who have successfully used the meditations on the Will and on the Rainbow Bridge as given in *The Science of Becoming Oneself.*[7]

7. Saraydarian, H., *The Science of Becoming Oneself*, pp. 141–156; 183–220.

Chapter XII

THE CYCLES OF SOUL INFLUENCE

"When the vitalizing force is contacting at stated periods a certain set of atoms, it will call forth from them a specific sound which will demonstrate objectively as environing circumstances."[1]

—The Tibetan

The Presence within man observes various cycles to make His guidance felt by man, who is active on physical, emotional and mental planes.

We have Planetary cycles, Lunar cycles, Solar cycles, Zodiacal cycles and many others that come into existence because of the different configurations of heavenly bodies.

One of the cycles that affects the average man more closely than others is the Lunar cycle. From the new moon to the full moon, the inner Presence makes a special endeavor to reach the unfolding human soul and evoke a greater response to light, to love and to divine Will. The moon cycle is also utilized by some churches and esoteric groups to create a new spiritual polarization, a higher sensitivity to spiritual energies released in such cycles.

Our Solar System is a unit. This unit is controlled, kept alive and directed toward a Cosmic goal through the instrumentality of energies. It is like an organism, which receives different kinds of energies, transmutes them, assimilates them, and then expresses them. It is this process that keeps the Solar System alive and furthers Solar evolution; the evolution of each atom, cell and being in the Solar field.

This great organism, which also acts as a single organ within a greater whole, exists in a Solar electromagnetic field. In this energy field there are many *problem producing factors*, which create disturbances within the field, cause difficulties within the Solar organism, and interfere with the process of receiving, assimilating and expressing these energies. For example, meteors, comets, electromagnetic storms in the Solar space, disintegrating bodies (of which we have quite a number in our Solar System)—all of these create an imbalance of energies and cause disturbances in the receiving mechanism. Bodies which are in process of growth and unfoldment have a different kind of radio transmission than the bodies that are in the process of decay.

Radiation coming from evolving and blooming bodies, creates health, alignment, unfoldment and freedom. Emanations coming from decaying bodies, or

1. Bailey, Alice A., *A Treatise on Cosmic Fire*, p. 273.

from "points of corruption," create disturbances, cleavages and disintegration. In human beings these emanations create selfishness, destructive speech, negativity and nationalism.

MOON INFLUENCES

The moons in our Solar System constitute one of the problem producing factors. Because of the fact that they are decaying and disintegrating organs in the Solar organism, they create tremendous complications and difficulties in the process which we call the energy receiving, assimilating and expressing process of the Solar organism. The same is true in a Solar sense, because there are many constellations which are in the process of disintegration and which, therefore, have a "malefic effect upon our System."

When various constellations or planets and the sun form a certain cyclic configuration, they channel powerful energies and produce ample insulation against decaying organs. In this way hindrances caused by disintegrating bodies can be overcome to a relative degree, and the energies safely received on earth without pollution. We have such powerful alignments for the Full Moon of Aries, Taurus and Gemini, and in lesser degree for each full moon.

Our moon is a decaying organ in the Solar System and, as such, it is a problem producing factor for the earth specifically, and for the Solar System in general. As a decaying organ within our body affects the body by hindering the circulatory flow of various electromagnetic energies, so the decaying moon disturbs, pollutes and hinders energies on their way to our earth. There are cycles in which this condition is met and handled in a way that the decaying body is insulated and the hindrance is relatively absent for a period of fourteen days each month. This starts at the *new moon* when the Solar radiation slowly overpowers the moon. At the time of each *full moon*, it is totally insulated, and energies coming from the different constellations or from various planets bypass the disturbing factors of the moon and reach our planet earth.

Throughout the ages, those who knew about the cycles, planned new moon and full moon meditation periods to help us reorient our whole being toward the Inner Light, the radiant Presence in each man, and to build a new channel of communication for light, love and power. This is the period when a man puts away all problem producing factors within himself, such as his illusions, glamours, inertia and negative emotions.

UNIVERSALITY OF CYCLES

In Cosmos, in the Solar System, and on the earth we have the problem producing factor of decaying bodies or organs. The same is true within our own spheres. A negative emotion, a criminal thought, a fear, a jealousy or an act of selfishness is nothing but a disintegrating and disturbing force-wave within our electromagnetic sphere. Starting with the new moon, because of inflowing Solar and stellar energies, a man can insulate these factors, and build a communication line between his physical, emotional, mental nature and the Spiritual Presence within.

He can then extend this communication line first toward the Wise Ones of all Ages, and then toward the Life ensouling our planet and using it as His body.

In some esoteric books we read that our Planetary Life enters into Its cyclic meditation at the time of the new moon. In the full moon period It reaches the highest point of Its tension, and at the exact moment of the full moon, It contacts the Solar Life, in the body of Whom our Planetary Life acts as one of Its centers. The ever extending golden bridge of communication does not end here. The Solar Life in Its turn contacts those Lives (constellations) that form a special configuration in relation to our Solar System. Thus a superb alignment is set up from man to the planet, to the Solar Life, and on to Cosmic Lives. When this alignment is achieved there comes a pouring down of energies from lofty Spiritual Beings and great Lives.

It is under such conditions that a window suddenly opens in our consciousness, and for a moment a flash of revelation strikes our Soul. We see, for a short moment, the reason for our being here and our responsibilities toward life as a whole. Relationships with greater spheres and energies expand our consciousness, expand our awareness and deepen our sense of responsibility, because these incoming energies are impressed by the Plan, the Purpose, and visions of Great Ones. The degree of our receptivity and assimilation depends on the degree of the alignment of our threefold personality with the inner Presence, and on the mental focus at the time of full moon meditation.

The same is true of the Planetary Life and Solar Life. If the kingdoms of nature have achieved better alignment and harmony, our Planetary Logos can draw more energy and distribute it into His system in a more beneficial way.

For the Planetary Life there is another reason for such contact. We are told that once a month the impressions that our Planetary Life receives are highly charged with Cosmic Revelations on which He appropriates His own plans for planetary life, and kingdoms. These new appropriations release new concepts, new ideas, new visions, and new responses in humanity as a whole. We are told that at the time of the full moon, especially the Full Moon of Aries, Taurus and Gemini, a globular and Solar meditation is going on. All advanced human beings and great Initiates are in intensive meditation at this time, taking advantage of this special planetary and solar alignment, to illuminate and charge Their nature, making it totally creative.[2]

INFLUENCE ON THE INDIVIDUAL

Esoteric tradition says that the highest alignment with the Solar Life is achieved at the time of Taurus Full Moon. The Hierarchy, the Brotherhood of the Masters, starts Its preparation for this occasion in December, at that time when the sun moves northward. This long period of preparation enables Them to absorb the incoming energies, to radiate them to humanity and to all kingdoms of nature.

2. Read *The Science of Meditation* by H. Saraydarian, pp. 333–364.

As the moon wanes during the period from the full moon to the new moon, the disturbing factors gain power, and their influence is felt by humanity, and other kingdoms. This influence can be avoided if, during the waxing phase of the moon, a man charges himself with enough energy to reject all negative influences with his own radiation during the waning period. Energy is accumulated through meditation which is a process of contact with the Presence in man.

Sometimes people wonder why, at full moon time, many violent disturbances occur in patients of mental hospitals and even in the average man. The reason is that, because of such cyclic alignment, the energies pour down upon humanity as a whole and stimulate its nature. These energies are attracted to and received by the more active and receptive etheric centers, causing them to become overactive and highly demanding. They also create friction if they are deflected and disturbed in the organism, due to decaying conditions and other problem producing factors, such as damaged nervous systems and glands or emotional and mental conditions which disturb the incoming energies, pollute them, and create a state of imbalance in the energy field of human beings.

All of these conditions affect the behavior of people and present them with difficult situations to be faced and handled. It is not the moon that is causing these disturbances. They are the result of the reaction of man's distorted physical and psychic mechanism to the incoming energies. The Tibetan Master says that

> "As the moon becomes small through the process of disintegration, its effect upon the Earth will be correspondingly lessened, and this stage will be paralleled by a consequent greater freedom from evil impulse of the sons of men." [3]

Ancient tradition tells us that the emotional sphere of the moon is also in the process of decomposition, and it is at the dark phase of the moon that this disintegrating astral body affects the emotional nature of our world humanity, because the astral body of our Planetary Life is still fused with the Lunar astral body. This is the reason that we have so many emotional disturbances which seriously affect our brain and nervous system and lead us to separative, hateful and criminal actions, when the energies precipitated at the time of the full moon strike us. Man can use the cycles for his own and global benefit by organizing group meditations during the full moon days, channeling these energies, and using them creatively.

At each full moon our Solar Presence within us observes these cycles, and tries to reach man, to kindle the flame that will light his way toward freedom, compassion, peace, and spiritual creativity. We must extend our hand to our Guide, especially at the full moon meditation period, and stand within His Light, expressing it as the energy of blessings to all humanity. It is through such a closeness that Soul-infusion can be achieved, and the path toward Mastery can be paved.

---

3. Bailey, Alice A., *A Treatise on Cosmic Fire*, p. 795.

Chapter XIII

EXPANSION OF AWARENESS AT WESAK

"No cost is too great to pay in order to be of use to the Hierarchy at the time of the Full Moon of May, the Wesak Festival; no price is too high in order to gain spiritual illumination which can be possible, particularly at that time."[1]

—The Tibetan

It is a great joy to us and to the Watching One, that people all over the world, individually or in group formation, are observing the Wesak Festival and building a channel to receive and pass to humanity the energy of spiritual will, love and enlightenment.[2]

ENERGY FIELDS

At this time, as the Full Moon is approaching, the Great Ones, the Initiates and disciples are forming a great field of energy in the Himalayas, through their meditation, contemplation, mystical and sacred rituals, and through Their great striving, invocations and contacts.

This is the field which will be charged more and more by the presence of Christ, and through the blessings of the Great Lord Buddha; it will provide a chalice for cosmic energy, and a channel through which these energies can pass to the kingdoms of nature.

This energy field is formed of the four cosmic ethers and, as a huge cloud formation, spreads itself all over the world.

All those who are sensitive enough to this energy field, will slowly notice that seeds of great beauty, truth and goodness start to bloom within their hearts. All those who love their fellow man, all those who really work for the unity of mankind, who really strive beyond their physical satisfactions to reach and touch this field of energy, will be impressed by new age visions, ideas and goals.

When all these people work in their own fields and in their own ways to express these energies, they will create another field of energy which we may call the "Hope of Humanity."

This second field of energy is created whenever a man with pure motives, through striving, opens himself to the energy field created by the Hierarchy. Eventually these two fields will fuse within each other and humanity will be flooded with new inspiration, and with new drives for greater creativity.

---

1. Bailey, Alice A., *Discipleship in the New Age,* Vol. I, p. 629.
2. For further information on Wesak see *The Science of Meditation* by H. Saraydarian, pp. 349–358.

From ancient times, great Sages have set aside definite days in the year for fasting, for prayer, for rest, for striving, for meditation, and They called these days "Holy Days." To make holy means to set something apart to be used for a greater purpose. On these holy days, people used to extend themselves beyond the limit of their past achievements. They tried to contact greater beauties, to bring more joy, more unity and peace to the world of men.

In the new age people will consider the New-Moon and Full-Moon periods as special days, and the three major Full Moons, namely, the Full Moons of Aries, Taurus and Gemini, the holy days of the year.

The greatest moment of contact of the year will be recognized as the Day of the Wesak Full Moon, the day on which the three great centers on the planet, Humanity, Hierarchy and the Father's Home are linked and fused with cosmic centers, thus releasing potent energies over our planet earth.

The energies about which we are speaking are coming from the sun Sirius, from the Great Bear, from the constellation of Taurus, and especially from that great star, Aldebaran, which is shining as the Eye of the Bull. Esoteric sources say that these are the Great Lives which are focussing Their energies at this time on our Planetary Logos, Sanat Kumara, Shamballa, and the Hierarchy through which the energies will be radiated out and spread throughout all ranks of Initiates, disciples, aspirants and humanity in general, as well as the lower kingdoms of the planet.

These three Great Lives, or Constellations, are channels for the energy of enlightenment, love, compassion, and will-power. This time is unique because of the combinations of these energies and the effect of these combinations upon the nature of the human being. Where these three energies are available, our whole nature responds to them. All three kinds of Monads (First, Second and Third Ray Monads) and all the other types of rays are involved and affected by such combinations.

EXPANSION OF CONSCIOUSNESS AND AWARENESS

The flow of energies and the registration of these energies, their assimilation by our nature and the measure of the expansion of consciousness, depend on the level upon which consciousness is focussed and active. For example, the expansion of consciousness of a Master will be, let us say, one hundred miles, but the expansion of the consciousness of a little man will be three yards—so to say.

As you stand on higher levels, on higher planes, you are more in touch with higher energies and because of the relationships of these energies with the higher planes, you experience continuity of consciousness, that great bridging process which opens before your eyes the oceanic splendor of your inner being. If you are focussed on the emotional level, expansion will be different than when you are focussed on the intuitional level.

The registration, the assimilation and the radiation of these energies depend upon the condition of the centers in our etheric body. When a man is focussed within the lower centers, below the diaphragm, these centers will be stimulated more, and become more active. If the higher centers are active, they will receive more energy and will be more active. When the higher centers are more active, you are expanding yourself into greater relationships, into better communication, and because of this communication you have more power, more energy, more enlightenment and more love.

As the processes of registration and assimilation of energies proceed, we build new relationships with the world, with the physical, emotional and mental worlds, and these relationships expand our consciousness. A man who is living a very simple life in a village has some degree of consciousness, but if he comes to a large city and involves himself with many activities, relationships and responsibilities, his consciousness does not remain the same. His consciousness expands because of many relationships and the problems that these relationships present to him. We may say that at these Full Moons, if we make the needed preparation, we will really expand our consciousness because we will see things more clearly and in better relationship on these three levels of human endeavour, the physical, emotional and mental fields.

What is happening today is not a means to expand only our consciousness, but also to expand our *awareness*. We hear much about expanding our consciousness, but very little about expanding our awareness. Awareness is a matter of direct experience, of knowing through identification, of opening to the sunshine and becoming one with it. It is an awakening to the Real Life, to the function of that Great Life. It is experiencing both the form side of life and the formless side; experiencing the manifested side of life and the unmanifested side; the blueprint of this manifestation and the energy of this manifestation. Actually we are building a bridge between the objective and subjective worlds, between the world of cause and the world of effect.

The cause is the realm of awareness. You become aware of the cause, and then you become aware of the effect through your consciousness. This consciousness necessitates reasoning, analysis, induction, deduction, comparison, and so on. Awareness does not need these things. You are aware because you are *in the world of causes*. Nothing from the world of effects, affects your clarity of vision. You can go from the effect to the cause, but the cause *is*, and from the causal plane you can easily see what is happening on the plane of effects, without being affected by it.

When your awareness expands more and more, you see the Divine Will behind the causes. You can see also the direct or distorted effects of these causes. When you become aware of energies, aware of immortality, aware of the continuity of life, aware of joy, peace, love and beauty, you see that they were there all the time, but that now you have awakened and become aware of their existence, aware of the fact that they belong to your own greater nature, that they are parts of your nature. Thus, awareness leads to realization. Consciousness puts into expression this awareness upon the three worlds of human endeavor, through creative living, and as the consciousness expands, it does a better job in translating the content, the beauty and the richness of awareness.

At the time of the Wesak Full Moon, we have a great opportunity to clean our etheric, emotional and mental bodies—to clean dark and blind urges from within our etheric body, the glamours or negative emotions and supressions from our astral body, illusions and muddy thinking from our minds, and to stand in the light of our spiritual awareness. At the time of the Full Moon of Taurus a window opens through which man reaches a very high level of realization because of a great revelation which dawns in his awareness. If he achieves the needed alignment and integration for a moment, infinity opens to him, speaks to him. He senses for one moment that he IS and that Cosmos IS; that he is part of Cosmos, that he is one with Cosmos; that all his despair and all his separativeness, which are the cause of his misery, disappear.

The steps which lead to this awareness are three:

ONE: *Man steps out of his mental consciousness through the help of his Inner Guide* and, for the first time, he senses tremendous synthesis, a tremendous sense of unity, a tremendous clarity of vision. This is a sign that he is entering into the awareness of the intuitional plane. As he enters into the intuitional plane, he feels the energy of the Great Lord Buddha because the aura, or the influence of that Great Lord, is penetrating and active at this time, especially on the buddhic plane, the intuitional plane.

The disciple senses not only the energy of the Enlightened One, but he senses also the great Light which is the source of the intuitional or buddhic plane, the Constellation of Taurus. For one second the Eye of the Bull radiates in his soul. This is the reason that Taurus is the powerful Bull, related to Buddha and the intuitional plane where the Plan of the Hierarchy substantiates. Symbolically then, the Plan is the Bull rushing with great light and power into manifestation.

We know that love is pure reason, enlightenment, and pure understanding. Actually, the word *buddhi* means understanding in the causal level. For this reason the Great Lord is called the Lord of Compassion, Understanding and Buddha, the Enlightened One.

Lord Buddha draws His energy from the constellation of Taurus, the Light Bearer. I would say that His permanent location is on a higher plane, but at this time of Wesak, He descends onto the intuitional plane and makes us aware of His existence; He builds a bridge for us for a greater contact.

TWO: *If a man has done the needed meditation and disciplining of his life*; if he has purified his heart and truly sincerely wants to serve humanity and to sacrifice for humanity, he will be granted accordingly a longer or shorter stay in a greater sphere of awareness which is technically called the atmic plane or nirvanic awareness.

When the Great Lord entered into nirvana, that was the sphere of awareness which He penetrated, and that is the goal of each human being in this Chain, in this cycle of evolution. As a man progresses into the ocean of such awareness, he registers the energy of the Great Bear and his life becomes a tremendous beauty of light and love, peace and serenity. Buddha has stood for ages as a path through which man may achieve, He has stood for ages as a beacon to lead humanity from darkness to light.

The atmic plane is the plane of compassion, peace, deep serenity, and divine harmony. As we develop these virtues, we prepare ourselves to enter into this sphere and eventually work there in total awakeness.

THREE: *If a man has done well; if he has disciplined his tongue, his body, his emotions and mind; if he has cleared his karma,* which means that he has paid his debts and that he owes no debts to others on the three levels, then he is granted entrance into the sphere of the monadic plane for a longer or shorter period of time where he receives the divine shock that *he IS*; that, *he is the Self, one with the Cosmos.*

At this stage, we are told that all that man has cherished throughout ages, all that for which he has spent his time, energy and life, disappears, and man enters into Freedom. He is now the detached one. The energy that he feels is the energy of Sirius, the rays of which guide him from the human kingdom to the Kingdom Divine; he becomes a member of the Hierarchy and a member of the Great Lodge on Sirius. He is now a Master because he has mastered his life.

BUILDING COMMUNICATIONS

Thus the Wesak Festival is building a golden bridge between the physical, emotional, mental, intuitional, atmic, monadic and divine planes. Actually, the Wesak ceremony is a great labour of building a communication line between matter and spirit, or among the seven planes of existence. The ceremonies that the Masters are performing with advanced Initiates and disciples is a process to create a tremendous electromagnetic field, to invoke, to evoke, to receive, to assimilate and radiate these energies on all planes, not only on the human level but also upon all the seven cosmic physical planes. For example, when They form the five-pointed star, chant certain mantrams, and expand Their antennas (Their antahkarana or the group antahkarana) into the higher cosmic ethers, They absorb the energy of Sirius.

They make seven formations as They form these seven symbols:

1. A circle.
2. A circle with a point at the center.
3. Two circles and a cross within the inner circle.
4. A triangle within a circle.
5. A triangle with three petals superimposed and extending beyond the three sides of the triangle.
6. The six-pointed star.
7. The five-pointed star.

These seven symbols also refer to the seven rays, the seven planes and seven centers. Basically these seven symbols are evolved from the three original symbols. We have three basic rays and three basic types of Monads:

— First Ray Monads and the First Ray
— Second Ray Monads and the Second Ray
— Third Ray Monads and the Third, the Synthesizing Ray.

The three basic symbols are:

— The cross
— The triangle
— The circle

It seems to me that the cross is the esoteric symbol of our Planetary Logos, our Divinity. The triangle is the esoteric symbol of the Buddha as He relates the Logos to Hierarchy, or Christ. The circle is the esoteric symbol of Christ, the perfect Man. Strangely enough, the cross placed within the circle, forms the symbol of our planet.

You remember, for example, Christ was carrying the cross on His shoulders and going to the mountain of crucifixion to be crucified on the cross. This is a very symbolic, meaningful ceremony, or event, in which Christ is carrying the Will of God, the Will of the Planetary Logos. On top of the mountain of achievement and sacrifice, He is giving Himself up totally, sacrificing Himself totally to the Divinity, to the cross. Actually churches erred when they held that the cross was the symbol of Christ or Christianity, because the cross was in existence many thousands of years ago, long before Christianity.

Now, the Masters, Initiates and disciples are using the three original symbols in different arrangements. Let us say They are arranging different "electron tubes" in different formations and relationships as they use these live symbols to attract energies of specific constellations, tuning in with these various super radio stations.

As they change the symbolic formations, they create different communications, or fusions. A constellation is active within a sphere of seven planes, and each plane has its own special frequency and radiant beauty. The Masters perform scientifically accurate symbolic formations so that they may draw energy from the level they wish; combine those energies that are needed at that particular moment of world conditions with those energies that can be used for future possibilities; appropriate and store these energies in special levels and centers to be radiated out or distributed in right proportion to all kingdoms of nature, according to their need.

We can see that these great ones are not dancing or performing artistic movements, but are creating channels of communication, selection and distribution. The main purpose of these ceremonies is to clear the channels of divine circulatory flow in all kingdoms, and to condition the progress of each atom of each cell, and each living form, on the path of liberation, expansion and initiation. They are breaking the barriers of limitation and disunity, barriers on physical, emotional and mental planes—dispelling the fog, the mist, the smog and letting the energy in for purification, progress and freedom.

EVOLUTIONARY PROGRESSIONS

I said that Christ is going to replace Buddha. Does this statement deny the Divinity of Christ? On the contrary. A Divinity Who is not able to progress and surpass Himself is dead and does not exist. A Divinity is sensed and recognized only through those who are progressing toward Him. We can see God when He is in the process of greater unfoldment; when upon each stage of His development He radiates more beauty, more power and more bliss. Every man is divine. Nothing exists in Cosmos which is not from Him. This is what He meant when He said, "Greater things you will do than I have done."

The Wesak ceremony will not continue in the near future as it now stands. Great Lord Buddha, Who is the Bridge between the center where the Will of God is known and the center which is formed by all Great Ones, will graduate from our planetary ring-pass-not and enter into Solar evolution. The Ancient Wisdom teaches that each atom, each cell, each living form, is advancing toward planetary, Solar and Cosmic evolution.

We are told in esoteric literature that Lord Buddha and Lord Christ will graduate in the very near future from the planetary "high school," enter into "solar college" and then into the kindergarten of Cosmic evolution. Again, we are told that Lord Buddha will leave this planet and Christ will not only be the bridge between humanity and the Hierarchy, but also the bridge between the Hierarchy and the Center where the Will of God is known. The Tibetan Master says that the Great Lord Christ decided in 1945 to stay with Humanity another two thousand years to push forward the evolution of humanity until humanity creates true peace and finds its way toward Infinity.

HOW TO PARTICIPATE IN WESAK

Can we participate in the living ritual in the Himalayas? First let me say that according to the Ancient Wisdom, events take place on various planes of existence. We have our physical world, a subtle plane which is called the emotional plane, a mental sphere, the intuitional sphere, and three other higher spheres. Now, to be able to communicate with these spheres you need two important things. First you must have the needed vehicle that can be used on that plane. For example, if you want to visit your friend in the city, you use your car. Your car is your transportation tool on the physical plane. If you want to visit a friend on an island, you can use your boat or an airplane. If you want to go to the moon or to other planets, you use your space ship. The same is true with the subjective travel. If you want to enter into the emotional plane you must know how to use your emotional mechanism. If you want to enter into the deeper worlds you must use your mental vehicle.

The Wesak Festival is performed in one of the sacred valleys of the Himalayas. It is performed on the physical, emotional, mental and intuitional levels. If you have only a physical vehicle you will see the physical part of it; if you have an emotional vehicle, and if your emotional world is pure enough, you will see the emotional aspect too; if your mental vehicle is built, you can see the mental equivalent of that event, but if your intuitional vehicle is built you can see the whole beauty of Wesak. You can see Cosmic beams of light operating; you can see the whole process of transformation taking place within the electromagnetic field which the Masters have created in the valley; you can see the radiation which is relating the event with all disciples everywhere; you can see the Great Lords attending in Their very subtle bodies, and eventually, you will be able to see the electric wall which surrounds the valley for many miles and repels all those who try to enter the Festival, but who are not ready.

The second prerequisite is continuity of consciousness. Some pure souls can watch the Festival from a distance led by their intense aspiration, but when they come back to their normal life they cannot remember anything, though they still have the bliss and joy within themselves. Continuity of consciousness is achieved when man succeeds in building that bridge which connects the psychological gap between the lower and the higher mind, or between the awakening consciousness and the superconsciousness. Now if you want to attend such events, you must start purifying your bodies and build the golden bridge, through esoteric meditation. I wrote about the technique of bridge building in the books, *The Science of Becoming Oneself* and *The Science of Meditation.*

If we are not yet ready to participate factually in the Festival, how can we draw some benefit from it and live a more meaningful life?

On our level of development it is not too important to be in the valley. It may even harm us if we force ourselves and we may develop psychological and physical problems as the result of overstimulation. The wisest thing for aspirants and disciples of the future to do is to set aside these seven days of Wesak as the most holy days of their lives and use them to work upon themselves. These seven days are the three days before the day of Wesak, the Wesak day itself, and the three days following Wesak.

I would suggest that the three days preceding Wesak must be dedicated to holy living, purification, sublimation and transformation. On Wesak day, total orientation towards beauty, goodness and truth must be maintained. This is the day of contact. First, you contact your own soul. Next, the eyes of your Master are focussed upon you for a second, and then you feel the great energies penetrating into your system, causing some degree of transfiguration, after which you will make great decisions to change your life into higher levels of living.

During the next three days you will bless others; you will radiate your love, your compassion, to all living beings, to the whole of humanity—accepting humanity as a great brotherhood, as the beloved child of God. If you do this year after year, you will see yourself going toward the sunny mountains of achievement and you will become a life-giver, a joy-giver, a giver of health, love and beauty.

RESULTS OF PARTICIPATION

How can we use the Will-to-Good energy which is pouring in at this time? This is a powerful energy emanating from the Center where the Will of God is known, or from the Father's House, as Christ said. This energy can be attracted and used by all those who love their fellow human beings and who are filled with compassion toward life as a whole. When a man touches this energy, he becomes a man of goodwill and lives a life of right human relations. You can touch this energy of the Will-to-Good, increasing the dynamic heart quality within yourself and cleansing yourself from all separative thoughts and negative emotions. Once you do this, you will be ready to touch the ray of that energy, absorb it according to your capacity and radiate it out to your fellow men, healing all separative walls and sicknesses of the mind, emotions and body.

This will pave the way for the New World Religion, which will emerge slowly. The most important step toward the New World Religion is removing all separative walls among the existing religions and seeing the common denominator, or the golden thread, running through all of them. When this is done, we will see that all religions were instructions to humanity from the same source. It is only the merchants of religion who spoiled the purity of religions, creating hatred and pollution among them. Eventually we will see that the New World Religion will be not only an emotional appeal but also a scientific and true spiritual appeal toward the Fountain of Life. We will scientifically communicate not only with the departed ones, but with Great Masters, with Great Lives in space, with the Lives living in great galaxies, and so on. This is what the New World Religion will be—an enormous expansion and communication with manifold Cosmos.

The Wesak Festival is the greatest step toward this achievement. As we are told, the great Founders of all religions are present in the Wesak Valley, chanting and performing the ceremonies which will bring Cosmic energies into our world. The Tibetan Master says that it will be at one of the Wesak Festivals that the reappearance of the Christ will occur. He will come and give us the new Teaching of the New Age. Actually the symbolic rituals create a tremendous communication line among humanity, and between Christ and the Center where the Will-of-God is known.

Without going into detail, we can say that different energies are drawn and expressed by different formations. Such formations act as magnets and transmitters. For example, the triangle, or pyramid, attracts different energy than the five-pointed star, and they each release the energy received into different levels or planes. These formations have various functions:

1. They attract energies.
2. They fuse them.
3. They radiate them in proper channels to further the evolution of humanity.

All these forces will be greatly accelerated after the year 1975. The Tibetan Master says that at the Wesak of 1975, "a powerful energy will be released upon humanity," and as the result of this release, man will be able to break through the wall of his ignorance, the chains of his hatreds and separativeness, and the prison of his physical limitations. These achievements will not happen at once; it will take labour and striving to cooperate with and use these energies. Great, sunny and beautiful ages are waiting for humanity, and humanity will make it! This is our belief.

Chapter XIV

WORDS OF CAUTION

"So many distortions, so many inaccuracies have been admitted into the Teachings. Verily, each purification is great Service."

—M. M.

THE YOGAS

On the path of self-development there are methods which can be used to enable man to contact his Soul and enjoy deeper experiences of expanded consciousness. These methods were created by great psycho-scientists who were highly clairvoyant and enlightened by great spiritual realizations. They used them in their temples or colleges with discrimination and knowledge. As ages passed, self-seeking teachers exposed the techniques to the public as a means of providing fruitful income for their own personal vanities and glamours. We wish to mention a few which are being misused in many countries and which have caused physical, psychological and spiritual damage to many.

1. Mantra Yoga
2. Hatha Yoga (Asana and Pranayama)
3. Laya Yoga (Kundalini, Third Eye and Sacral Center Yogas)

Mantra Yoga

Mantras are verses or phrases which carry power and produce an effect upon the mind, emotions and body, and which start energies of space in motion. Mantras are used chiefly in chanting. We are told that there is a real science of chanting, but that the key to this science is lost for the average man. It is held by the great Enlightened Ones who are called Masters of Wisdom.

Unless a man is admitted as a disciple and is supervised by such Great Ones, Mantra yoga, the chanting method, may create unending difficulties and hinder progress on the path of the aspirant. Chanting is a technique to evoke energies. Each word, each tone, each rhythm creates corresponding vibrations and colors of different frequencies in space, according to the level of consciousness and the *beingness* level of a man.

Energies thus evoked are fiery and if they are not manipulated consciously and scientifically, they will, more often create destructive results when unconsciously directed to the centers, the glands, and to their corresponding organs. These damaging results cannot be detected in a short time. Their effects may be felt in one life or in many lives, depending upon the strength of the cause activated by the use of chanting to invoke energies.

Chanting can be safely used if one knows the condition of the bodies, their stage of development on the path of evolution, their habit patterns, diseases through which they have passed and the degree of sensitivity and responsiveness of these vehicles. To these conditions must be added knowledge of the environment in which the man lives. To know the conditions as they exist is very important, because only through such knowledge will we be able to foresee the result, either constructive or destructive, as energies evoked (responding energies) create different results when they come in contact with different types of bodies in different states.

Chanting in groups is less dangerous in the beginning, but when the saturation point is reached; when the overall reaction and response is out of control, you will witness degeneration of principles and disintegration of great goals, intentions and service. Immediately following this moral destruction, the form side of the group begins to show signs of degeneration or disintegration through many physical, emotional and mental complications. These signs can easily be seen by a member who reaches a safe degree of "dis-identification" with the group.

Sometimes it happens that these results do not appear for a long period of time because a few members or one highly developed person absorbs the shocks (so to say) and protects the group members. Eventually, however, this person either withdraws from the group or falls into the whirlpool of group difficulties. Group chanting is safe when the members are highly developed and are under the guidance of an Initiate.

Individual chanting is more dangerous because the energy thus released can easily cause disturbances in one's bodies if there is any kind of defect in them. It often happens that an individual, through chanting, clears some obstruction from his vehicles by stimulating them. When this occurs he feels relaxed and happy, but he should be warned that this is the right time to escape from danger, providing that he has not already made connection with the deva kingdom through chanting. In the event that the connection has been made, escape will be more difficult, because the devas do not like to lose the one who chants.

Masters of Wisdom warn us to clear our physical, emotional and mental bodies before we try to use Mantra yoga to invoke energies. The greatest protection, the greatest shield, is a pure heart and service.

Hatha Yoga

In the west, especially in the United States and Canada, Hatha yoga found fertile ground to expand and spread. This is natural because at the present time the West is focussed on the form side of life and Hatha yoga works for the form side, for material values, for physical well-being and beauty; not merely for the sake of individual interest, but mainly for the social and economic interests of man.

Hatha yoga has two main branches: (1) *asana* means bodily postures, and

(2) *pranayama* means literally to hold back the breath. These two methods are very dangerous tools when in the hands of a man who plays the part of a master without having the needed knowledge to clear away resultant complications. Hatha yoga brings rapid changes in the physical body—changes in the glands, nervous system and blood. It first affects the etheric body by fusing it more closely with the physical body, giving a feeling of energy, upliftment and good health. When its use is continued, the inpouring energy from the etheric body via the centers slowly stimulates various glands unevenly. First it creates imbalance in the harmonious functioning of the centers, and then highly stimulates certain centers and affects their corresponding organs. Again, this is registered as an energizing feeling, but when complications begin to exist in the glands and surrounding organs, various diseases eventuate.

Over-stimulated centers cause over-activity or low activity in the glands, creating a condition which welcomes many kinds of germs or growths. Of course such results do not appear suddenly. They start in the subtle levels and gradually express themselves on the physical plane.

Another effect of Hatha yoga is the creation of subtle walls in the etheric, astral and mental passages through which man withdraws himself and enters into the fiery world. Hatha yoga chains a man to his physical body and his physical environment, which eventually makes spiritual flights of the human soul impossible. It densifies the aura and shuts off communication with the higher realms. Thus, sooner or later, the Hatha yogi cuts himself from communion with the higher worlds and becomes an automaton.

The health of which the Hatha yogi speaks is an illusion. Most Hatha yogis have died very young or if death did not occur early, it was because they were able to balance in some way the harm done, by using Bhakti or Rajah yoga.

Hatha yoga is millions of years old. It was used in the Lemurian Race to bring fusion between the physical and etheric bodies, making it possible for the command, (the wish or desire) the volition of the man, to be passed immediately to the nervous system through the *nadis*, the etheric nerves. This purpose was fulfilled ages and ages ago. There is no need for it today. To use a method which is not needed creates undue pressure and leads to complications in the system. These results can be seen in the social life of those races which have continued to use Hatha yoga over a long period of time as a way of life.

Pranayama, the science of breath, is even more dangerous than Asana. Breath is fire and the best way to use this fire is in normal, deep breathing. We need no other breathing exercise than this. Pranayama can be used to heal certain diseases and to expand the consciousness, but it should be done under the guidance of a Master who *sees* through His third eye and controls the dosage, the focus and the duration of the exercise.

Breathing is not a physical activity. Through breathing it is possible to bring in powerful energies from higher realms and let them loose upon the lower levels. If the nature of energies thus released is not known; if the technique of controlling and directing them is not known; if the correct point of focus is not known, the man is in danger. He may become the victim of the forces that he releases through his breathing exercises.

This actually is the case of all those who with good intention submit themselves to teachers who are blind to the real Teaching. A fifth Degree Initiate, a true Master, who can see with the third eye may, if He deems it wise, prescribe certain breathing exercises which can help in regulating certain etheric centers, and glands, astral or mental energies within the system. Such a Master is not found in bazaars or in wealthy institutions, but in a highly elevated consciousness.

The dangers of Hatha yoga can be recognized by the following symptoms:

For Women—

1. Desire for sex, but physical dissatisfaction or even repulsion.
2. Insomnia.
3. Trouble in sex glands and organs.
4. Trouble in kidneys, stomach, liver and throat.
5. Breast trouble.
6. Lack of energy.
7. Diffused state of mind, lack of concentration on higher ideas or actions.
8. Lack of self-initiatory action.
9. Indifference to the needs of others.
10. Emotional instability, over-sensitiveness or dullness.
11. Forcefulness.
12. Stubborness.
13. Lack of broad understanding.
14. Fanaticism or narrow-mindedness.

These and many other related symptoms do not appear in the beginning, but slowly come into existence in such a manner that the yogi becomes used to them and in time his life is completely dominated by them, making his escape impossible.

For Men—

1. Over-stimulation of the sex urge and a thirst for sex.
2. Heart palpitation.
3. Stomach and kidney trouble.
4. Prostate gland trouble.
5. Less sensitivity in the five senses.
6. Inability to pass to subtle levels in meditation, thinking or sleep.
7. Increasing sense of pride.
8. Increasing attachment to matter or form.
9. Growing irresponsibility.
10. Growing indifference toward real spiritual values.
11. Sensitivity to the thoughts of others coming from their lower minds.
12. Totalitarianism.
13. Development of the mechanism of escape.

In place of Hatha yoga we must encourage various physical activities involving the whole body, such as hiking, mountain climbing, swimming, surfing, skiing, volleyball, basketball, etc. These kinds of sports place our whole body in motion causing deeper breathing and greater fusion with prana, the life-giving energy of the universe.

The first stage of development of our physical body is the result of our consciousness. As our consciousness grows and expands, the brain, the glands and all organs pass through changes in adapting themselves to respond to and express the expanding consciousness.

Whenever we work on the *mechanism* to try to expand our consciousness, to secure greater energy or to improve our health, we disturb the balance of our electromagnetic energy system and pay the price with ill health or other complications on many levels. Hatha yoga is one means by which people try to expand their consciousness and assure good health and longevity.

What does Hatha yoga actually do?

– It artificially stimulates the many organs in the body before they are ready for that stimulation.
– It hardens the corresponding etheric and astral centers of the organs, making it difficult if not impossible for the human soul to pass from one plane to another. Thus the first obstacles noticed are on the astral and etheric centers, making the development of continuity of consciousness very difficult. The results may extend to the mental nature and cause fossilization of the mental centers.

The best method of achieving growth and expansion is to *start with the consciousness*. Try to enlarge and refine it, opening it to greater horizons and lifting it to higher mental planes. When expansion of consciousness is accomplished in this manner, the body will adjust itself, because consciousness comes first; the body is the shadow which takes form after the consciousness.

The real and healthy development for the Aryan race starts from within. The consciousness expands and upon the expanded consciousness the bodies are built. The expansion of consciousness purifies and unfolds the centers from above, downwardly, gradually changing the etheric and physical bodies and leading them to transfiguration.

Hatha yoga bears a close relationship to the use of drugs for development. It is the same *reversal* method—from matter to consciousness rather than from consciousness to transformation of matter. The use of Hatha yoga and drugs are both obsolete, because body development has already been accomplished and we need no longer work on it. To do so would be a turning back.

Hatha yoga also tightens the link between the physical and etheric, intensifying the substance of the astral body to the point of crystallization. Thus obstacles are created which block the path of Soul contact, and which hinder the process of externalization of the unit of consciousness from etheric-astral into higher mental and buddhic planes.

A Hatha yogi is chiefly a wanderer on the etheric and astral levels where he collects many glamours under which he often carries on his activities. It is difficult for him to pass to higher mental planes or into the Ashrams of the buddhic plane where the true Teaching can be given to him. Should he by chance pass into these higher levels, the result would be greater illusions in his conscious life.

There are a few who, being Lemurian in their conscious orientation, may escape the dangers of Hatha yoga in this life, but in future reincarnations, when their focus of consciousness changes to Aryan consciousness, they will have to pay the debt for their heedlessness and folly.

Laya Yoga

Kundalini Yoga is another menace which is causing great damage to our young adults who are attracted to this yoga by their vanities and love of power. There is a center at the base of the spine which contains tremendous, fiery power and controls the thermostat of the body and the body organs. Actually, it has a triple fire: one fire controls the heat, another is the cooling system, and the third is the link between matter and spirit. This fire slowly climbs the etheric spine as a result of the expansion of consciousness and as a result of living a clean, harmless and sacrificial life. It ascends because of our spiritual aspiration and practical service, and as it ascends it dissolves the etheric web that divides the centers on the spine, stimulating them into greater rhythmic and harmonious activity. The energy thus flowing into the centers creates no complications because of the purification process through which each center has passed as the result of spiritual discipline, meditation and sacrificial living.

Thus, from one center to another, the fire of kundalini climbs, bringing forth greater blooming and radioactivity in the centers, which in turn, bring into the system greater energies from their corresponding higher centers and planes. At last the fire reaches the highest, the head center and fuses with that center. At this stage a man is in full illumination; he is a Serpent (kundalini fire) of Wisdom, as the Egyptian Hierophants were symbolically known.

The exploitation of Kundalini yoga is taking place in many cities and yogis are teaching people how to raise the fire and create extraordinary experiences in their lives. The result in most cases is that they are forcing the fire to rise and prematurely burn the etheric webs, the protecting network between the etheric centers. After destroying it, the fire rushes into the centers, over stimulating them, creating pain, disorders and illnesses that cannot be cured by modern medical means.

Strive to bloom as the lilies of the field bloom in full beauty, without forcing the form side of life, but rather by aspiring toward light and living a harmless life, dedicating yourself to a great service for humanity. As a result of your aspiration and service your sense of responsibility will grow; you will be quite ready for sacrificial living. In so doing the fire will rise naturally and glorify the man.

For those who are victims of Kundalini yoga, we suggest absolute rest in a place surrounded by the beauty of nature, and a simple, pure diet of vegetables and fruits for at least three years.

Third Eye Yoga. This yoga is another gopher that is eating at the roots of well-intentioned aspirants. The third eye results when two magnetic fields in the brain come together and fuse with each other. Activity in one of the fields is started by the spiritual activity of the pineal gland, and the other by the spiritual action of the pituitary body. These energy fields are created in the brain as a result of personality integration and fusion with the spiritual nature. As the spiritual, sacrificial, loving life of the disciple deepens and expands, these two fields form, intensify their radiation and eventually fuse. At the center of fusion a point of light appears and grows as the man advances on the path of service and realization. This small light eventually becomes an eye which slowly moves away and comes to rest twelve inches above the head. We are not speaking of the ajna center, nor of the eye that sees clairvoyantly, etherically or astrally. We are speaking of the true third eye which directs energies, controls forces and matter and builds or destroys.[1]

The so-called "third eye yogis" teach their victims to force the opening of this eye through certain meditations, postures, breathing exercises and even by chanting. This is as wrong as it would be to stimulate a three year old child to sexual activities.

The results of this yoga are very dark. The victim's suffering starts with headaches and ends with his being imprisoned in an asylum, if he has really followed the instructions given by his "guru." Such instructions and exercises, if carried out, overstimulate the greatest treasures of nature, the pineal and pituitary glands, causing unpredictable and unimaginable complications in the physical, astral and mental bodies, the causes of which cannot be detected or the condition relieved by modern medicine.

The karma of such teachers will be very dark, because eventually they will not only have to pay back the money they have collected from their victims, but they will also have to pay for the pain and suffering they have caused, through their own pain and suffering. Let harmlessness be the keynote of each teacher!

Sacral Center Yoga. Another widespread practice is sex yoga or the technique used to stimulate the sexual centers for greater physical pleasure. The victims of this yoga experience much pleasure in these activities for a time. In a few years, however, they lose all sex sensation, but retain the burning desire for sex. In a short period of time the burning desire heats their sex organs and

1. Please read about the third eye in *The Science of Meditation*, H. Saraydarian, pp. 167–185 and about the Yogas, pp. 240–264.

they start developing growths as well as many other disorders. This yoga is practiced under different names in many places where human sex is freely displayed and enjoyed under many kinds of stimulants, such as music, dance, touch, films, jokes and others.

Sometimes such freedom releases accumulated tensions and gives a healthy feeling to the participant, but it causes greater accumulations to be released in the future. Because of the fact that tension and the human body follow different paths, the tension increases and the sexual ability declines through the process of aging. Thus man confronts an insurmountable difficulty in attempting to release his tensions sexually. As time goes on, this creates great depression and often leads him into suicidal action. Esoteric Wisdom teaches that sex energy can be enjoyed, controlled and elevated into greater creativity through right meditation, right living and right service. Only a fool will waste his money in ridding himself of his sex energy through following the teachings of blind and ignoble teachers or through excessive sexual activity.

In *The Essene Gospel of Peace* Jesus says to his listeners: ". . . for the whoremonger is like a tree whose sap runs out from its trunk. And that tree will be dried up before its time, nor will it ever bear fruit."[2]

ASTRAL PROJECTION

Astral projection is another practice which is causing unending psychological and physical problems.

Astral projection is a new name for an old method by which it is possible to detach the awareness unit from the physical body and send "him" to any location to procure information or to perform a service. People have used many different methods to master this technique. They have used hypnotism, anesthesia, suffocation, the threat of great danger, pain, worship, intense aspiration, concentration, meditation and contemplation.

The four states in the process of astral projection are those in which:

1. The unit of consciousness is out of the body, but there is no registration in the brain and the experience is not recalled in waking consciousness.
2. The unit of awareness is out of the body and the brain registers all of the experiences.
3. The unit of awareness is out of the body and the body is used by another of higher or lower order while the subject is completely unconscious.
4. The unit of awareness consciously hands the control of his body over to a high-grade entity to use for a given period throughout which he witnesses and shares all experiences, offering no interference in the work thus performed by the entity.

Whenever a man falls into an unconscious state of being, his body is an open house which can be occupied, possessed or obsessed by low-level entities.

2. Szekley, Edmund Bordeaux, *The Essene Gospel of Peace*, p. 58.

When this happens, the man upon regaining consciousness, finds that he has totally lost control of his mental and nervous mechanisms and that they are often used by forces about which he knows nothing and over which he has no control. The man becomes a multiple person and is in grave danger because his body and mind are used for purposes often contradictory in his nature. For example, a decision is made and action is taken, but the next moment the decision is changed and action is postponed. The man is completely bewildered. Such a state of mind not only creates a problem for the subject, but also for the society in which he lives. Very often he is led off to an asylum for possible recovery or for life-long imprisonment.

This unconscious state can be caused by hypnotism, shocks, accidents, anesthesia or various methods of astral projection. It is true that anesthesia is the least dangerous, because in this case the awareness unit is not thrown out of the sphere of the body. The communication line between the awareness unit and the body is merely suspended. The greatest danger in anesthesia is that a patient under an anesthetic for surgery can pick up all conversation carried on around him and later use it as post-hypnotic suggestion. After he has awakened and returned home, he may develop strange behavior as he attempts to obey hypnotic suggestions put into his consciousness by words spoken while he was under anesthesia. Anesthesia can be relatively safe when all precautions are taken to protect the patient from the time the anesthetic is administered to the moment when he is fully awake. There should be no conversation and a minimum of noise in the operating room. If doctors and nurses would heed this warning, many complications and much suffering on the part of their patients could be avoided. Unfortunately, in most of our hospitals the regulations are a far cry from this standard.

Hypnotism is a major cause of physical and psychological problems. The subject not only registers the suggestions given to him as orders and commands, but also, very subtly, he registers the thoughts and desires of the hypnotist. He may even register thoughtforms floating in space which have some association with the moment and relationship to the suggestions given. Thus, after he is returned to consciousness, he may be loaded with many post-hypnotic suggestions of which the hypnotist has no knowledge and for which he apparently holds no responsibility! The most dangerous thing about hypnotism is that it is possible for the subject to be occupied by low-level entities. This may or may not happen immediately, but in time, when the experience is repeated again and again, earth-bound entities may slowly make room and settle themselves in the aura of the unfortunate subject. Speaking about hypnotism, Helena Petrovna Blavatsky says,

> "There is a danger of black magic, into which all the world, and especially America, is rushing as fast as it can go. Only a wide knowledge of the real psychic and spiritual nature of man can save humanity from grave dangers.

> . . . Do you not see the tremendous evils that lie concealed in hypnotism? . . . Whoever lets himself or herself be hypnotised, by anyone, good or bad, is opening a door which he will be powerless to shut, and he cannot tell who will be the next to enter! If you could foresee what I foresee, you would begin heart and soul to spread the teaching of universal brotherhood. It is the only safeguard!" [3]

Accidents may cause the same condition as does anesthesia. Great care must be taken to place the victim in a comfortable position and maintain silence until his consciousness returns.

Constant fear may cause a gradual withdrawal of the occupant from the body, thus opening the door for invasion by thoughtforms, glamours and entities. Ancient and modern Initiates and Sages have exercised the technique of withdrawal from the body to render a special service or to contact Beings found on higher levels. They have given hints concerning the technique in various occult writings. We have summarized some of the information which outlines preparation for the use of this technique. To establish the proper condition it is necessary:

- To practice daily meditation for at least fourteen to twenty-one years, unless one is a high degree Initiate.
- To build the bridge between the mind and the Spiritual Triad.
- To unfold the head center through abstract thinking and sacrificial living.
- To have the needed build-up of the nervous system and a purified, transformed body.
- To be shielded by a Great One to assure that attacks by the dark ones will be repulsed.
- To know the mechanism and the laws of etheric, astral, mental and intuitional planes.

When these conditions have been fulfilled, a Great One will help the pilgrim learn to fly out of the body as the mother eagle teaches her children to soar over the vast abyss. Before these conditions are met, so-called "astral projections" can bring fatal consequences. The intense desire to come out of the body rends protective etheric webs and may overstimulate the heart, the solar plexus and throat centers. It may lead to many organic problems such as serious eye and ear trouble.

I would suggest that my readers visit some of our asylums and witness the terrible, unhappy existence of the patients. Seeing the mental conditions of these patients might serve to make people more cautious about entering into activities in which they give up or lose control of their own minds.

Out of body experience is the inheritance of every man as fruit is the inheritance of a healthy tree. The tree must be planted under the best possible conditions; it must grow for years before it is able to open its flowers and bear

---

3. Blavatsky, H. P., *Collected Writings*, Vol. VIII, pp. 406–407.

fruit. The same is true for a human being. When he creates the right conditions for his physical, his emotional and mental nature; when he lives a life of continuous sacrificial service and high aspiration; he will bloom as the lilies of the field. He will have higher psychic powers and will use them consciously and constructively. Before a man has built the golden Chalice, he should not invoke and play with fire. The Chalice is built not by exercises of various kinds, but by transfiguration of his nature and by acts of sacrificial service.

SUPPRESSIVE MEDITATION

Self-hypnotism and hypnotism in general have a close affinity with the kind of "meditation," in which you repeat a mantram for from twenty to twenty-five minutes twice daily, rendering your mind totally passive and making you feel very peaceful.

A "meditation," such as this, creates a state of *thoughtlessness* in your mind, because of the repetition and because of the power that any mantram can evoke within your system. A thoughtless mind is, indeed, in true peace, *providing it is not under suppression*; if it is under suppression you may have "peace," but it is only temporary; you are inviting great danger to yourself in the coming years.

When you try to negate thoughts by mechanically repeating a mantram instead of concentrating your mind upon lofty thoughts, visions and ideas, two things happen:

– You create a magnetic vacuum in your mind which can be filled with any suggestion telepathically reaching your mind, creating there an unobserved, unrealized urge or drive for its fulfillment.
– You suppress the thoughtforms found in your mental sphere, but at the same time you are creating tremendous power in those thoughtforms by the force built up through mechanical repetition of the mantram.

A thoughtless state of mind can be achieved through the practice of contemplation, which is fusion with the Inner Light, the Inner Being, but this can be accomplished only after the mind is totally purified by the fire of true thinking—*true meditation.*

Contemplation is a state in which man is no longer identified with his own mental plane, or mental substance, but is free to communicate with the Inner Being, and to reflect the beauty of this contact in the mirror of his mind. Agitation in the mind occurs when a man identifies with his illusions and thoughtforms. Once he is freed from this identification, his mind is as tranquil as a beautiful lake in the mountains on a windless day.

The great Lord Buddha held that his method of mindfulness and His achievement were the result of His mental labour, of His untiring search for the laws and causes of all that makes man either a master or a slave of life.

Most of our troubles are the result of our identification with our negative, destructive, separative thoughts and illusions. When these thoughts and illusions are *suppressed*, we will have a period of peace and tranquility; we will not even be concerned about our duties, responsibilities and problems, but I would call such "peace" psychic intoxication—not a solution to our problems.

When your mind is suppressed and rendered neutral, your pranic energy will rush to your bloodstream and nerve channels, creating a feeling of power and supremacy. This feeling of strength and power makes you think that you are removing psychosomatic disorders in the body. This may be true for the time being, but results which appear to be favorable are only on the surface. The real danger will start when the suppressed thoughts start to exercise tremendous pressure on your etheric centers and your brain centers, affecting the corresponding organs and glands. This will be the physical effect.

When the suppressed energies can no longer be contained under your conscious control, they will flood your mind creating total upheaval and grave mental disorder. These effects will not occur in one day, one month or even in one year, but the effect is accumulative and is proportionate to the effort you have been putting into the exercise. Sometimes it takes five to ten years for full recovery from the effects of this kind of "pseudo-meditation."

The question will be asked, "How does it happen that the teachers of such mental techniques, seem healthy and joyful?" The answer is that many people in the East have used this technique from childhood; they have become accustomed to it and have, perhaps, devised some methods of releasing the pressure, allowing them to lead their normal lives. Those in the East who practice this technique usually live quiet, peaceful lives in the mountainous areas away from congested cities. They experience none of the physical, emotional and mental pressures of the western world. Even their body composition and structure are different, because of:

- Their simple diet, consisting largely of fruit, nuts and herbs, grown in unpolluted areas.
- The absence of air and noise pollution.
- The leisurely, simple life they live.

These conditions are in direct contrast to those of people in the West, whose physical, emotional and mental natures are tuned to the faster, stimulating pace of industrial nations, of western civilization and culture. They have not received the necessary early training and practice in the mantram method which would enable them to handle energy invoked, and their systems, already burdened by the pressures of daily living, cannot withstand the added pressure.

It is only recently that the young people of the western countries have been exposed to this technique. Many of them have been deceived into believing that they have found the way to true meditation, and are completely unaware of the future danger. In true meditation, step by step, through an active thinking process, we build a line of communication with higher planes to achieve continuity of consciousness on all planes.

Suppressive exercises, by whatever name, will eventually lead you to slavery, loss of self-determination, and weakening of any true creative ability, because you have been conditioned by post-hypnotic suggestions thrown into your mind at a time when you were doping it with the repetition of mantrams.

People aspire toward peace of mind and relaxation, but true peace of mind is not achieved by quelling the mind and making it totally *passive* through power generated by verbal repetition. True peace of mind can be reached through an *active* mind, capable of working out a problem that calls for analysis and logic; a mind that can take the solution and refine it by formulating lofty impressions coming into it from the intuitional plane.

Actually, the ultimate goal of a disciple is not the finding of peace and health for himself; his goal is the great service that he can give to humanity in spite of his own condition. Meditation for him is the search and labour to learn more about the laws and energies in nature; to translate and use them in ways that will help people progress on the path of evolution toward the purpose of life.

People are often amazed at reading accounts of how this mantram-intoning exercise lowers the blood pressure. It is a cheap way for its advocates, or "teachers," to advertise. In truth, you will have more relaxation and lowering of blood pressure when you *engage your mind* in thoughts of gratitude, serenity, love, forgiveness, unity, solemnity, etc.

A suppressed mind results in peace to the nervous system, but once the suppression reaches a stage in which you can no longer control it, the peaceful nerves will crack, causing serious problems in your mental and physical health.

We are also informed that drug and criminal habits are curbed through this technique. No doubt this is true, but it is accomplished through suppression and not through *purification*. In true purification or release we know the reasons for not being criminal, the reasons for not using drugs; we have a mighty will to start purification and to sustain purity throughout our life. Forbiddance and suppression, in whatever form they may appear, are the enemies of true evolution and healthy unfoldment.

SELF-HYPNOTISM

Questions have been asked as to whether meditation is related in any way to self-hypnotism, or if the invocations and prayers which people are using can be a kind of self-hypnosis? To give detailed answers to such questions would require a whole volume, but to keep it as short as possible we can say that meditation is diametrically opposed to self-hypnotism.

Meditation is a process of awakening; in other words, a process of conscious mastery of the physical, emotional and mental bodies. This is achieved through sublimating, energizing and transmuting the substances, the living atoms of these bodies, so that eventually they obey the command of the central unit of consciousness.[4]

In meditation you are trying to bring the bodies and their conditions under the control of your Inner Self, gradually transmuting and transforming the little lives of your vehicles and making them responsive to your highest good. This is like a true democracy which educates and expands the consciousness of people to help them see the highest good and live their lives accordingly.

In meditation you are expanding your consciousness and learning about your inner being, the laws through which it works, and the laws by which you can transform and master the physical, emotional and mental bodies.

In meditation you try to see things as they are, the overall picture; you try to discover areas where you can use these things in such a way that they will improve your responses and relationships in the wider scope of your life.

In self-hypnotism the nature of the bodies does not improve, the cause of distress is locked in, and the recording mechanism is disconnected. Of course, here we have release, but it is illusionary. As for example, your enemy hides himself in your home and in due time makes an attack, this time with a hammer instead of a revolver. The suspended causes of distress remain as they were in our etheric, emotional and mental spheres, and there they create psychic tumors, or tightly wound coils of force which, with any appropriate association, escape and express themselves in the weakest parts of the body; or they accumulate with other locked in forces and attack us in many ways. Many, many emotional depressions and problems are the result of the pressure of such accumulated psychic tumors. It is also possible that such inner tensions exercise a tremendous pressure upon the cells, causing growths of various types.

In self-hypnotism you are forcing a command upon your bodies, but you are not eliminating the deep seated problems within. You are not expanding your consciousness, and you are not really mastering your vehicles; you are deceiving them.

In meditation man prepares himself to reach a goal, to utilize it, and enjoy it consciously. In self-hypnotism a man is forced to his goal without having the needed preparation to utilize that goal and enjoy it consciously.

In meditation you are purifying all your vehicles and reaching enlightenment. In self-hypnotism you are closing the windows and doors to keep the house clean and undisturbed, without taking into consideration that decay may start from within. Through self-hypnotism, man's will, consciousness and body are not improving; he is finding "release" from things he likes or dislikes personally, but they will still harm him in various ways.

He is telling his vehicles that the pain will be there, but he will not feel it; the cause for the desire of smoking will be there, but he will hate smoking;

4. See *The Science of Meditation* by H. Saraydarian, pp. 23–35.

the cause for the dislike of sexual intercourse will be there, but he will enjoy intercourse; the cause of insomnia will be there, but he will sleep well. The man, assuming that all of these things are good for him, will feel successful, without realizing that the hidden causes will once again exercise their power more forcibly than before because of having been suppressed.

In the dentist's chair, through self-hypnotism or hypnotism, you may enjoy painless surgery or the painless filling of your teeth, but your nerves will record the pain, and it will be passed on to your subtle bodies, although your brain will not record it. You will have static in your atmosphere creating disturbances which will disrupt communication and response. Those who follow self-hypnotism gradually lose their sensitivity to respond and to record subtle impressions coming from higher sources. If this continues, man becomes his own victim; his initiative weakens and he loses touch with practical life.

As was stated in a previous chapter, through the act of hypnotism "the dweller in the bodies" moves out—sometimes totally, sometimes partially. If partially, the dweller withdraws its conscious influence from the physical, astral or even from the higher mental planes, leaving the lower sheaths prey to incoming entities, thoughtforms or suggestions, which invade and possess them. Thus new stations are created which control the nature of man, and he becomes the battlefield of intense conflict. The conflict starts when the dweller returns to its habitation and finds strangers—invading commands, thoughtforms, post-hypnotic suggestions, and many kinds of entities—possessing the mechanism. In psychological terms, man is in intense conflict within his nature. The tragedy is that very often the dweller in the bodies assumes that he is responsible for all low-grade or sinful separative deeds performed under the influence of these invading hosts, and he develops an intense guilt complex which leads to great depression, mental confusion and breakdown.

If the withdrawal of the inner dweller is total, the invaders have complete possession; the personality and the individuality are kept out of the bodies, and the bodies are used by strangers who will not tolerate the return of the owner. This constitutes a great failure for the dweller on the path of his evolution.

Actually the word self-hypnosis is an incorrect term. A man who tries to hypnotize himself does not know what the *Self* is. To him, his "self" is his body, and perhaps the dominating urge of his body, or it is an emotion, an illusion, a glamour, a desire or thought. How then does a man dare to hypnotize his vehicle if he does not own it, and if he does not know who he is? When he tries to hypnotize "himself," he is injecting into his nature a dominating wish, an urge, a dream, an idea, which can become a part of his total illusions and glamours. So it is not the real "you" that hypnotizes your vehicle, but a thought, an urge, a drive, a postulate, a decision which, in its turn, could be a product of a former hypnotic suggestion.

This means that the self-hypnotist, after being hypnotized a thousand times by life events themselves and by his environment, tries to "re-hypnotize" himself again and again, and here we see the comedy. Suppose "you" continue to hypnotize "yourself" with ever-changing, and possibly conflicting selves. Can you imagine what will happen to your mechanism under the impact of such hypnosis?

Imposition Versus Transmutation

Hypnotism is imposition. Self-hypnotism is an imposition upon your thoughts and feelings, upon your physical, emotional and mental vehicles. This imposition can be totally negative, which may lead you to depression or to the asylum. It may be a positive imposition, but in any case, it is an act of imposition, not *transmutation.*

Imposed knowledge is not knowledge; it is a tape recording. Imposed morality is not morality, because man has no choice. Imposed virtue is a vice. When knowledge is the result of greater incoming light and refinement, it is real knowledge. When morality is the result of seeing greater goals, laws and beauty in life, it is real morality. When virtue is the result of unfolding the higher centers and fusing oneself with the Soul and Spiritual Triad, it is real virtue.

This means that imposition, which is hypnotism itself, does not lead us to true values but toward artificial values—and artificial values create conflict in our nature.

Post-Hypnotic Suggestion. Through hypnosis the glamours and illusions of the hypnotist may flow into the sensitive, electromagnetic atmosphere of the subject, as post-hypnotic suggestions. The hypnotist may be able to erase his verbal, past hypnotic results, but he will never be able to erase the post-hypnotic suggestions formed in the mind of his victim through the inflow of his own glamours and illusions. Once the subject is under hypnosis, he is like a magnet that absorbs verbal, emotional and mental expressions, and registers them as blind commands. The following story may serve to illustrate:

> A steamship landed on a shore near the jungle and the captain left it to visit a village nearby. During his absence many monkeys came out of the jungle. They boarded the ship, climbing wildly over the equipment, trying all the wheels, levers and buttons. By chance they lifted the anchor and the huge vessel sailed slowly out to the open sea. The monkeys, happy over their success, continually changed the speed and direction and eventually struck a rocky island, destroying the ship.

This is what happens when a man practices any kind of hypnotism. The monkeys in this story represent post-hypnotic suggestions which act and re-act under associative impulses and eventually destroy the man's rudder, his self-determinism.

Act of Will. There is a very subtle difference between hypnotism and the act of will. In the act of will you are releasing a powerful energy from your highest centers, clearing away hindering materials in the etheric, emotional and mental bodies. This is the technique of true healing. When the Real Man is able to release the healing energy within himself by an act of will and determine the manner in which his bodies are to live, true healing is realized. Hypnotism works on the bodies. Meditation works on the consciousness, and the bodies adjust themselves to the purified and expanded consciousness. The act of will is an act of releasing the healing energies within the man, and restoring the free circulation of energies in the etheric and other subtle bodies.

Relaxation. Hypnotists often speak of their claim that hypnotism relaxes all our nerves and muscles, and that it helps us to rest and feel serene. The fact is that hypnotism more often exercises an imposed quietness upon the body, but creates greater tensions in the etheric, astral and mental planes. These tensions, in due time, come down to the physical plane causing great upheavals and great damage to the nerves and glandular systems.

Real relaxation is a process of tuning in with the harmony of nature and with the harmony of the creative principle in man. In this process the bodies are integrated and aligned with the inner beauty which radiates out as peace and serenity. True relaxation and peace are states of beingness; they are results of the expanding consciousness, in the light of which reality is contacted and timelessness is sensed.

Healing—Hypnotism Not Recommended. There is another method of healing which is used by great Masters. It is called the *technique of suggestion.* People confuse *suggestion* with *hypnotism* and think that they refer to the same technique.

The suggestion technique is used by Great Ones in the following manner. We are told that through Their spiritual eye They see the conditions of our etheric, astral and mental bodies. They see also in those vehicles some deep seated hypnotic suggestions which may read:

— I am sick.
— I am paralyzed.
— I have some unknown sickness and I cannot work.
— My eyes cannot see.

The Great Ones see these blocking glamours and illusions or commands in the atmosphere of the subject, and through a suggestion they wipe them away and restore health. This is done in the following way:

After They see the aberrant form (astral, etheric or mental) which is the cause of the trouble, they construct in their mind a health-giving-form, and through Their spoken words They project that form into the related vehicle, cleaning and wiping away the trouble-causing-form, restoring health. All this is done while the subject is wide awake or conscious. For example, after seeing in the aura of the subject an image of a sick heart, they visualize a very healthy heart and say:

"Your heart is healthy, get up and work"—or,
"Pick up your bed and walk."

This is not hypnotism. This is the using of visualization, will and projection, which transmutes, changes, sublimates and transforms the inner, subjective nature of man, the result of which is seen on the physical body as good health. The healing done by Christ can be placed in this category, for He healed by direct suggestion—"You are healed."

Of course there is the problem of Karma involved in the act of healing, but the Great Ones do not heal if the sickness is Karmic. The healing is done when the Karma has run out, or when the sickness is imposed by dark forces or hypnotists.

In anesthesia, your nervous system as a whole does not register the pain because the etheric counterpart of the nervous system is suspended.

Under hypnosis, the recorder of pain, the unit of consciousness, is suspended, but the nervous system as a whole records the pain and passes it on to the subtle bodies. Under hypnosis, the house is vacant and the commands given may carry on their destructive work with the furniture, the water, electric and communication lines, etc., without being noticed by the owner. Every command, every suggestion acts as the householder.

In self-hypnotism, the owner of the personality—the mental, emotional and physical bodies—is in the process of withdrawing, and in the process of identification with his own suggestions or dreams, as a form of psychic insulation. Thus the real Self is creating an illusionary self—a false image—which is acting as a real Self, or as the owner of the body. As the self-hypnotism continues, the man sooner or later becomes a split personality, or one "body" with two heads.

In case of surgery, through the use of hypnotism, the pain is not recorded by the *owner*, but the astral and lower mental bodies register it as pain because of the disturbed condition of the nerves and muscle tissue. If by chance, through some associations, the hidden pain in the astral and lower mental bodies is restimulated, the man feels the pain without finding any physical causes for it.

Auto-Suggestion. There is a great difference between self-hypnosis and auto-suggestion. In auto-suggestion you are holding a healthy and shining picture of yourself, creating a magnetic attraction. This magnetic attraction is slowly molding your body, or bodies, according to the desired pattern of health and beauty. This is an act of conscious transformation through transmutation. The substance of your vehicle is transmuted primarily by your will power.

The magnetic pattern serves three main purposes:

– To lift your level of beingness and open a new avenue toward the future.
– To release certain kinds of energy from higher sources within your nature.
– To use this energy to purify, eliminate and to build.

Looking Backwards. Some psychoanalysts and physicians use a very dangerour approach in treating their patients. The analyst stirs the memory of unhappy events, the "rubbish of the past," stored in the dark layers of the patient's mind, hoping that in so doing he can release the factors causing the trouble, and thus heal the patient. Certainly we would not consider our homes clean if someone were to stir the contents of the rubbish barrel. We would see that ventilating the debris in the bottom of the barrel would cause hundreds of flies and other insects to be released into the air, spreading many kinds of germs throughout our dwelling places.

A similar thing happens when the psychologist or psychiatrist focusses his and the patient's attention upon past happenings. Such procedures serve to restimulate past fears, sins, misdeeds and many other actions in which the patient believed himself to be at fault, forcing him to occupy himself with the painful past.

Some physicians have similar methods based on *fear* and exploitation. After they diagnose the malady, the patient immediately feels that he has a very serious problem. The physician approaches him with his findings and gives the disease a technical Greek or Latin name, building more fear. He goes on to explain that in a certain part of the body a condition exists which needs immediate attention or serious results are unavoidable. Fear continues to mount and the "tonality" of the patient is lowered tremendously because of the huge "dose" of fear which has been injected into his system. All of his thought energy is focussed on his illness.

Those who understand human psychology are aware of what a potent factor the mind is in the healing process. Once the energy of the mind is directed to the diseased part of the body, it pours into that area a kind of force, poisoned by fear, and the patient's condition becomes more serious.

The best technique for the physician is to approach the patient with a smile, with humor and joy, giving him the needed medical and surgical care, but shifting his attention as much as possible, from the diseased parts of the body, turning his thoughts to healthy vehicles and their activities. Thus, the doctor can be instrumental in bringing cheer and hope to his patient.

A similar method should be used by those practitioners who work with the human emotions and thoughts. Instead of wasting their own and the patient's valuable time by digging deep into the buried past, they must draw the patient's attention toward goodness, beauty and the glory within their nature and within the nature of those to whom their problems are related.

Just sitting and imagining moments of joy or a moment of great ecstasy, uplifts people and gives them courage to face their problems. Where there is fear, events of fearlessness must be cultivated; where there is a "hang-up" from the past, the *future* must be emphasized; where there is ugliness, beauty must be visualized in dramatic fashion; when there is illness, the thoughts must be turned toward an image of radiant health.

All unhappy experiences of the past have served to form a mental image which causes us suffering and distress. These mental clouds must be worked out and dispersed by creating more joyous, acceptable and electromagnetic thoughtforms—thoughtforms to oppose, to melt and to assimilate the unwanted cause of trouble. Thoughts heal when they are charged with joy and the concept of the future. The great sage, M. Morya, in one of his books entitled *Fiery World*, says:

> "During every illness one can apply thought as a means of healing or relief, but such thought should eject the sickness from the organism with full force, without hesitancy or delay. However, if such force be lacking it is generally better not to think about the sickness at all, but to leave to the lower Manus the carrying on of the inner battle. It is most harmful to waver in thought and to visualize a victory of the sickness. In such cases it is better to distract the attention of the patient from his condition. When people speak of the fatal outcome of a sickness, they themselves bring it closer. The least serious sickness can assume dangerous proportions if nourished by thought. Observations should be made in hospitals concerning the effect of thought upon the progress of illness. Even the healing of wounds depends upon psychic energy. Thus we arrive again at the very same Fire generated by thought. All treatments by rays, thermal action, and applications of light comprise the same fiery influences, which are weak in comparison with the power of thought. Hence, the most vital advice is to develop fiery thought."[5]

Confession of the observer. Ancients used the method of confession, but it was not the kind of confession found in our churches today. Their confession was made without identification or self-pity, and without expectation of forgiveness or anticipation of Paradise. It was a clear, cold observation of what the personality did because of ignorance, an unconscious drive, or an hypnotic condition. The confessor used to help the confessing one to keep himself detached from the deeds of the personality. He faithfully watched him as he created detachment, and "dis-identification" between the observing consciousness and the performer. Thus the upliftment of the consciousness was hastened.

Movies and Television Are Hypnotic. It is a psychological fact that whenever a child or an adult is in a painful, emotional condition; when he is extremely excited by fear or desire, and is tense with expectancy; he is in a state in which post-hypnotic suggestions can be planted abundantly—suggestions which may eventually form the motivating power behind all of his actions in his future life.

Such conditions are created everytime we watch a criminal movie, or a dramatic commercial on our television sets. Most of the commercials, advertisements, movies and other striking presentations actually mold the future of a nation through hypnotic suggestion. They cause people to become sleeping fools who because of their having been saturated with post-hypnotic suggestions,

---

5. Agni Yoga Society, *Fiery World*, Vol. I, par. 99.

act without self-determinism. The events of their lives control the "push-buttons" and lead them into actions which otherwise they never would have taken.

When we think of our beloved little children who, hour after hour, watch criminal films involving shooting and killing, we can well understand what their own future behavior might be and the reasons for that behavior. They are retarded in their striving toward their educational goals. In one hour of viewing television programs thousands and thousands of destructive images are forced into their virgin minds. Ugly images and deep seated impressions, which may eventually destroy or curb the possibility of sound thinking and healthy responses, are implanted in their young minds. Doctors have found that the radioactivity of television has a detrimental effect on their brain, nervous system and overall health.

In the future it will be possible to prove scientifically the fact that post-hypnotic suggestions are creating a race of sleeping fools with a defective sense of morals and misguided sense of responsibility.

Television can be used as a great channel for communication between the individual and the world as a method of education, and as a field of challenge to awaken in us the sense of responsibility. Love for others, the urge to heroic action, self mastery and striving toward one humanity are themes which can be effectively presented through the medium of television.

In the very near future television will replace many high schools and colleges. The new age teacher will present his subject matter before the camera and millions of people will have the opportunity to study in their private homes. Indeed, teaching by television is a method already being used to some extent.

Talents

We know that it is possible to create pseudo-talents. Very often such "talents" are the result of strong commands impressed on our minds at a time when we are in an hypnotic state of mind.

For example, when a man is under hypnosis, he can be told that he is a painter. If this suggestion is repeated over a long period of time, he will develop an urge for painting and will have a strong conviction that he is talented in this art. He will think that one day he will grow to be a great genius!

The fact is that in every man there is a tremendous creative ability which will express itself as his consciousness expands and his realization into higher levels develops. It is possible to awaken such abilities prematurely by mechanical means, but the result may be one or more of the following:

- The victim of this forced creativity will never pass average or common creativity.
- If he starts to go above average, he will feel a tremendous pressure on his nervous and glandular systems, which will lead him into various physical and psychological complications, or into total disability.

- He will often be a split personality, having deep seated doubts in his mind about himself; about his creative talents and his goals.
- In any event, he will feel that he is not creating as expected, or if he becomes "de-hypnotized," he will fall into a heavy depression which may lead to suicide or insanity. People lose their will to live when their dreams and expectations with which they are identified, evaporate.

A true artist is the flower of an age-long labour, through which his Chalice is filled with rare experiences and beauties; his consciousness is focussed within the Lotus and eventually within the Spiritual Triad. Creativity is the result, or the effect of the unfolding, blooming and radiating human soul, as he gradually tunes in with the Solar and Cosmic harmonies.

Past Lives

In self-hypnotism, very often we are guided to explore our past lives or future possibilities. Through self-hypnotism it is possible to come in contact with ever-changing dramas in the astral body, reflected from many sources. Our astral body, being a part of the astral body of humanity, reflects continuously the "movies" of past lives, especially of those who are associated with us in any way. These movies can be reflections of real lives, but they are distorted by a mixing together of many lives, or they may actually be motion pictures, dramatizations of many minds engaged in imagination and day-dreaming. Self-hypnotism leads us into the astral plane, where we do not have the slightest power to discriminate the real from the unreal.

The true facts of our past lives are found in the causal body, and the causal body can be approached by expanding our consciousness and purifying our bodies through meditation. Nature hides our past lives with great wisdom because the release of the facts of some past lives can exercise tremendous pressure, causing destructive explosions within our mental, emotional and physical vehicles. If the bodies are not purified enough to absorb the shock, if the consciousness is not refined and expanded enough to understand the facts of the past lives and relate them to the present, complex disorder and confusion will be the effect upon the three lower bodies.

Many pseudo Cleopatras or Napoleons have been created through such methods when the self-hypnotized person has come in contact with the life "movies" of such people. He has identified with them astrally and started to act as the personification of his own illusion. The suffering and embarrassment of such persons, when they start to communicate with relatively sane people, is great and deeply humiliating. The unhappy situation will react upon their personal, family and social life and will create real suffering for those who love them.

Psychic Powers

Sometimes people even try to develop psychic powers through self-hypnotism It is possible to put into action some astral powers, such as astral clairvoyance astral clairaudience and sensitivity to the thoughts of others. People, after having gained such powers, regret it tremendously and try to rid themselves of them if they can. Once the astral ears and eyes are opened, without having achieved the conscious control of the voices and visions, they completely dominate the life of a person and lead him into hospitals or asylums when the corresponding physical organs are affected because of inflaming pressure. Self-hypnotism has caused many people to hear noises and voices. Most of these people cannot control or stop them and they fall into a chaotic state of life.

Higher psychic powers are developed when the higher etheric centers start to function as a result of cultivated major virtues, meditation and service.

Conclusions on Self-hypnotism

There is the Law of Cause and Effect, the Law of Compensation; hiding yourself from your Karma does not help you. Karma must be paid and the best way to pay it is by consciously facing yourself and walking the path of transmutation and transfiguration.

In prayers and invocations people may fall into a state of light self-hypnosis. For this reason mechanical repetition of prayers is not recommended. Prayers offered consciously will create thoughts, thoughtforms, greater aspiration and manipulation of energy, bringing transmutation into the nature of man. Through prayers and invocations man sets goals and visions to be achieved. Every goal and every vision will create great upliftment and transmutation when a man sincerely aspires toward that goal or vision.

The use of self-hypnotism to cultivate virtues and to eliminate vices, resembles a situation in which a man puts a record on to play, and then knocks himself unconscious. When the music is over he comes to, but he has not been able to enjoy the music and the upliftment that could have come with it. The virtues are ours and will remain with us if we cultivate them consciously with labour and battle. The vices that are defeated will remain defeated if they are mastered by our labour consciously carried on. Their defeat will bring great transmutation in our nature and great expansion of consciousness.

Self-hypnotism resembles the writing of checks without having the capital in the bank.

There is great richness of experience in consciously conquering our nature through our developing will. There is great progress in facing pain, suffering, misery and many other complex circumstances. They are all part of the lessons we must pass through and learn.

Conscious suffering creates heroes. Self-hypnotism creates slaves.

Chapter XV

GUIDEPOSTS

"The Raja Yoga seeks to control the changes in consciousness, and by this control to rule the material vehicles.

"The Hatha Yoga seeks to control the vibration of matter, and by this control to evoke the desired changes in consciousness."[1]

—Annie Besant

The following quotations are the viewpoints of noted Teachers in the esoteric field.

> "The weak point in Hatha Yoga is that action on this line cannot reach beyond the astral plane, and the great strain imposed on the comparatively intractable matter of the physical plane sometimes leads to atrophy of the very organs, the activity of which is necessary for effecting the changes in consciousness that would be useful. The Hatha Yogi gains control over the bodily organs with which the waking consciousness no longer concerns itself, having relinquished them to its lower part, the 'subconsciousness.' This is often useful as regards the prevention of disease, but serves no higher purpose. When he begins to work on the brain centres, connected with ordinary consciousness, and still more when he touches those connected with the super-consciousness, he enters a dangerous region, and is more likely to paralyse than to evolve."[2]

In *The Secret Doctrine,* H.P.B. comments: "Anugita explains, says Arjuna Misra, pranayama, or regulation of the breath in yoga practices. This mode, however, without the previous acquisition of, or at least full understanding of the two higher senses, of which there are seven, as will be shown, pertains rather to lower yoga. The Hatha so called, was and still is discountenanced by the Arhats. It is injurious to the health and alone can never develop into Raja Yoga."[3] She continues in other writings:

> "The Hatha-Yogi either becomes a sorcerer, or learns practically *nothing*; or more frequently yet, kills himself by such an injudicious practice. The *mantram* ignorantly employed may, and often has proved a treacherous weapon, whose mystical power has caused it to turn and *stab the user.*"[4]

1. Besant, Annie, *An Introduction to Yoga*, p. 43.
2. *Ibid.*
3. Blavatsky, H. P., *The Secret Doctrine*, Original Edition, Vol. I, p. 95.
4. Blavatsky, H. P., *Collected Writings*, Vol. IV, p. 166.

> "It is not that among the Hatha-Yogins—men who at times had reached through a physical and well-organized system of training the highest powers as 'wonder workers'—there has never been a man worthy of being considered as a true Yogin."[5]

The author of *The Mahatma Letters* paints a dismal picture: "Suby Ram—a truly good man—yet a devotee of another error. Not his guru's voice—*his own.* The voice of a pure, unselfish earnest soul, absorbed in misguided, misdirected mysticism. Add to it a chronic disorder in that portion of the brain which responds to clear vision and the secret is soon told: that disorder was developed by *forced* visions; by Hatha Yoga and prolonged asceticism."[6]

> "A bad trainer will sometimes terrorize a horse. He will never after that get really good work out of him. You do not want that, you want to have a friendly agreement with the creature. Your body is exactly like that; you ought to find out the best way to deal with it. It is of no use to try to use Hatha Yoga methods, that is a great mistake. You must be kind to it, but you must be the master; it must not manage you. You must treat it intelligently and get out of it the maximum of work it can do. Get as much out of it as you can, comfortably; never over do it, never overstrain its powers, you may do harm in an hour that it will take years to repair. You will do very much better by trying to understand it, trying to find out what it needs in the way of food and drink. They do not all need the same—they all want carbon and hydrogen and that sort of thing, but the proportion in which they can take them differs very much. Within reason, give it what it wants and likes, but never things which are bad for it, like alcohol and meat. Keep up a friendly relation with it; in that way both of you will get on far more satisfactorily. But never set yourself at variance with it as the Hatha Yogi does, thinking you can dominate it by cruelty or by starving it, or by self-repression. That is never the way to manage anything, but always try to get what you want by understanding what you are dealing with, and inducing such intelligence as the creature may have to work along with you. That is the way to get your result."[7]

> "You have heard of certain children who can see through solid bodies. Seek the solution in the karmic fiery nature. Actually, this is an entirely specific physical phenomenon, usually not conducive to the higher fiery attainments. Hatha Yoga intensifies separate centers and it can only be regretted that these partial endeavors do not lead to Raja Yoga and Agni Yoga. Thus, physical and fiery exercises are harmful, disturbing the surrounding equilibrium. Fire is the highest element, and the approach to it must be by way of the higher consciousness. One can understand and learn to love Fire only through this higher consciousness."[8]

---

5. *Ibid.*, Vol. II, p. 463.
6. Sinnett, A. P., *The Mahatma Letters*, p. 225.
7. Leadbeater, C. W., *Talks on AT THE FEET OF THE MASTER*, p. 91.
8. Agni Yoga Society, *Fiery World*, Vol. I, par. 13.

Volume I of the *Letters of Helena Roerich* states: "One should not overestimate the achievements of Hatha Yoga and think that 'the adepts of Hatha Yoga are equal to those of Raja Yoga in ability to awaken the kundalini and to acquire various siddhis,' and that 'they reach bliss and liberation from matter.' It is not so! The degree of bliss reached by such adepts is very relative, and they *never* reach liberation from matter (in the sense which is meant by the Great Teachers) by means of Hatha Yoga. As it is said in the Teaching, 'We know of no one who reached the goal by way of Hatha Yoga.'

"Even the development of the lower siddhis, to which the Hatha Yogis come by stubborn and terribly difficult mechanical exercises (Western literature has no idea about even half of these horrors), is not lasting, and in their next incarnations they may lose all these siddhis. Only those achievements are valuable and permanent that come naturally, for then they are the result of inner spiritual development and can never be lost. Only in such way can the all-powerful manifestations be reached. Exercises in Hatha Yoga should not go beyond a slight and very careful pranayama, which strengthens health, as otherwise they might be dangerous and could lead to mediumism, obsession and insanity.

"Quite correctly, the Hindu people of high spiritual development consider Hatha Yoga most undesirable, and they say that at best it is useful 'for fat and ill people.' Even Vivekananda, who is so often mentioned now, though he cited examples of fearful demoniac persons whom he knew who were able to perform the most amazing miracles and cure the hopelessly sick by a glance, was very much against the so-called siddhis and these miracles.

"Therefore, the main test for all spiritual Teachers is the magnet of their own hearts, their occult ability to change spiritually the surroundings and to transform the consciousness and the very nature of their disciples. It is by no means their ability in so-called miracles. This requires the fiery ray of synthesis, which is inherent in the opened centers but not in the lower siddhis. No pranayama can give the necessary purification and high results if the consciousness does not correlate with the High Ideal. The higher forms of Yoga do not need pranayama. Every coolie in India knows about pranayama; the average Hindu performs it every day, but nevertheless they are far from spiritual achievement. Therefore, do not rely just upon pranayama!

"The highest achievement of a Yogi is the opening of the eye of Dangma, and it is not what we call clairvoyance. It is the awakening of perceptions which never can be developed by any mechanical means but which comes as the result of accumulations of uninterrupted spiritual aspirations and self-sacrifices over thousands of years; and these results are manifested in the most subtle energies, which are stored and preserved within the Chalice. A true Yogi should try his very best to awaken these old accumulations and to preserve and protect the new ones; otherwise, he is a mere book-taught occultist.

"It is also quite wrong to think that 'the occult sciences would never have obtained the correct idea of the astral plane, had it not been for the selfless work of the Hatha Yogis. . . .' Such an assertion is equivalent to a statement that the foundations of physics and chemistry would have been unknown to Ruhmkorff and Crookes without the work of present-day college freshman! Or that an agriculturist knows less about the chemistry of the soil than an ordinary ploughman.

"Moreover, the difference between Hatha Yoga and Raja Yoga is precisely qualitative, and not quantitive, as you think. Hatha Yoga can never rise above the lower psychic phenomena. And there never has been a case when a Hatha Yogi became a Raja Yogi—their paths are entirely different. The true efficacious pearls include Raja, Jnana, Bhakti and Agni Yoga, but not Hatha Yoga, as some ignorant people think; just as artificial pearls cannot be compared to real ones. Furthermore, I cannot quite understand the following thought: 'But nevertheless, Hatha Yoga gives to its adepts efficacious pearls of high achievement, and in the same manner every occultist must look upon the achievements, of Agni Yoga as a similar tremendous victory of spirit over the flesh.' Here again, Agni Yoga is put on the same level with Hatha Yoga, whereas these two Yogas are *diametrically opposite*. As it is said, 'Verily, Agni Yoga *has nothing in common with* Hatha Yoga; this must be thoroughly realized.' Agni Yoga deals with the highest fiery transmutation of all the centers, which cannot be achieved by any mechanical methods but requires the direct controlling influence of the Great Teacher. The high attainment of Agni Yoga can be reached only by a spirit which possesses agelong spiritual accumulations, collected in the center of the Chalice, while the latter is not absolutely essential for the Hatha Yogi. Another thing that is characteristic of Agni Yoga is that its achievements must be attained during everyday life, while all the other Yogas (except Karma Yoga) demand isolation from ordinary life, and thus are not sufficient for the present and future evolution.

"It is also a mistake to call every beginner of any of the Yogas a 'Yogi'. Yoga, or *communion*, is achieved by hard and *constant* spiritual practice, and can be hastened, as it was said above, only by karmic accumulations. Therefore, it is wrong to say that 'a Raja Yogi sometimes becomes a fanatic; a Jnana Yogi an intellectual speculator; and a Bhakti Yogi a religious zealot who rejoices at the 'righteous' punishment of heretics.' Rather, it would be more correct to say that 'those who have certain inclinations which may lead them to become in their later incarnations Raja Yogis may first manifest themselves as fanatics; those with tendencies toward Jnana as intellectual pedants; and those with Bhakti tendencies as religious hypocrites.' Once, however, a high degree of true Yoga is achieved (either Raja, Bhakti or Jnana), there can be no real perversion of the guiding principles in such an intense way. A king of Spirit cannot become a fanatic, and a Jnana-Philosopher possessing the eye of Dangma cannot become an idle intellectual pedant; neither can a Bhakti-a lord of the cosmic magnet of the all-embracing heart-rejoice at 'righteous punishment.' When the Teaching mentions there are 'signs of the Hatha Yogi in the unbearable athlete, signs of the Bhakti Yogi in the hypocrite, and signs of the Raja Yogi in the fanatic,' it is pointing out characteristic inclinations which, if transmuted by spiritual fire, would lead into one or another of the different types of Yoga. But not vice versa!

"One should also take into consideration that Hatha Yoga is dangerous because, in a peculiar way, it strengthens the astral body and holds it for a very long time in the lower astral spheres, which prevents the evolution of the spirit. In the temples of India there was, and still is, a custom of keeping Hatha Yogis for certain lower phenomena of the astral type. They are supposed to lead a very pure life, but even then are never initiated into the higher spiritual powers. And if such a Hatha Yogi leaves the temple, he is not accepted back again, for, by becoming free from the higher control while having an easy access to the lower strata of the Subtle World, such a yogi becomes a victim and sometimes even an instrument of the darkest forces. Here is also the reason why Hierophants of Egypt never accepted mediumistically inclined disciples, and even avoided lymphatic servants. Not a single medium, not one lymphatic, can become a true Agni Yogi.

"The Great Teachers are grieved because of the predomination of lower psychism at the expense of true spirituality. Without the understanding and application of the Living Ethics, without spirituality, the lower psychism can lead to the most grievous results. Therefore, in order to be accepted as disciples it is necessary, first of all, to practice self-perfection, to improve morally and spiritually, and to apply the Teaching in life. This will broaden the consciousness and bring the necessary balance. The Teaching is beautiful and true when it is realized, but no tricks of pseudo-occultism and magic will lead to true discipleship. In order to fill one's vessel from the High Source, one has to establish the corresponding high vibrations. The application in life of the Living Ethics is the quickest way to reach the goal.

"Great is the mission to kindle the consciousness of people by 'podvig' (great deeds), which can change the whole essence of people. Perhaps never was the idea of podvig so necessary in life as now. What a beautiful word—*podvig*! How expressive! And note how remarkable it is that it has no equivalent in any other Western language. So please remember that communion with the Teacher is achieved through the heart, through purified thinking, and by way of the long, tireless work of self-perfection.

"And now one more warning: theoretical occultism is most dangerous. Many most harmful books flood the market. Perhaps (and fortunately) not all of them are translated into the Russian language. As it is said, 'Many of them are the creation of hands that are lacking in beauty, knowledge and honesty.'

"It is said by the Great Teacher, 'Only Blavatsky knew,' and it is our duty to rehabilitate the memory of this great woman martyr. If you only knew all the slanderous literature about Mme. Blavatsky, all the betrayals and the perfidy around her, you would be horrified. So much ingratitude, viciousness and ignorance. Of course, all hideousness results from the latter."[9]

The Master M. has said:

> "Hatha Yoga cannot be regarded as an independent form. The growth of the spirit changes it into Raja Yoga. It is impossible to name anybody who attained through Hatha Yoga. Besides, in the astral world the accomplishments through Hatha Yoga may even bring harm, by stressing especially the astral body. The fakirs may adapt themselves to the astral plane and unwittingly weaken the ascent of thought. Even an immobile person, meditating, can attain further; because thought is the Raja of all that exists. Beauty is born through the lightning of thought. Truly, a flaming Bhakti can kindle new worlds with a thought. And the step of a Jnana will be but the smile of a Raja-Bhakti. Therefore Hatha and Jnana are not self-sufficient. What sage of wisdom would not be the lord of love?"[10]
>
> "It might be of interest here to note that it is the problem of establishing a relation between the animal and himself which was the original basis of what is called Hatha-Yoga and tantric magic. The link was sought in this yoga with that which was known to be similar in the two kingdoms (the physical body with its activities and purposes) and that which should be negative in the human kingdom was stimulated into a positive agency through the power of the will. That followers of Hatha-Yoga are not aware of this purpose may be true, but the originating exponents of the Hatha-Yoga mysteries were well aware of this objective, and in their zeal for unity between the two kingdoms, sought unity in the lower aspects, and neglected the real method.
>
> "In establishing group relation with the superhuman kingdoms, man has not so erred, though relatively little progress has as yet been made, and few are the human units who have merged their consciousness with that of the greater directing Intelligences and yet remained in the human family. This is the true Raja Yoga."[11]

In explaining the work of the Hierarchy, the Tibetan states: ". . . The Ibezhan adepts had to deal with a humanity which was in its infancy, whose polarization was most unstable, and whose coordination was very imperfect. There was very little mentality to be found and men were practically altogether astral; they functioned even more consciously on the astral plane than on the physical, and it was part of the work of these early adepts, working under instruction from Shamballa to develop the energy centres of the human unit,

9. Roerich, Helena, *Letters of Helena Roerich*, Vol. I, pp. 203–207.
10. Agni Yoga Society, *Agni Yoga*, par. 28.
11. Bailey, Alice A., *A Treatise on Cosmic Fire*, p. 1213.

stimulate the brain and make him fully self-conscious on the physical plane. Their objective was to bring about a realization of the kingdom of God within, and little attention was paid (in Their training of Their disciples) to the bringing about of the realization of God in nature or in other units. It was necessary in those days to employ methods more definitely physical than are permissible now, and these methods of physical stimulation were employed and the laws of energy as they work through the various centres were taught until the time came when another big change was made in the hierarchical methods, and the door from the animal kingdom into the human was closed and the door of initiation was opened. It was felt at that time that man was then self-centered enough and individualized enough to permit of a drastic change in method and practice. All this took a vast period of time and it is the remnants of the earlier Temple practices which have come down to us in degraded phallic teaching, in Tantrik magic and the practices of Hatha Yogis. The infant humanity of Lemurian and early Atlantean days had to be taught what they were by means of symbols and methods which to us would be crude, impossible and of a nature which the race should have transcended for many millions of years."[12]

> "Now you can the better understand why Hatha-Yoga has not been indicated by Us. Less than the others does it direct man to the fundamental energy. True, through the perfecting of muscular control and will power, it slowly advances a man, but the most basic factor with which one ought to begin remains neglected.
>
> "Why proceed only from below when the best gifts come from Above? Will not cognition of the most basic energy constitute the most speedy advancement? Not a Hatha-Yogi said, 'The world is thought.' "[13]
>
> "What has forced the poisons toward the earthly spheres? The occurrences of disruption of the elements give rise to a powerful poisonous gas. Usually this gas is easily assimilated in space, but the chemical rays of the sun are driving the gaseous waves into the layers near to the planet. A dangerous reaction results, but those forewarned can overcome the poison. Irritation and its offspring, imperil, combine easily with the poison of space, which is called 'aeroperil.' The laws are like in all things.
>
> "The Teacher sometimes wears a mask against the gas. Of course the action of the poison is not always the same. But sensitive apparati are responsive. Cold considerably minimizes the action of the gases."[14]

The Master M. continues: "Regard the relation between Teacher and disciple. The Teacher gives indications within those limits which are permitted. He uplifts

---

12. Bailey, Alice A., *A Treatise on White Magic*, pp. 380–381.
13. Agni Yoga Society, *Aum*, par. 540.
14. Agni Yoga Society, *Agni Yoga*, par. 23.

the disciple, cleansing him of the outworn habits. He warns him against all kinds of treason, superstition and hypocrisy. He tries the disciple openly and in secret. The Teacher unbars the gates of the next step with the words, 'Rejoice, brother.' He may also close them with the words, 'Farewell, passer-by.'

"The disciple chooses his own Teacher. He reveres Him as one of the Highest Beings. He trusts Him and brings Him his best thoughts. He cherishes the Name of the Teacher and inscribes It upon the glaive of his word. He shows diligence in labor and flexibility in achievement. He meets trials as the light of morning and directs his hope to the lock of the next gates.

"Friends, if you wish to approach Us, elect a Teacher on earth and place in Him your guidance. He will tell you in time when the key may be turned in the gates. Each one should have a Teacher on earth."[15]

> "It might be generally laid down that an upright position in a comfortable chair, with the spine erect, the feet crossed naturally, the hands folded in the lap, the eye closed, and the chin a little dropped is the best posture for the occidental aspirant. In the East there is a science of postures and about eighty-four different positions, some of them most intricate and painful, are listed. This science is a branch of hatha yoga and is not to be followed by the fifth root-race; it is a remnant of that yoga which was necessary and sufficient for the Lemurian root-race man, who needed to learn physical control. Bhakti yoga, or the yoga of the devotee was the yoga of the Atlantean or fourth root-race man, plus a little hatha yoga. In this fifth root-race, the Aryan, hatha yoga should fall into desuetude altogether where the disciple is concerned, and he should occupy himself with Raja Yoga plus bhakti yoga—he should be a mental devotee.
>
> "The *Lemurian* disciple learned to control the physical body and to devote it to the service of Ishvara through hatha yoga, with aspiration towards emotional control.
>
> "The *Atlantean* disciple learned to control the emotional body and to devote it to the service of Ishvara through bhakti yoga, with aspiration towards mental control.
>
> "The *Aryan* disciple has to learn to control the mental body and devote it to the service of Ishvara through Raja Yoga, with aspiration towards knowledge of the indweller, the soul. Thus in this root-race, the entire lower man, the personality is subjugated and the 'Transfiguration' of humanity takes place."[16]

Volume II of the *Letters of Helena Roerich* continue the topic: "It is, of course, exceedingly difficult to describe in words the inexpressible. But still, 'Thought reigns above all Samadhi. The higher, the more powerful. The more flaming the thought, the more useful the manifestation. Truly, thought is all-

15. *Ibid.*, par. 103.
16. Bailey, Alice A., *The Light of the Soul*, p. 214.

powerful and limitless.' Moreover, on our planet the attainment of Samadhi is accessible only to a high Arhat who lives in completely different conditions. Certainly Vivekananda did not achieve complete Samadhi, but, not being sufficiently prepared for it physically, even the degree of Samadhi in which he was immersed brought its sad results. His early death was the result of this premature and forcible experience.

"The human organism of our planetary cycle is still far from such perceptions, and therefore lengthy preparation is needed, not only for this kind of manifestation but also for lesser fiery ones. The very finest vibrations of the unregulated force of Kundalini may destroy a body which is not trained or tempered for its acceptance. Let us bear in mind that the so-called 'yogi,' Ramacharaka (an American by the name of Atkinson), certainly was never a yogi even if he was amongst the listeners of Vivekananda. Hence the freedom with which he writes about mechanical methods without clarifying all the dangers connected with such forcing.

"Thousands of books dealing with easy mechanical methods of developing the hidden lower psychic powers are now thrown upon the world book market. In truth, these ignorant and irresponsible writers are collaborating with the forces of darkness. The latter want nothing so much as to open certain centers in people and thus get hold of them, and through them to join in earthly life in order to fulfill their dark plans. Indeed they are trying to retain around Earth an atmosphere polluted by the very low emanation necessary for their existence.

"Without doubt, simple, rhythmic breathing is in itself quite beneficial. People forget not only the benefit to be derived from fresh air but precisely how to breathe correctly, which actually is the foundation of our health. However, the pranayama of Hatha Yoga has nothing to do with such rhythmic breathing. The pranayama employed by the Hatha Yogis has as its purpose, by means of suspension of breath, rotation, and other gymnastics, the arousing and calling forth of an influx of blood to certain centers, thus causing their increased activity. But one can well imagine how harmful it can be for a man to arouse the centers that are in organs which, for some reason, are weakened or even diseased; certainly their diseased condition will only be intensified. That explains why there are so many unfortunate cases among those who practice pranayama under ignorant and irresponsible teachers. The opening of the centers can safely take place only under the guidance of a Great Teacher, who sees the true condition of one's organism in all its complexity, and who knows what can be applied or permitted, and when. Let us bear in mind that precisely during the transmutation of the centers, a tremendous tension and influx of blood toward them take place. The Teacher must know how, at times, to transfer these tensions to a less dangerous place, or to divert the excess of blood, in order to avoid general conflagration and even fiery death. Believe me, the Teacher will not lose a single moment if a disciple is ready for such transmutation, and will provide whatever is necessary for his organism in accordance with his way of life.

"I have written enough to my correspondents about the harm of mechanical ways, and about the danger of the development of mediumship. For true discipleship, it is essential to apply the strength of the spirit and to know the truth, rather than to be tempted by all sorts of tricks, accessible to any medium." [17]

"It is most essential to point out the difference between mediumship, psychism, and true spiritual development. Much harm has been done by books about all kinds of Hatha Yoga exercises. What ignorance is displayed in thinking that the highest and subtlest can be achieved by purely mechanical methods! You are quite right when you say that people, in striving for spiritual development (which to them so often means the achievement of psychic powers), forget that without active service to the General Good this development will be one-sided and unstable. Our inner fires are kindled only through contact with people. Only thus can we test ourselves; only thus shall we be able to sharpen and temper the blade of our spirit. Undoubtedly, certain isolation and *periodic* retreat is essential for the restoration of our forces. However, constant seclusion will never provide that tension of our forces which alone can bring their refinement. Many statements in the Teaching confirm this. For example, in the second book of *Leaves of Morya's Garden*, on page 47, it is said: 'Christ, Buddha, and their closest co-workers did not use magic formulae but acted and created in full blending with the spirit. Therefore, in the new evolution the former artificial methods must be *abandoned. . . . The mechanics of yogism are no longer suitable for the regeneration of the world.*' And further on, 'Many times have saints returned to Earth because they had conveyed to the crowd too much of their exaltation instead of the structure of life. We are absolutely averse to monasteries, for they are the antithesis of life. . . . *Indeed, through life one must attain.*' Likewise, in the book *Agni Yoga* it is said, in the middle of paragraph 161, 'Raja Yoga, Jnana Yoga, Bhakti Yoga are all isolated from their surrounding reality [from active participation in life]; and because of this they cannot enter into the evolution of the future.' And in paragraph 163, this most unifying Yoga [Agni Yoga] exacts an obligation *to construct* the entire life in conformity with a discipline externally imperceptible.' This means that while constructing and working, one should take certain precautions and should follow the indicated regimen for maintaining health. Thus, if we study the lives of the Great Teachers of humanity, we shall discover that none of them *shut themselves off* from life, but poured all their forces, spiritual and physical, into the service for the General Good. Thus, in everything let us follow these great examples in a lofty attainment of self-renunciation. The crown of self-renunciation is glorious!" [18]

"As for pranayama, you overestimate its significance. Correct breathing is always beneficial, but those exercises which are advocated by irresponsible self-styled yogis are extremely dangerous. I thought I had already written sufficiently

17. Roerich, Helena, *Letters of Helena Roerich*, Vol. II, pp. 21–22.
18. *Ibid.*, pp. 27–28.

about this, but apparently it is necessary to return to this question again. Therefore I shall once more remind you that only he who has completely purified his heart and his mental body from all earthly dross is able to enter the Holy of Holies of Yoga. *Without this purification, no pranayama, will help one to reach even the first gates of true knowledge.* Pranayama can develop mediumship, which would close the Gates. Long exercises in pranayama or in Hatha Yoga make the study of Raja Yoga *impossible.* All the psychic faculties that are developed by means of pranayama, means of the artificial stimulation of the physical and astral bodies, are limited to *a psychic plane,* and not by far a high one; this is proved by the quality of the visions of psychics and mediums. It is important to realize that psychism is *not spirituality.* Precisely, as is said in the Teaching, 'Psychism is the antithesis of spirituality,' and it only hinders the possibility of approaching the Great Teachers. That is why the Teaching begins and ends with the realm of spirit and so severely condemns all exercises for the development of lower psychism. No doubt, the path of spirituality, the royal path, is much more difficult and slow, but it is the only one that deposits all achievements in the Chalice. Those who follow this path have their psychic powers awakened *naturally* and they are developed on all the seven planes, *from the highest* to the lowest; and by fusing them into one this path upholds the great synthesis. No true Teacher will help a disciple to enter the astral spheres by way of mechanical exercises. One should have *no illusions* about this, for otherwise it might be easily possible to contact an entity from these spheres impersonating a Teacher. So many warnings about this were written by H. P. Blavatsky! This very fact created many enemies for her among mediums and psychics, but she fulfilled her ordained mission and pointed out the harm of spiritualism, due mainly to the ignorant approach to it of all classes of society. From my personal experience I know with what hostility all such indications and warnings are accepted."[19]

> "Since Hatha Yoga demands certain bodily exercises, the question may be raised as to whether such exercises are also needed for other Yogas? Neither Arhats nor Great Spiritual Toilers practiced these. Verily, theirs are the trials of the spirit, which not only subdue the body but take the place of all exercises of the flesh. Only the avowal of spirit can replace all else."[20]

> "The process as carried on by the Dark Brotherhood is the reverse of this. They centre the attention upon the form, and seek to shatter and break that form, or the combination of atoms, in order to permit the central electric life to escape. They bring about this result through external agencies and by availing themselves of the destructive nature of the substance (deva essence) itself. They burn and destroy the material sheath, seeking to imprison the

19. *Ibid.*, pp. 194–195.
20. Agni Yoga Society, *Fiery World*, Vol. I, par. 380.

escaping volatile essence as the form disintegrates. This hinders the evolutionary plan in the case of the life involved, delays the consummation, interferes with the ordered progress of development, and puts all the factors involved in a bad position. The life (or entity) concerned receives a setback, the devas work destructively, and without participation in the purpose of the plan, and the magician is in danger, under the Law of Karma, and through the materialising of his own substance by affinity with the third aspect. Black magic of this nature creeps into all religions along this very line of the destruction of the form through outer agency, and not through the liberation of the life through inner development and preparedness. It produces the evils of Hatha Yoga in India and similar methods as practised in certain religions and occult orders in the Occident also. Both work with matter on some plane in the three worlds, and do evil that good may come; both control the devas, and attempts to produce specific ends by manipulation of the matter of the form. The Hierarchy works with the soul within the form and produces results that are intelligent, self-induced and permanent. Wherever attention is centred on the form and not on the Spirit, the tendency is to deva worship, deva contact and black magic, for the *form* is made of deva substance on all planes."[21]

"Concentration upon the physical body only serves to enhance its potency and to feed its appetites and bring to the surface of consciousness that which should be securely secluded below the threshold of consciousness.

"The true aspirant should be occupied with emotional, not physical control and with the effort to focus himself upon the mental plane, prior to achieving a stabilized contact with the Soul."[22]

---

21. Bailey, Alice A., *A Treatise on Cosmic Fire*, pp. 490–491.
22. Bailey, Alice A., *Esoteric Healing*, p. 579.

Chapter XVI

CRISIS IN MAN AND ON THE PLANET

"When the Lord said that He brought to Earth not peace but the sword, none understood his great truth. The purification of the spirit by fire is that sword!

"Can purification be accomplished without striking blows? Is it possible to purify the striving without annihilating the dross? Is it possible to manifest achievement without striving of the spirit? Only the sword which smites egoism can link the spirit to the higher world. The one who rests upon a false peace verily builds self-destruction. Thus, the word of the Lord about the sword furnished the symbol of purification."[1]

—M. M.

When natural calamities, in the form of earthquakes, fires, floods, hurricanes and epidemics, occur in certain places, much of the heavy load of Karma is lightened or burned away in those places. After such disasters, a new beauty and a better life begins there. These disasters help people to realize the greatness of the might of Nature and the insignificant power of the human being, with all of his scientific knowledge and accumulated wealth, to find protection against them.

The substance of the three worlds moves toward involution, toward manifestation, toward materialization and diversity, and man gradually falls into the inertia of matter, covering himself with a thick blanket of material possessions. He enters into the dream states of his pleasures and uses his mind to satisfy his separated life. Natural calamities or disasters may serve to give him a stormy shock which often cracks the shell of identification with the material and lets light flow into his consciousness; light which may lead him into more freedom, more complete detachment from the three worlds, and which may shed more light upon the path of his eternal journey.

For many centuries people have thought that natural calamities or disasters were:

- Warnings of the Greater Power.
- Punishment for our wrong way of living which is against the Will of that Great Power.
- The result of the Law of Cause and Effect.
- The result of our own thoughts, emotions and deeds.

There is great meaning behind these views.

1. Agni Yoga Society, *Infinity*, Vol. II, par. 169.

We know that all globes and systems, including our earth, are floating in and are operated by electromagnetic forces. This ocean of electromagnetic forces is the sphere in which our planet evolves through all of its kingdoms toward a planned destination. The electromagnetic sphere is built, basically, of three kinds of energy which in common language are known as "intellect," "love" and "fire" or "will."

These three energies are the source of our existence, life, and evolution. They make up the field in which all life-forms on the planet, live and move and have their being. They balance and lead the total planetary life into progressive development under a greater Plan of the Solar System. We are told that around the planet, these energies have their centers and their geometrical network through which they reach each living being, each man, endeavoring to keep the way of evolution, the path toward greater consummation, open within and before all forms.

Man is a replica of our planet. He moves in the same kind of individual atmosphere, has the same energies and corresponding centers to make contact with the greater whole. This is the reason that man reflects or responds to all *events* that occur in the great energy field, as an inseparable unit of that global field. His thoughts, his emotions, his deeds make an immediate impression upon the energy field and eventually bring forth response in various forms.

These thoughts, emotions and deeds are actually charges of energy which not only penetrate the great ocean of energy, but which also build cloudy formations around the globe. When such formations reach a certain point of density, power and radioactivity, they cause great destructive or constructive effects upon the kingdoms of the globe. The nature of their content, or their polarization, determines whether the effect will be destructive or constructive. These cloudy formations either channel global energy or hinder its flow, for good or for destructive purposes. When they disappear by *exhausting themselves*, we see again the rainbow in the sky.

An interesting story in the Old Testament tells of three Great Beings who came to the cities of Sodom and Gomorrah. There they found a righteous man and warned him that They were going to destroy the two cities. They said that the cities were to be burned because of the wickedness of their people, and it came to pass. Those cities and ". . . all the inhabitants of the cities, and that which grew upon the ground,"[2] were burned.

What has wickedness to do with the destruction of cities by fires or earthquakes? The answer is that wickedness, a life lived against love, against light, against the purpose of the globe, creates disturbances in the spheres, charging the negative formations and eventually spurring them into action. Natural catastrophies are the result of this action.

2. Genesis 19:25.

We must understand that the result of this action is not limited to our globe, but extends toward the Solar System. Our Solar System is a unit and we share the results of all that transpires upon the other globes. Progress upon any one globe is progress of the Solar System in its totality. We further each other's progress, or we create hindrances, slowing progress. Very soon we will be able to prove that all the globes of the Solar System are a unit held together by the forces of the electromagnetic field, which serves as the basic means of communication and relationship. In other words, all of the globes serve a greater purpose *together*, actuated by a Greater Life.

Millions of years ago, in Lemurian times, through the advent of the Solar Lords, our Spiritual Hierarchy came into being. The purpose of the Hierarchy was to help humanity grow and evolve in harmony with the timetable of the Solar System.[3] Due to a great failure in the moon, our humanity was not progressing at the same pace as the rest of the Solar System. It was becoming a blocking stone on the path of Solar progress. The Hierarchy invoked the help of millions of advanced Beings, who came and eventually incarnated in man to further human progress on the evolutionary path.

People sometimes think that because of spiritual pressure within man, we should be able to do better than we are now doing on a global scale. This is true if we, under the law of freedom of choice, wish to do so. Very often, however, human beings, instead of listening to the small voice within their hearts, live a life harmful to themselves and to others. Thus originates imbalance, which eventually becomes the cause of various disasters.

When humanity creates obstacles on the path of harmonious development of the global life, its own obstacles form a charged cloud of negative energy which in due time comes down and strikes its originating source and place in the form of volcanic eruptions, earthquakes, fires, the submerging of continents, and other natural calamities. The result of such catastrophes is a clearing away of hindrances and the establishing of harmony within the energy field of the globe and of the Solar System.

A parallel happening takes place in our individual lives. Our physical body is floating within the etheric, emotional and mental bodies which are under the rhythm of the Inner Presence. When things go wrong in any of these bodies through our lies, hatreds, jealousies; in wasting precious energies; or in wrong mental activities and negative attitudes; we create disturbances within these bodies. These disturbances, sooner or later, come down and effect the condition of our physical body. In a sense our physical body is the shadow of our etheric body. Any change in the etheric body reflects on the physical body. Because of this fact, we are told that in the coming centuries, medicine will deal, primarily, with the etheric body in the healing of the physical body.

3. Saraydarian, H., *The Science of Meditation*, Chap. XXX.

Each man has (as does the whole of humanity), according to his own level of consciousness, a certain quota of energy which he uses according to his own power of discrimination. He may waste it through excessive sex, or he may try to raise it for higher creative purposes to produce masterpieces of art, scientific discoveries or healing radiations. When he changes his level and stands upon a higher plane, his quota of energy increases because of the increasing efficiency of his etheric and higher centers. At this point his responsibility to these energies increases. If he misuses them, he burns his lower centers and disturbs the corresponding glands of the physical body, inviting pain and suffering upon himself. To misuse means that, instead of using energies on their own levels, man uses them on lower levels to satisfy his physical and emotional desires. For example, you are a king who has ten great scientists working for you, but instead of letting them do their scientific research, you use them for digging or for carrying stones to build pleasure houses for you. You are misusing energies.

The individual and perhaps all of humanity misuse energy—particularly the sex energy. This energy is one of the most valuable in the mechanism of man. It stands between spirit and matter and can enrich the spiritual life of man when sublimated, or impoverish it, if wasted. The wasting of sex energy creates great disturbances in the subtle bodies and these disturbances come back to the physical mechanism causing complications. For this reason great emphasis is laid upon the importance of sexual moderation and its creative use. In those places where this energy is actually wasted in great quantities, destruction occurs through natural calamities.

Sex energy is a very valuable energy because it proceeds to become vitality, sensitivity in the brain cells, impressionability in the aura, creativity in the mind, magnetism and healing radiation in the centers. Through it we provide the materials or substance to build our higher vehicles on individual and global scales. For this reason it should not be wasted, but should be used for procreative purposes, and to create beauty, transmutation and bliss. When wasted in massive quantities by nations or large groups of human beings, the entire mechanism of human beings or nations cannot respond to creative energies, but rather, distorts them, causing imbalance which invites destruction. Many nations and groups have been destroyed in this way.

People sometimes think that the source of energy is inexhaustible. This is true if you are at a stage in which you do not use the energy for any personal pleasure and satisfaction, but use it only to further the Divine Purpose. Below this level your quota of energy is limited. This accounts for the fact that when people feel a lack of sexual energy, they consume more food and use more alcohol or other stimulants to fill the vacuum. Those who are engaged in higher meditation and magical works of the Soul are creating a great fire within themselves. It sometimes happens that fire is created, but we do not have adequate protection around the fire because of the misuse of our valuable substances. Thus, the fire burns our vehicles, causing many physical disorders. Imagine how this will effect the planetary balance, if the majority of people are using etheric, emotional and mental energies against the ordained Will of the Cosmic Magnet. The great Rajput Sage, M.M., says:

"The more anyone renounces, the more he receives. But nations have forgotten how to renounce; even the smallest thinks only how to receive. Meanwhile, the planet is ill and all is sinking in this sickness. And someone wishes to evade the final battle through infection of the whole planet. And some hope to be setting sail in broken fragments, forgetting that the ocean is also departing. It is easy to picture that the planetary body can be just as sick as any other organism, and the spirit of the planet is affected by the condition of its body. How to name the illness of the planet? Best of all as a fever from poisoning. Suffocating gases, from the accumulations of the lower strata of the Subtle World, cut the planet off from the world which could send assistance. The Earth's destiny can be ended by a gigantic explosion if the thickness of the cover be not pierced. A stupendous acceleration is forcing all lines to shake. It could have been expected that acceleration was urgent for a certain country, but it is needed for the whole planet."[4]

"Agni Yoga is not only a progressive development of human possibilities; it should effect the combination with the cosmic energies which reach our planet at a prescribed period. This fact must be understood with surety. Otherwise a seeming succession of sicknesses will spread, and their cure by external measures will bring on most disastrous results.

"How can one be cured of this manifestation of fires? They can only be utilized as a useful psychically active force. How can one cure pains in the spine, if they are correlated with the awakening of Kundalini? He who knows will but welcome it, and will aid by rubbing in mint. How can we stop the burning of the third eye if it begins to function? Is it not more rational to give it development, shielding it from the sun? Long ago people knotted their hair on the crowns of their heads, in order to protect this channel. Can one stop the functioning of the solar plexus if it begins to rotate? Each outrage of the solar serpent may culminate in injury to the brain. Equally dangerous is an interruption to the functioning of the center of the Chalice. Of course, poisoning by opium intercepts the movement of the centers; but then, decapitation would be simpler!

"One may realize what consternation will be provoked by these inexplicable movements of the centers if we do not approach them through the channel of psychic energy. Strangely enough, all study of the physical traces of imperil may compel the understanding of the precipitations of psychic energy. One can observe the traces of imperil in any nerve channel. But one may remark that around the granulations of this poison is gathered some sort of substance which absorbs this virulent viper. The precipitate of psychic energy will be discovered, because each energy has its physical crystal.

---

4. Agni Yoga Society, *Community*, par. 49.

"Whoever has seen the crystals of Fohat and Materia Lucida knows how visible are the crystals of even the most subtle energies. The combining of the physical plane of energies with the invisible saturation of space will be the true direction of study. The way of the metaphysicist has not effected evident results. The alchemist is reposing in his coffin. But chemistry will disclose the tangible reality if it will meet the true understanding of psychic energy and all-binding fire.

"I consider it necessary to provide possibility, but the freedom of the will must not be violated. Whosoever wishes, he will understand! Never give an all-exhaustive formula. Permit place for the free will."[5]

"The disturbance of climatic conditions is evident. But people superficially remark about the sun spots or the shifting of the earth's axis. Such assertions are made by the most cowardly, but they also do not realize what they are saying. The wiping out of civilizations, the annihilation of life, by which the planet was visited more than once, was encountered by precisely the same arguments. Thus, also, people did not care to notice the signs of distress, and superficially continued to argue about prolonging the sapped-out conditions of life. Thus also, among innumerable misconceptions, people ask why in studying the highest knowledge the heightening of sensitiveness and peculiar pains are inevitable. If they were told that the chosen ones are suffering because of their heedlessness, they would not believe it. They will not admit that they in themselves represent condensers and transmuters of energy. Thus, when numerous such apparatuses are damaged, the distribution of energy is disturbed, and only a few sensitive hearts take on the pressure which should have been apportioned throughout the entire world. The Solar-natures take upon themselves the pressure of the fiery energy, and must be responsible for millions of drones."[6]

There are cycles in which new energies are poured into the sphere of our globe, or into the sphere of our Solar System. They provide great opportunities for progress and initiations. Within these cycles, occur cycles of crises which must be handled wisely to preserve the equilibrium or harmony of the planetary Life. The energies pouring in are impersonal energies and can be destructive or constructive in their immediate effect, according to the level of consciousness upon which they make their impact. At the time of their release, if they contact harmful and destructive thoughtforms, thoughtforms that are against Light, Love and Divine Will, they create great upheavals, revolutions, wars and natural calamities. If, however, these energies contact thoughtforms of unity, love, cooperation, and gratitude, they become sources of tremendous creativity in the seven fields of human endeavor.

---

5. Agni Yoga Society, *Agni Yoga*, par. 220.
6. Agni Yoga Society, *Heart*, par. 463.

Therefore, in these cycles, it is imperative that the aspirants, disciples and Initiates of the world be alert, wakeful and that they live sacrificial lives of great beauty, making it possible for these energies to create right-human-relations, foster good-will, further the idea of unity and synthesis, and thus break down the barriers existing among nations, paving the way to one humanity. Each created form is a transformer and a transmitter. If the form is not in the right psychic condition, the whole apparatus or "set" fails to perform without distortion and error.

Most people think that flowers and birds are created to be used by man for his enjoyment and satisfaction. They may be used for these purposes, but they have greater roles to play. They are "electron tubes" which transmute certain healing energies to human beings, without which the human kingdom would suffer tremendously. They also cleanse from the atmosphere, heavy layers of base thoughtforms, criminal or ugly thoughtforms. They serve to establish harmony and rhythm. The singing of birds and the fragrance of flowers have a destructive effect on negative emotions and base thoughts floating in the atmosphere. It is important to purify the atmosphere of your garden with fragrant and colorful flowers. Fragrance and color are vibrations which have a great effect on the psychic world. You must also try to attract as many birds as possible to your garden, because their songs will open pure channels between you and the deva kingdoms. It is not advisable to keep birds in cages. An imprisoned bird does not sing as does a free bird. It is the hymns and songs of free birds that should fill the air around us.

Smog and many poisonous gases, the result of human greed, are destroying our flowers, birds and trees. Thus, they are leading us to sickness and disease, and are producing a fertile soil for the growth of the dark forces on our planet. Spiritual energies can express themselves in pure air, in the beauty of nature, in fragrance and in the mountains and forests that are clear of poisonous gases. Spiritual energies need healthy birds and flowers of thought, emotions and deeds, that they may pour down the more abundant life of joy and bliss.

One of the greatest tasks of educators is to prepare human beings to serve as healthy "tubes" transmuting benevolent energies into living acts. Only by heightening the quality of sensitivity to spiritual impressions, and by purifying our thoughts, feelings and acts through the fire of love, can we create the needed equipment for safe absorption, digestion and expression of these energies, and thus condition the evolution of life on our planet. In the event that we fail in this preparation, the incoming energies will not reach us, or if they do succeed in penetrating through the pollution, they will destroy us because of the pollution of our own low quality development. Even the shifting of the North Pole which may cause earthquakes, is a means of focussing new energies upon the planet. Everytime this shift occurs, we are being given a new opportunity to move ahead on the path of evolution. The destructive effect is not caused by the shift, but by the friction between new energies and dark formations of human crime, greed, glamour and illusion.

Spiritual energies pour down more abundantly during the full-moon period. The Tibetan Master strongly advises that at each full moon, disciples and Initiates come together and meditate to absorb these energies and turn them into creative activities and uplifting aspirations. This is accomplished by right thinking and lofty prayers, invocations, meditation and contemplation, expressed through a life of right-human-relations and good-will.

One point must be stressed here; when natural calamities occur, we may assume it to be the punishment of God. This is not true. When a man is stricken by sickness, that sickness is there to establish order, equilibrium and, eventually, health in his system. Many people think in terms of one life. We believe that each life of ours is but a day in the great life period. All suffering, pain and catastrophes eventually awaken us and cleanse our system of all impurities, establishing light, love and power within us. Indeed, our obstacles must be blessed. The same holds true on planetary and solar scales.

Potent energies are handled by the group of Great Initiates to protect humanity. For example, we are told that in 1939 the energy of Will was released upon humanity, and the immediate effect was a great war, because of the human state of consciousness in which greed, hatred and selfishness ran rampant. The same energy will be released again in 1975. The result will depend upon the way in which we react to that energy, the manner in which we handle it. It is imperative, therefore, that we think and live in terms of one humanity, peace, cooperation, and understanding, if we are to prevent a great catastrophe.

Sunspots are the heartbeats of the Solar Being. When such Solar energies are released, great upheavals may occur because of the chaotic condition of the thought atmosphere surrounding the planet. This same Solar energy may also become great creative energy if it is received, assimilated, absorbed, and expressed. Besides the energy released through the sunspots, there are extraplanetary currents of thought energy which may come from lower or higher spheres. They, too, can create positive or negative effects, depending upon the condition of the receivers, users and transmitters.

The Rajput Prince asks again:

> "Is a deluge possible which can wash away entire regions? Can there be an earthquake which destroys whole countries? Can there be a whirlwind sweeping away cities? Can there be a fall of enormous meteors? All these are possible, and the swing of the pendulum can be increased. Does the quality of human thought have no significance? Thus let people reflect about the essence of things. It is very near to thought and many thoughts are directed here from other worlds. Let us not blame sunspots alone. A single thought about Brotherhood is already salutary."[7]

7. Agni Yoga Society, *Brotherhood,* par. 250.

We are told that in 1945, in an effort to stop the suffering of humanity, the two Great Lords, the Buddha and the Christ, shifted the Will energy and channeled it through the love center of the planet, the Hierarchy. This act was performed in *response to the cry for help by humanity*. A human being, equipped with Light, Love and the Divine Will, can consciously cooperate with Nature. Several incidents which illustrate this fact are set forth in the Bible:

– Noah built the ark before the deluge.[8]
– Elijah prayed and the rains came.[9]
– Moses divided the waters of the great river.[10]
– Jesus ordered the winds and the waves to calm.[11]

It is time, now, to prepare Group Disciples, Great Initiates, who understand Nature and who cooperate with it for evolutionary ends.

The New Age, because of great incoming energies, needs group "tubes," group "transformers" and group "transmitters." Through their mode of living, meditation, love and service, they will absorb the many energies, refine the atmosphere, and purify the globe of pollution. Thus, will they condition the beneficial effects of the incoming energies.

Very often, after great natural disasters, we turn to spiritual practices, renouncements, disciplines and love. Suddenly we recognize spiritual values, and the urge to serve and protect increases within us. We realize that some of the losses suffered through such crises have great educational value which can be stored as treasures and used throughout the ages.

You may lose money, property and many other things, but the lesson learned may prove to be of much greater value than the losses. One minute of right orientation toward the Cosmic Magnet saves your life a thousand years of pain and suffering, and leads you toward a life of love. Hatred leads to death. The other name for death is hatred. It leads to darkness, to suffering and to natural calamities.

Your actions and words, then, must be charged with Love energy, to cause higher, deeper and more inclusive responses. Your type of being conditions the type of energy which you will bring in and put into action. If you do not work on the principles of Love and harmony, you will ruin the harmony and balance of the forces. The result will be that natural phenomena will work against your existence. If we do not have right responses between the parts and the whole, we call the condition *sickness* or *illness*. Right response is the right method for assimilation of the energies of the universe, and for expressing them in creative action. The Tibetan Master in his book, *Esoteric Healing* says:

8. Genesis 6:14.
9. Kings 18:45.
10. Exodus 14:21.
11. Matthew 8:23.

> "If you were to ask me what, in reality, lies behind all disease, all frustrations, error and lack of divine expression in the three worlds, I would say it was *separativeness* which produces the major difficulties arising in the etheric body, plus the inability of the outer tangible form to respond adequately to the inner and subtler impulses."[12]

We must know and understand that *everything exists*. We can discover it only when we start to respond. The light is there, but we are unable to see it if we are blind. Until we register the light, we cannot see the light. It was a tremendous shock to me when suddenly one day, I realized that everything *is there*! We need only to *grow*, to love, to understand, to know, to unfold and *be*! Thus, the answers to all of our problems can be found through deeper and higher responses to the greater Life within us and within the Cosmos.

As we come into closer harmony with our Soul, the energy of Love and the expression of Love increase. Love gives life; Love brings joy; Love creates harmony. Within that harmony, man is born as a Soul, and is ready to set his face toward his Eternal Home.

---

12. Bailey, Alice A., *Esoteric Healing*, p. 82.

Chapter XVII

THE COMET AND 1975

"The purifying fires of the Universe penetrate all regions of the planet. The sparks of conflagration spread along all channels of karmic action. As volcanoes, these affirmed fires explode. The force of karma shifts and transfers power from hand to hand. The cosmic course is directed toward those purifying conflagrations; hence the comet, speeding through the Infinite. The tensity of the currents is very great and the effect corresponds to the fires of the planet."[1]

—M.M.

The unfolding human soul grows and reaches maturity through crises. Every crisis is an opportunity and a test. As awareness expands, life after life, the soul passes individual and global crises. Each time achievement is tested, new horizons are opened before the evolving soul.

At this stage of history the unfolding soul of humanity is facing a major crisis which is global and especially involves our political, educational, religious and economic fields. The highest point of this crisis will be the Full Moon of Taurus 1975. As esoteric history shows, before major points of crisis are reached, humanity witnesses numerous signs such as wars, celestial configurations and comets.

It is interesting to note that we have had several wars in the Far and Middle East; we have had many interesting astrological configurations; serious energy and economic crises have occurred; and on March 7, 1973, two or three days after the new moon, Dr. Lubos Kohoutek at Hamburg University discovered a comet.

Comets are called "dirty snowballs" by some astronomers. For esoteric students, they are fiery lives or messengers playing a great role in the framework of the whole existence.

Comets have a center by which they are controlled. They are links or communication lines among Solar Systems and galaxies, and open a passage through which extra systemic energies or rays may flow. Functioning under the Law of Evolution and the Law of Economy, they distribute or generate energy as they pass along their own particular routes through the various spheres.

They create friction in the atoms of the whole Solar System, releasing energy waves. As energy waves fall upon our Earth sphere they bring great revelation and insight. Before a comet enters a Solar System it creates tremendous pressure on that Solar System as a whole. After passing through the ring or sphere of

1. Agni Yoga Society, *Infinity*, Vol II, par. 4.

the System, it creates a great vacuum which becomes a field of chemical explosions and transmutation.

As a comet enters any organized sphere such as a Solar System, it creates an ever flowing process of stimulation, transmutation and atomic release. The energies produced are psychic, electrical and magnetic. They reach and affect the bodies of the planets and act on every form upon the planets, charging them with new energies. These energies create changes in the atoms and cells of all living beings and may even affect the genes.

The pressure and resulting process of stimulation, transmutation and atomic release affect the mental, emotional and etheric nature of living beings, causing:

1. Expansion of consciousness, upliftment, enlightenment and release.
2. Destruction of things which are not in line with cosmic prospect.
3. Revelations of new laws and elements through which new *intentions* (IN-TENSIONS) can be reached. IN-TENSIONS are the result of new energies being active in a given field of consciousness.

The comets burn and clean, to some degree, the spheres which are polluted by all formations resulting from wrong thinking, negative and separative emotions, and selfish and criminal drives and actions.

The whole energy system is in the process of adjustment. The comets themselves are not evil. They adjust and tune the Solar System through their new energy supply, pressure and purification. When planets are out of harmony with the sun, they become out of balance; comets serve to put the planets back on their axes and into proper orbit. It may also happen that comets take away moons or planets which are considered great hindrances on the path of Solar or Cosmic evolution. They burn such obstructions in space through the process of intense friction.

The present comet has arrived here just before the release of Shamballa energy in 1975. It may be that it is purifying the Solar System and the sphere of our earth, to some extent, to eliminate the great catastrophic effect that the energy of Shamballa may have upon our planet, due to physical and moral pollution.

People often think that comets are without influence. Actually, they deeply influence the psychology of people for good or for bad, depending on the level upon which the people are focussed, or from which they react.

A comet which appeared in 1811 was visible for 17 months, and in 1811 there was a great war between Russia and France in which France was defeated. There was also the war of 1812 between America and England. Another comet which came in 1910, called Halley's Comet, heralded the great war which lasted from 1914 to 1945.

War is a phenomenon of conflict between two series of man-atoms, differently polarized. This conflict is started and often stimulated by great comets which cause tremendous friction within the sphere of the Solar System. Every form shares that friction, and expresses it in various ways at that given moment.

What might we expect from this comet? Is it a messenger from space? Do we lack spiritual and intellectual fuel? Is the passing of this comet to replenlish our supply and restore law and order? Are we in danger of atomic war? Is this comet the messenger of the New Age and the vanguard of the fiery energy of the Stronghold?

The answers to these questions will be given by humanity itself. The answers will depend upon the way in which humanity reacts, the reaction of the human mind, the way man lives and expresses his emotions, the way he responds to his fellowmen, the way he functions upon the earth.

After the comet has completed its task, we will face the critical year—the momentous year 1975. At the Wesak Full Moon of that year the Great Ones will release the energy of the Will Center over humanity. *Will* energy is fiery, highly dynamic and penetrative. Again, the effect of this energy will be conditioned by humanity itself; humanity— through its activities, emotional reactions and mental responses—will decide the effect of this energy. Some possible effects may be that:

1. It may annihilate the sense of separativeness on the mental plane if enough men and women of goodwill strive toward unity and stand for brotherhood of humanity. Should this happen, we will see the bloom of the human soul; unity and human brotherhood with all the political, religious and economic consequences, and *Christ may appear.*
2. If humanity keeps its hatreds and exploitative attitude, its greed and totalitarianism, it may create total destruction of our civilization through the "fire." This does not mean that the human race will be annihilated, but the externalization of the Hierarchy will be delayed for thousands of years, until humanity learns its lesson and turns to the vision of Christ.
3. If humanity does not respond to the virtues of the New Age—simplicity, beauty, love and unity—if humanity continues to live a selfish life, this energy may strike its physical, emotional and mental vehicles, creating many degenerative diseases for a long time to come.

We are entering into one of the major crises which may last a few days, a few years, or decades. Its effect may start immediately after 1975 like a thunderbolt or through a slow process.

With the energy of Shamballa, however, there are other available energies, which are already penetrating into our Solar System. The first is the energy of the Seventh Ray, and the other is the energy of the constellation of Libra which will increase in power toward 2025.

These energies are impersonal and their effects will be conditoned again by the various responses of all kingdoms of nature, especially by the response of humanity. If humanity takes those steps which will make the form more responsive to the unfolding of spiritual values; if humanity creates harmony between the *above* and *below*, then the energy of Shamballa will pave the way for greater revelations, and the Seventh Ray energy together with the energy of Libra will inaugurate an age of outstanding creative activity, beauty and harmony.

Let us also mention that this comet will transfer energy to our Solar System, particularly from two other great Lives which are called Capricornus and Aquarius. We know, too, that the equinoctial sun is moving into the sign Aquarius for the next twenty-two centuries.

Capricornus releases in man the conquering will by which he "uplifts" himself above his mundane life with its personality reactions, and enters into the domain of his spiritual will and universal awareness. This same thing may happen for the planet and for the planetary life, because by using this capricornian energy the Earth may tune in with the will aspect of Cosmos, and finally become a *sacred* planet.

The energy of Aquarius reveals the inner urge to serve, to cooperate, to move toward synthesis, and to expand into group and universal awareness. It leads toward cooperation and closer communication.

All indications are that we have a unique opportunity to change this planet of sorrow and death into a planet of joy and liberation. Man must choose between life and death. This great opportunity invites all of us, at this time, to do our utmost to bring in positive effects:

1. By daily meditating and brooding upon the concept of harmony, mastery, unity and synthesis.
2. By daily speaking, writing and thinking about the brotherhood of humanity, about peace, about non-possession, about the highest good for all humanity.
3. By daily repeating the Great Invocation and blessing the United Nations and humanity.
4. By keeping silence for one hour daily, and one day each month.

Thus, we will meet the crisis, and make it a door of initiation into the life "more abundant."

Chapter XVIII

KARMA—THE LAW OF CAUSE AND EFFECT

"Metaphysically, the law of retribution; . . . There is the karma of merit and the karma of demerit. It is the power that controls all things, the resultant of moral action, . . ."[1]

—The Tibetan

Karma is a Sanskrit word which means action, work, causation, retribution, and accumulated causes for future actions. It is defined as the Law of Cause and Effect. "Whatever a man soweth that shall he also reap" is a biblical expression of its meaning.

Edwin Arnold, in his wonderful book, *The Light of Asia*, explains it in poetry:

". . . my Brothers! each man's life
The outcome of his former living is;
The bygone wrongs bring forth sorrows and woes,
The bygone right breeds bliss.. . .
This is the doctrine of Karma."[2]

The Law of Karma functions on all levels of the human being and on all planes of our Solar System. It functions automatically. Automatically it creates reaction to any action; it selects the dates, the environment, the conditions, the intensity of the reactions, and the personnel.

In nature we have a super electronic computer (symbolically speaking) which works as the Law of Cause and Effect, registering all *motion* on any plane, and deciding the reaction on the basis of when, where, how, and the persons involved. This is a very complex mechanism, the operation of which is always extremely complex, adapting itself to the slightest act on any level. It is the Creator's instrument of Justice and Love.

The Law of Karma functions through the all embracing field of electromagnetic energies in space. Our physical-etheric, emotional, and mental natures are fused with this field and the slightest motion in them is registered, impressed and acted upon individually or in total. All of our actions on these three planes have their special frequencies, wave lengths, tonality, and other unique characteristics. Each of them is performed in conscious motivation, or as an unconscious reaction. Those that are performed in conscious motivation carry with them

1. Bailey, Alice A., *Letters on Occult Meditation*, p. 351.
2. Arnold, Sir Edwin, *The Light of Asia*, p. 143.

a greater charge of energy. Their impression is greater and deeper on the electromagnetic field, because their reaction is proportionate to their action.

The intensity of action differs from plane to plane. For example, if an action is motivated from the physical plane and expressed by the emotional or mental plane, in each case it will have a different wave length, frequency, and intensity to impress the electromagnetic field of space. Simple actions have simple reactions; complicated actions have complicated reactions and effects which can run as chain reactions. Each action creates a reaction not only on its own level, but it also starts in motion other levels through the corresponding points in them. This accounts for the chain reaction within the levels and within the responding levels of the space field. Thus, each action builds the future, your self-created home, in which you are going to live. In a sense, we can say that a human being is creating his own future through the life he is living *now*. Our future is the accumulated answer to the actions that we express now. The totality of these actions, reactions and inter-actions is called in Sanskrit, Karma.

Reincarnation is the result of the Law of Karma. If there is no karma, there is no incarnation. The goal of evolution is to liberate us from the wheel of incarnations, from the process of birth and death. This is accomplished when our good karma totally obliterates our "bad" karma.

The Ancient Wisdom teaches that the Solar Angel is a representative of the Karmic Lords and of the Hierarchical Plan within the man. Karmic Lords are four Great Beings, three of Whom deal with the three fires: electric fire, Solar fire, and fire by friction. These are the names of electricity, the lowest of which is the electricity we commonly use. In the Ancient Wisdom it is called "fire by friction."

The Fourth Karmic Lord systematizes the work of these three Great Beings and "attends to the uniform blending and merging of the three fires." In the Ancient Wisdom these Great Beings are called Maharajahs, the Lipika Lords, (the registerers), or the Lords of Karma, Who function under the rule of a greater Lord in the Sun Sirius. Further, we are told that this *Law of Karma* is rooted in or operated on the Third Subplane of the Cosmic Mental Plane. There are also:

> "Four devas, who are the *plane* representatives of the four Maharajahs (The Lords of Karma) and are the focal points for karmic influence in connection with man. The four Maharajahs are the dispensers of karma to the Heavenly Men [Planetary Logoi], and thus to the cells, centres, and organs of His body necessarily; but the whole system works through graded representatives; the same laws govern these agents of plane karma as govern the systemic and cosmic, and during plane manifestation they are, for instance, the only unit *in form* permitted to pass beyond the plane ring-pass-not. All other units in manifestation on a plane have to discard the vehicle through which they function before they can pass on to subtler levels." [3]

3. Bailey, Alice A., *A Treatise on Cosmic Fire*, pp. 468–469.

> ". . . KARMA is imposed upon the ensouling entity through the medium of matter or substance itself . . . and . . . this matter or substance is *intelligent material composed of deva essence.*" [4]

We are told that there is Cosmic Karma, Systemic Karma, Planetary Karma, Karma of the Chain, Globe Karma, Plane Karma, Karma of a Subplane, the Karma of the Kingdoms of the Nature (the animal, vegetable, mineral kingdoms), the Karma of the Human Hierarchy, which is subdivided into:

> "World karma. (The seven root-races.)
> Racial karma, . . . each root-race.
> Subrace karma, . . .
> National karma.
> Family karma.
> Individual karma." [5]

The Tibetan Teacher also says that: "All these different types of karma are intermingled and bound up in a manner inconceivable and inextricable to man." [6]

In view of such an oceanic picture we can feel only the depth of responsibility of each unit, for the whole stands as an inseparable unit in which every cell affects every other cell in that whole.

We all share each other's karma. A pain in our heart can be a distant echo of some disorder on any plane in the Cosmic whole, and the accumulated karma of a nation can strike as lightning upon a hero who is ready to sacrifice his life for the whole.

This reminds me of a game which was played in Asia. Two deep pools of water were connected underneath by a three inch pipe. In each pool five boys were chained by their feet in water up to their jaws. They all had buckets in their hands. Each team had to empty its own pool into the other pool to save its own life. Thus, each of us tries to get rid of our own karma, but always we are faced with the karma of others. Some of us increase the karma of others by the way we live, some of us decrease the karma of others by the way we serve and suffer.

While I was meditating on this subject, I found that the way out of karma is possible, not by running out of karma, but by preparing oneself to face greater karma in greater fields. I wonder if this is the way the world Saviours work: Is the path of the Cross, of suffering, a path of facing greater pressure of karma, lifting greater burdens from the shoulders of little ones, and giving them a chance to grow and enter the path of a "heroic" life?

It seems to me that as one faces greater karma of greater wholes he creates less personal karma, and thus helps to decrease the total karma. Freedom from karma on the three levels of personality will be possible when a man enters

4. *Ibid.*, p. 469.
5. *Ibid.*, pp. 470–471.
6. *Ibid.*, p. 471.

into the World of Causes and thus controls the effects within the world of personality. Such a man can suffer only for others and lift their burdens.

As we think about the Law of Karma, it becomes clearer to us that the liberation of humanity is possible only when the sense of responsibility is accepted, the brotherhood of humanity is worked out, and the life of each human being is a life of service and sacrifice for others. The whole task of our Solar Angels is to remind us of this Herculean labour and to lead us into the light of Cosmic Awareness in which a man lays down his life for others.

Once we understand the will and purpose of our Inner Lord we enter into the World of Causes and are liberated from the karma of the three lower worlds. Such an achievement is the result of a life lived sacrificially for others. Thus at the Crucifixion Initiation, "the Initiate has escaped permanently from the personality ring-pass-not," and we are told that only a seventh degree Initiate can escape the Solar ring-pass-not and its karma.

There was a time when man was speaking about his personal freedom. Then he realized the importance of his family group and national freedom. Now it is dawning in his mind that freedom is possible only if all humanity is liberated as a unit from its physical, emotional and mental slavery.

Will it be possible one day even to look beyond the planetary karma, and take steps for the liberation of humanity in a Solar sense? This must be the goal of Solar Heroes.

Chapter XIX

THE PROCESS OF DEATH AND LIFE AFTER

"*The Law of Sacrifice and Death* is the controlling factor on the physical plane. The destruction of the form, in order that the evolving life may progress, is one of the fundamental methods in evolution."[1]

—The Tibetan

We are told that the Real Man is the Monad, the Spark, the innermost Self. He has a physical body with the etheric double, the astral body and mental body. If a man is far enough advanced, he also has higher and subtler bodies through which to communicate with the higher realms.

Between these two poles—the Spark and the vehicles—he has the Eternal Guide, the Solar Angel, leading the sleeping Spark back to Himself through the process of gradual awakening, or through a series of initiations.

The Eternal Guide is anchored within a subtle mechanism, which in the Ancient Wisdom is called the Temple of Solomon, the Chalice or Lotus. This mechanism is a very complicated transister, transmitter, accumulator and recorder of experience for all incarnations. It is formed of twelve petals in the process of opening. Three of the petals are called knowledge petals, three are love petals and three are sacrifice petals. The three innermost petals are "valves" for the electric fire at the very center.

The energy of will expresses itself through the sacrificial petals, the energy of intuition through the love petals, and the energy of intelligence through the knowledge petals. These energies are the basic energies of the Solar Angel.

Communication with the physical world, with the emotional world and with the world of thoughts and ideas is carried on by the human soul through this mechanism. In this mechanism:

- Physical sensations are classified, translated and transmitted to the human soul, and reaction to the communication is brought back to the physical world.
- Impressions on the emotional body are translated and classified as feeling and emotion, and right reaction is given by the human soul.
- Impressions from physical, emotional and higher spheres are translated into concepts, into ideas, and the response given as thoughts, knowledge and understanding.

1. Bailey, Alice A., *A Treatise on Cosmic Fire*, p. 569.

The Lotus with its petals controls not only the metabolism of the body through the etheric centers and glands, but it also controls the emotional and mental metabolism. The Lotus with its petals is the agent of transmutation and sublimation; lower forces are refined through the heat (aspiration) it creates. Through this heat, forces are transmuted into emotional, mental and spiritual forces and energies. We must remember that activities and powers of the Lotus petals are relative to their unfoldment and development. There are people who have only a few petals functioning and others who have more. This is the factor which accounts for the difference between an average man and a man of great creativity, a man of great enlightenment.

The unfolding or developing human soul is the divine Spark in the process of being educated. He communicates with the Inner Guide according to his degree of development, through the knowledge petals. Later, as he proceeds on the path of Initiation, he will be able to communicate with Him through the love petals and, eventually, through the sacrificial petals. The Inner Guide serves as a bridge between the unfolding human soul and his Future—the human Soul in his Monadic awareness.

The vehicles of the human soul are the physical, emotional and mental bodies plus the etheric double. All of these vehicles, together, form the personality of the unfolding human soul. When they are truly integrated and controlled by the human soul, they become a Personality, the reflection of the Monad. The Personality is held together by the etheric vehicle and is connected to the Soul and the Spark by two energy lines which in the Ancient Wisdom are called the *life thread* and the *consciousness thread.* The consciousness thread branches off from the life thread which originates in the Monad, in the core of the man.[2]

The life thread extends to the heart center of the mental, astral and etheric vehicles, to the two lung centers under the breasts, to the spleen, and terminates within the heart. The consciousness thread passes through the Solar Angel, or Soul, to the head centers of the mental, astral and etheric bodies, terminating within the pineal gland in the brain.

THE PROCESS OF DEATH

From the viewpoint of occultism, the process of death takes place when the life thread withdraws in a certain sequential order: from the heart, the spleen the two lung centers, (the etheric heart center of the astral body, from the solar plexus on the fourth mental plane).[3] During this process, "Some physiological changes take place at the seat of the disease in connection with the heart, affecting the blood stream, the nervous system and the endocrine system." The connection between the nadis and the nervous system is severed. The glands "inject into the blood stream a substance which in turn affects the heart." The etheric body detaches from the physical body.

2. Read *The Science of Becoming Oneself* by H. Saraydarian, Chap. XVIII.
3. In case he is leaving both the astral and physical bodies.

A similar withdrawal is made by the consciousness thread in the following order: from the pineal gland, the head center in the etheric body, (the head center of the astral body, the base of spine center on the fourth mental plane, finally terminating in the Lotus, or Soul).[4]

When the sutratma, or life thread, withdraws, the man passes away and the consciousness thread registers all that occurs during the process of the life thread withdrawal. When the consciousness thread withdraws, the man still lives, but enters into a coma. We are told that there are two kinds of comas:

1. There is the coma in which an opportunity is given to the physical life by the Soul to repair its mechanism and restore health. The unconscious state causes the man to be unaware of the pain and complications which the body is undergoing. For example, if you are in a sudden accident and suffer serious injury, you may go into a coma. Such an unconscious state would be caused by the withdrawal of the consciousness thread for a short period during which you would feel no pain.
2. There is the coma caused by the withdrawal of the consciousness thread through a decision made by the Soul to dissolve the physical body. In this instance it would mean that a great battle is taking place between the physical elemental, or physical life, and the Soul. The physical life still wants to hold on to the life thread and avoid disintegration, but the Soul's plan is in direct opposition. This conflict, of course, ends in victory for the Soul's decision, but it may take hours or even a few weeks.

This latter kind of coma occurs if the physical elemental is tightly interwoven with the etheric body. Hatha Yoga contributes greatly to this condition, as it crystalizes the astral body and tightens the grip of the etheric body on the physical body.

If the coma is for restorative purposes, the light of four etheric centers will be glowing, but if it is for withdrawal of the life thread, the light of these centers (the heart center, the spleen and the two lung centers below the breasts) will fade away.

If it is withdrawal of the Soul from the physical plane, the light of the spleen will grow dim and go out, the light of the two lung centers will fade away and finally the flame of life will pass out of the heart.

Sometimes the battle with the Soul is carried on by a disciple (the unfolding human soul) when he thinks that he has much yet to do for the plan. He does not want to die because of numerous needs of his friends and his followers. His rejection causes some delay, in the form of a coma. When an Initiate passes on, however, there is no fight, no rejection. There is only blissful acceptance of the will of His Soul.

---

4. In case he is withdrawing from the astral and mental bodies.

After the life and consciousness threads are withdrawn, the physical body is apparently dead, but real death occurs when the life and consciousness threads withdraw themselves from the etheric body, causing complete disintegration of that body. This is accomplished by an act of the Solar Angel and at that time the physical man is dead. H.P. Blavatsky says:

> "At the solemn moment of death every man, even when death is sudden, sees the whole of his past life marshalled before him, in its minutest details. For one short instant the *personal* becomes one with the *individual* and all-knowing Ego [Solar Angel]. But this instant is enough to show him the whole chain of causes which have been at work during his life. He sees and now understands himself as he is, unadorned by flattery or self-deception. He reads his life, remaining as a spectator looking down into the arena he is quitting; he feels and knows the justice of all the suffering that has overtaken him."[5]

The consciousness thread withdraws itself on many different occasions. It may occur, for example, when a man grows very old; when he has some mental disorder or brain damage; when he "passes out," or faints, for various reasons. Under all these circumstances, the life thread continues to remain anchored in the heart and the man continues to live in spite of the absence of the consciousness thread in the physical and etheric planes.

The etheric body is formed of energy threads radiating from the sutratma, from the life thread. Actually, it is a coil of four grades of luminosity in the shape of the physical body. This thread of energy comes out of the center of the Lotus, and as a spider spins its web, the Solar Angel spins it into the etheric body upon which the Lunar Pitris build the physical body. The physical body is formed around this etheric coil. It is the real shadow of the etheric body.

At the time of death this coil is drawn into the Lotus, and all magnetically attracted cells and atoms, or physical substance, is dissolved into the general reservoir of force and matter. When the etheric coil is withdrawn, it passes into the Lotus and there it serves as a link between the physical permanent atom and the Lotus, keeping the permanent atom alive. Thus the life impulse for the physical body is centralized in the Causal body, the Lotus, and rooted in the first mental plane, the atomic plane.

When continuity of consciousness is achieved, the process of dying will be a conscious act and the man will be aware, step by step, of the experience of leaving the physical consciousness and entering into the astral consciousness. Such people often know when they will die because the Solar Angel informs them through special contact, and prepares them for the transition. The Tibetan Master says, "For the unevolved death is literally a sleep and a forgetting, for

5. Blavatsky, H. P., *The Key to Theosophy*, an abridgement, pp. 102–103.

the mind is not sufficiently awakened to react, and the storehouse of memory is yet practically empty."[6]

When a man passes away, he has a form the same as the one he had on the physical plane. The etheric body is an exact replica of his physical body. Later, when he has entirely entered into the astral world, he still has the same appearance, but when he enters into the mental world, he slowly changes into a lotus. Concerning the lotus, there are varying degrees of unfoldment and development. There are lotus buds, slowly opening lotuses, half open lotuses, and so on. The fully open lotus is very rare on the mental plane because a man no longer need stay there, whether he incarnates immediately after he passes away, or enters into the intuitional plane to continue his advanced evolution. The developing human soul is connected to the Lotus and his awareness is proportionate to the unfoldment of the Lotus.

The Inner Guide hovers over the Lotus and watches the human soul. He controls his cycles of incarnation and the type of body he must have for each incarnation.

In some esoteric books the mental plane is called the Master's garden where the real beauties start to sprout, grow and bloom.

Ancient tradition tells us that immediately after death, the *Messengers of Death*, the Angels of Death, meet the man and take him to the *Seat of Evaluation*, the *Seat of Judgment*. Some traditions hold that the judge is not really a separate entity, but the light of the Solar Angel under which, for a very short time, the human soul clearly sees the causes he released and the effects which they created upon the physical, emotional and mental planes. After he has seen these causes and effects, he is led by the Law to the level upon which he belongs. It may be the lowest astral plane, between the etheric and astral, beyond the astral, or mental. It is all according to his merit.

If a man lives a "life of gross misdeeds, of cruelty and greed, of murder and robbery, of slander and debauchery"—through all these acts—he predetermines the level to which he must go. Such people are led to a reformatory sphere, or into a sphere of rehabilitation, to impress upon their innermost being that, "Crime does not pay." This is the purgatory of which the Catholic fathers speak.

Those who are not far enough developed and are below average see all these things as nightmares, but those of average or above average development are more or less conscious of occurences on these planes. It may sometimes happen that they meet with those astral shells which were influencing them, leading them into crime and vice, and they are filled with fear, seeing in them the spirit of hell so colorfully described by the Church.

We are told that in all these situations the love of the One Life prevails; total justice with infinite compassion is given to lead man toward the path of

6. Bailey, Alice A., *A Treatise on White Magic*, pp. 300–301.

spiritual evolution. After a period of rehabilitation, a man is led to higher astral planes.

Zorathustra gave special teaching about life after death and said practically the same thing as did the apostle of Jesus when he said, "As you sow, so shall you reap." In *Yasna*, Master Zorathustra says,

> "Evil for evil and good reward for good.
> Affliction to the wicked,
> Happiness to the righteous,
> Woe to him who oppresses the righteous,
> Salvation to him who upholds righteousness."

He adds, "One should prepare and carry provisions for the spiritual world from the material world so that the soul may not be in trouble."[7]

THE THREE EXITS AND AID IN PASSING

The Ancient Wisdom teaches that there are three doors or orifices through which the unfolding human soul passes out of the sphere of the body. These doors are situated:

- At the top of the head.
- Below the apex of the heart, which we are told is a temporary exit.
- In the solar plexus.

These three doors are protected by a web of etheric matter, and keep the unfolding human soul within the sphere of the physical body.

A low-grade man is focussed in his solar plexus and we may even say that he lives and functions through that center. An average man, a man of good-will, a well-meaning man, a philanthropic worker is focussed in his heart center, and that is the focus of his activities. An advanced man, a disciple or an Initiate is focussed in his head, in the head center; that is his dwelling place, the headquarters of all his activities.

At the time of death, when the life and consciousness threads are broken, or withdrawn, man exits from one of these doors according to his level of evolution. These three doors lead the human soul into three different states of existence. The first door takes the disciples and Initiates directly into the higher mental planes and beyond. Through the second door one enters into the astral and higher astral planes—for a short time. The third door opens to an area between the lowest astral plane and the earth. This state is called the earth-bound sphere, where mostly earth-bound souls are trapped. They are those who exit through the orifice of the solar plexus.

These doors are used not only at the time of death, but also at the time of sleep. Under anesthesia or drugs, only the lower astral door, the solar plexus

7. Masani, Sir Rustom, *Zorastrianism*, p. 72.

is used. Man becomes conscious on the plane for which he is ready by his own merit, or level of beingness.

In occult literature we have information concerning aid that can be given at the time of passing. We are told that the following attitudes and procedures will be helpful:

1. There should be total silence in the sick room to help the one who is passing concentrate on his experiences, and consciously release himself from the physical body. A dying person is aware of all that is happening around him, though he may not be able to let it be known by any outer sign.
2. When the physicians know that there is no possibility of recovery, they should arrange to have orange light in the room. Orange light or color helps the person to focus his consciousness in the head, perhaps between the eyebrows or at the top of the head. It may also be of help to those who are advanced enough to pass away through the orifice of the head. For a less evolved person it is better to have a red light, which releases the man through the solar plexus. If he is a humanitarian, whose heart quality is evolved, it is better to use a green light.
3. Another way to help one at the time of passing is to sound or chant the OM or Om Mani Padme Hum, at least seven times. The one who chants must be an able man in the spiritual field, capable of guiding the dying person out of the physical plane. To awaken or clear the consciousness of the dying one, the following mantrams are highly effective:

   Avira, Verma Yedhi.
   O Self-revealing one,
   Reveal Thyself in me.

   and

   Lead us O Lord,
   From darkness to Light,
   From the unreal to the Real,
   From death to Immortality,
   From chaos to Beauty.

   In so doing, we are keeping him company with our imagination and deep love.
4. There should be no crying, no hysterical screaming; nothing but silence, peace, love, gratitude, and blessing must fill the atmosphere of the room of the dying person.
5. It is very good to repeat or read mentally the second chapter of the *Bhagavad Gita*, which is of supreme help for dying ones.
6. It is also important to anoint the person in transition with sacred oil, putting it on the head, ajna, throat and heart centers. It will be of tremendous help in releasing the anchorage points of the etheric body.

7. The top of the head of the dying man should be toward the east, and the hands and feet should be crossed. The reason for this position is related to the electrical currents of the energies controlled by the etheric body.
8. The burning of incense is good. Sandalwood is highly recommended. The Tibetan Master says that "no incense of any other kind is permitted." Sandalwood helps to separate the nadis from the nervous system and thus release the etheric body.
9. Care must be taken that those close to the dying person do not express with grief and tears, wishes or thoughts of seeing him back to normal physical life. Such actions may create great conflict between the plan of the Soul and the dying person who, in some cases, can be caught within the network of such thoughts and wishes. The best approach is to bless the laws of Nature, and to express love and blessings at the time of the farewell.
10. In the future it will be possible to accompany the dying person to the subtle levels, while he is still in his physical body. This science must be taught to all those who are related to such duties. They will be instructed as to how to come out of their physical bodies, and consciously guide the person as he leaves his body. The average priest, minister or officers of other religions are unaware of such facts. They repeat traditional prayers or chants, or formulate their own, according to their level of experience.
11. Following cremation, sandalwood should be burned for three days in the study or private room of the departed one, and group or individual meditation should be performed in his room, using seed thoughts taken from the *New Testament, Bhagavata Gita,* and *Dhammapada.* The atmosphere must be charged with radiating love, blessings and gratitude.

CREMATION

The Tibetan has stated:

> "Before so very long, burial in the ground will be against the Law and cremation will be enforced."

Throughtout the ages the corpse of the human being has been buried in the earth, polluting the soil with the germs of diseases, which in turn were passed on into vegetables, animals, water and then to human beings. Cremation helps to minimize this pollution and prevent many diseases from spreading. The use of well constructed, sealed boxes does not guarantee that germs, the tiny lives which cause disease, will not escape and pollute the soil.

The Tibetan Master states that if we use cremation, we will be able in the next million years to stamp out syphilis and other diseases, both from the human family and from the Soul of the planet. This seems like a long time, but if we remember that we will return many times yet to this planet, we will be eager to take action to clean the planet, that we may have a better home and better living conditions in the future for the ever unfolding human soul.

There is another reason for cremation. It helps to detach the subtle vehicles of the soul from the etheric body, and thus release the unfolding human soul to proceed on its own way toward higher realms. Without cremation the soul is attached to the etheric body for more than six days. Occultism holds that a man is not dead until he is separated from his etheric body, after leaving his physical body behind.

We are told that the etheric body is perpetuated through mummifying or embalming. This creates a very serious problem for the developing human soul. Sometimes the etheric body is kept in existence for ages, and if the person lived a wicked life, dark forces enter into such an etheric body and use it as a distributing station for their evil intentions. The Ancient Wisdom warns that we must be very careful not to touch mummies, or to get too close to their graves or tombs because their etheric bodies can still be active and used as vehicles by dark forces.

Cremation not only eliminates such attacks, but also purifies the astral plane by burning some forms of low desires, seeking expression through the etheric body. Thus cemeteries which are fields of germs, polluted by psychic forces, will eventually disappear.

People will soon realize that burying the body within the grave is exactly the same as accumulating your soiled clothes in your home. "Clothes" that cannot be used any more must be eliminated, and not perpetuated within marble boxes as magnets of psychic pollution.

Cremation must take place as soon as possible after a qualified physician declares that the body is *truly* dead. Some great Teachers suggest that cremation should take place within twelve hours, and must be delayed no longer than thirty-six hours. The unfolding human soul rejoices when he is released from the etheric body, which subtly relates him to the physical prison in which he has acted and suffered.

We are careful not to pass our germs to others, and if we know that our clothing is contaminated with germs, we try to disinfect it by using certain chemicals, or by burning it. After such an act we feel released. The unfolding human soul experiences the same feeling when his body is burned away, and can in no way harm any living form.

THE ASTRAL PLANE

After the etheric body is dissolved, the average man enters into the astral plane, which in some oriental books is called Kama-Loka. Kama means desire, and Loka, the sphere or plane.

The degrees of consciousness on the astral plane are as varied as the consciousness of all grades of men on earth. Some of them have a very dim consciousness on the astral plane, some are just awakening to their situation; others are totally asleep; many are very busy with their desires and imaginations and some of them live a dream life having no initiative to move forward and overcome the plane of glamours.

It is the unevolved man, wrapped in astral matter, who is totally asleep on this sphere. When an average man dies, he loses all of his memories or recollections. This lasts from a few hours to a few days. Sometimes people float in Kama-Loka, in the astral world, as sleeping corpses, and advanced disciples who have continuity of consciousness help them to awaken and understand the situation.

Jesus performed a tremendous amount of this service in a short period when He visited Kama-Loka, while His body was in the grave. He released most of the sleeping ones and also those who were caught in their glamours.[8]

When the time arrives for a man's entrance into the mental plane, the events of his life slowly pass before his spiritual eye, branching out into two series: those that belong to the mortal man, and those that belong to the immortal man. Very soon the life events of the mortal man totally fade away and those experienced by the immortal man remain.

We are told that at the Seventh Round, all memories come back to the unfolded human soul for right judgement of *merit* or *demerit*. They then melt away into the ocean of substance or are cleansed away just as we erase our tapes when the recordings are no longer needed.

The astral body is a disintegrating corpse which gradually fades away in the sea of the astral plane. Often this astral body is used by astral entities or dark forces to mislead people in their dreams, or by mediums and astral clairvoyants. The astral body resembles the physical body, and some devas or evil forces use this body to mislead people, giving them the impression that they are the same persons who passed away and now are anxious to lead or to give certain messages to the surviving ones.

In this way many well intentioned sensitives are misled and thrown off the path; groups are disbanded, and the work of Christ is hindered. This is the reason that the Masters warn us not to go to diviners, to mediums or lower psychics, and not to put faith in apparitions and visions, because the dark forces can work by hiding themselves in the astral body of any dead person, and mislead us by giving wrong information, impressions of fear, hatred, jealousy, and by stimulating our glamours and illusions. Master Morya calls mediums the "inns of disembodied liars."

Many people will say that sensitives or mediums helped them, and their visions and dreams came true. They are right, but the clever method used by such destructive forces is to first gain your confidence and then mislead you, just as expert gamblers lose a few dollars at first, to win all your riches later.

8. I Peter 3:19 and 4:16.

once you are caught in their grip. To avoid such dangers it is suggested that we use our logic, pure reason, and develop our intuition, which is the most dependable faculty latent within the man.

Those who act and react on their emotional level, and are conditioned by their desires and wishful cravings, very soon are caught by such entities and lose their way on the path of spiritual development. True occultism has nothing to do with black-magic, with mediums, with astral clairvoyants; it is the teaching of the way to develop our mind, our innate faculties, and to use them for the benefit of all mankind.

Occultists have often observed that the materializations in the seance rooms are dark forces using the astral forms of departed ones, and manifesting themselves by drawing more astral substance from the medium and from those who are present. It even happens that the astral corpse itself is attracted to the medium or to those who are tuned in because of many associations, and who are misled into thinking that it represents the real departed man.

Let us not forget that the astral shell has the memory of all that happened to the man on earth. This memory is like a recording on film or on a tape; when it finds the proper instrument, a projector or tape recorder, it plays its own memories. The instrument or tape is nothing else but the medium, whose brain is used to play back the memories of the astral shell. It is interesting to know that certain questions stimulate and release different portions of the tape, giving the impression that we are dealing with a self-actualized being, but all this is mechanical and of no value. Most of the mediums attract such astral corpses and are used by them as tape recorders.

Advanced people are not caught in the astral plane. While they are living in the dense physical body they slowly disassociate themselves from the astral world, focus their consciousness on the mental plane, and when they pass away leave their astral body as quickly as they leave their etheric body. In the most advanced people, the whole astral body has already disintegrated while they were still living in the physical body. This was the case with Helena Petrovna Blavatsky.

Astral entities often move, speak and give messages, using the brain of the medium or the brain of one of those present. It happens also that the medium can frequently control an astral entity unconsciously and project through it his own desires and intentions, causing the illusion that the materialization is a living individual coming in contact with those present.

When the time comes for the astral release, the Sutratma is withdrawn from the astral form and the energy for the astral body is centralized within the astral permanent atom. Thus the "future becoming" of the astral body lies dormant in the permanent seed.

Immediately after the Sutratma withdraws itself from the astral body, man steps out from the astral plane and enters into the mental plane. The sphere into which he enters, in ancient writings, is called Deva-Chan.

"DEVA-CHAN," HEAVEN

The next step, after experiencing the astral world or Kama-Loka, is entrance into another plane, called Deva-Chan. Deva-Chan is often pictured as seven golden mountains, into which you enter upon the golden bridge, built from the lower to the higher mind. These seven golden mountains represent the seven states of the mental plane, or seven spheres of heaven.

Deva-Chan is a Sanskrit word meaning "the abode of gods." Deva in Sanskrit means the shining one, an angel, or a god, but here it refers to the unfolding human soul, after he leaves behind the physical and astral bodies with their attachments, and enters into the mental plane. Chan means the abode, but a closer meaning in the usage here, would be the inn, a place of rest on your journey, where you may remain for a while before you travel on. Deva-Chan here refers to that sphere of greater light and joy into which the human soul enters after he is through the astral plane, and before his next incarnation.

In Deva-Chan the human soul may be on higher or lower mental levels, but it is still in the mental body. If higher, he has closer conscious communication with the Solar Angel through the Lotus; if he is on the lower levels of the mental plane, he will be unconscious of the existence of his Guardian Light, Who, nevertheless, will watch over him faithfully.

Christians call this place "paradise" or heaven; occultism holds that it is divided into seven states according to the seven planes of mental substance. Those who are more advanced in pure and clear thinking pass to the higher planes. The average intellectual falls in the middle section and the lesser developed one lives within the lower planes. Master K.H. says:

> "In the Deva-Chan the Ego sees and feels but that which he longed for. He who cares not for a continuation of sentient personal life after physical death will not have it. He will be reborn remaining unconscious of the transition."[9]

The human soul enters into Deva-Chan after much purification accomplished within the astral world, the Kama-Loka, or as some Christians express it, in purgatory. In one of His letters, Master K.H. says,

> "Every Ego [developing, unfolding human soul] . . . reborn into the Deva-Chan, is of necessity as innocent and pure as a new born babe. The fact of his being reborn at all, shows the preponderance of good over evil in his old personality. And while the Karma (of evil) steps aside for the time being to follow him in the future earth-reincarnation, he brings along with him but the Karma of his good deeds, words, and thoughts into this Deva-Chan . . . those who have not slipped down into the mire of unredeemable sin

9. Blavatsky, H. P., *Collected Writings*, Vol. III, p. 295.

> and bestiality—go to the Deva-Chan. They will have to pay for their sins, voluntary and unvoluntary, later on. Meanwhile, they are rewarded; receive the *effects* of the *causes* produced by them.
>
> ". . . He is completely engrossed in the bliss of all his personal earthly affections, preferences and thoughts and gathers in the fruit of his meritorious actions. No pain, no grief nor even the shadow of a sorrow comes to darken the bright horizon of his unalloyed happiness: for, *it is a state of perpetual 'Maya'*. . . . Since the conscious perception of one's *personality* on earth is but an evanescent dream that sense will be equally that a dream in the Deva-Chan—only a hundred fold intensified."[10]

In occultism there is another very meaningful word about which Master K.H. gives some explanations. He says,

> " 'Bardo' is the period between death and rebirth—and may last for from a few years to a kalpa [great period of time, a cycle]. It is divided into three sub-periods: (1) when the *Ego* delivered of its mortal coil enters into *Kama-Loka* . . . (2) when it enters into its 'Gestation State'; (3) when it is reborn in the *Rupa-Loka* [formless world or higher mental] or Deva-Chan. Sub-period (1) may last from a few minutes to a *number* of years. . . . Sub-period (2) is 'very long'; . . . proportionate to the *Ego's* spiritual stamina; Sub-period (3) lasts in proportion to the good KARMA, after which the *monad* [the developing human soul] is again reincarnated.
>
> ". . . Every effect must be proportionate to the cause. And, as man's terms of incarnate existence bear but a small proportion to his periods of inter-natal existence in the manvantaric cycle, so the good thoughts, words, and deeds of any one of these 'lives', on a globe are causative of effects, the working out of which requires far more time than the evolution of the causes occupied."[11]

When the time comes to step from the lower mental plane into the higher mental plane, the life thread withdraws itself from the mental unit and lower mental planes; it centers itself in the mental permanent atom.

Thus the physical, emotional and mental bodies pass away and their seeds of the future, raised up to the first plane of the mental plane, remain in the Lotus.

Sometimes this state in the abstract levels of the mind, especially the highest, is called the plane of nirvanic consciousness, where the Soul experiences great joy and bliss before reincarnation. The stay on this plane is of long duration for those who have lived a creative and sacrificial life, with pure thoughts and motives. Its duration is but an instant for those who are unevolved, and are

10. Sinnett, A. P., *The Mahatma Letters*, pp. 100–101.
11. *Ibid*, pp. 105–106.

still living a life of savagery. When such people briefly touch that plane, they come back immediately and do not taste its joy.

We are told also that very advanced Initiates have no interest in Deva-Chan; they do not stay there, but come back as soon as possible to continue their service and unfoldment until ready for mastership. Such people never enjoy the rest period of Deva-Chan. Their main goal is not to reach personal nirvana, which is found on the atomic subplane of the mental plane, but to enter into the buddhic plane; this is the state of nirvana of the soul.

During all these periods of out of body experience, the Solar Angel observes the activities and responses of the human soul. The Tibetan Master says that "on the inner side men *know* that the law of Rebirth governs the experiences—process of physical plane living, and they realize then that, prior to the elimination of the desire, (desire-mind, mental bodies) they are only passing through an interlude between incarnations."

After the period of Deva-Chan, man prepares himself to incarnate again, to learn lessons left unlearned. He is taken out of Deva-Chan by the force of his karma, accumulated in his permanent recording seeds.

In occult literature we are reminded that in after-life experiences we live in a dream, or we sleep, remaining unconscious of our existence. This seems very true, as our physical life, which we think of as a real life, or a factual life, is nothing more than a heavy dream, in which we are totally conditioned by the karmic forces we created in the past, or by the forces set into activity through our unconscious, mechanical actions, reactions and responses. It is nothing more than a dream acted out in the land of sleep walkers. A few people are aware of this. For them, too, life is a dream, but the difference is that they know it is a dream and they are trying to awaken from that dream. Death is not an awakening, because the same sleep with more subtle and colorful forms will continue in the hereafter.

To awaken means to enter into the path which leads to the real Self within, and to gradually experience mastery over the illusion of life with its pleasures and pain, its fears and expectations.

The Ancient Wisdom teaches that the physical, emotional and mental planes are the planes of sleep and dreams. Our awakening starts when we penetrate with the light of the intuitional plane. This is the reason that the intuitional plane is called the buddhic plane, and those who are awakened on that plane are called Buddhas, or enlightened ones.

Here starts the world of Reality in the Cosmic physical plane. Reality is an ever progressing awareness of Self, in man and in the universe, plus the awareness of the responsibilities of that SELF in Cosmos and in man, upon all planes. Any attachment to any part of existence creates slavery and loss of reality, but all these planes of dreams and our various attachments can eventually awaken us, because as incarnation succeeds incarnation we bring some impressions with us to the brain consciousness and in so doing we evaluate things differently. We learn by seeing the effects of causes on the emotional plane—

causes created upon the earth, and sooner or later we become more careful not to create undesirable causes.

On the mental plane we enjoy the fruits of all our creative aspirations, as they bloom into colors, music, movements and organizations. We see the actualization of our hopes and plans; we see the beauty of greater communication, love and scientific, economic, political and religious improvements, and all these impress us. When we come again to face our karmic jungle, we are more aware of higher realities and we try harder to liberate ourselves from our negative karmas, pay our debts and try to organize our life in such a way that we are able to fulfill our higher urges and higher dreams.

The Deva-Chanic period mainly impresses upon us the mystery of joy, harmony, and simplicity. You can see these three pearls shining in the eyes of a baby, in the tears of the baby, in the smiles of the baby, but slowly, slowly, the dust of life comes and covers these three pearls, and they sink into the heavy layers of our fears, hatred, and greed—but they have not been lost! Again and again our Inner Guide will remind us of the three pearls, and if we listen to the Inner Voice, we will start searching for them at all costs. This search is the path which leads us toward discipleship, Initiation and mastery.

INDIVIDUALITY AND PERSONALITY

Individuality, individualization and the unfolding human soul are important terms in occultism which need definition at this point, to further clarify our subject.

The Solar Angel here on earth, is the door to Infinity. It was through the Solar Angel that the developing human soul achieved individualization and started to live as a self conscious entity.

Individuality is the result of age long evolution and Initiation. It is achieved after the human soul has infused himself with the light of his Inner Guide and is functioning within the realm of the Spiritual Triad. The Monad, as a potential gem, is changing into a diamond in the divine light of the Inner Presence, as He passes through the laboratory of experience in the three worlds. Unless a man enters into the process of becoming a diamond, an individuality, he will never gain conscious immortality.

Individuality is that stage reached by the human soul in which he is advanced enough to be an awakened, self-conscious, self-determined being, free from imprisonment by his three lower vehicles. He is one who stands in the light of the Spiritual Triad. Individuality at its highest point of development is the Self, the Spark or the Divine Self within the phenomenal man, purified of his attachments and free from all lower identification.

At the time of *individualization*, the Solar Angel passes the third aspect of divinity, the fire of intelligence, to the human soul imprisoned within the three lower substances of the human form. At this point, for the first time, the man becomes aware of himself, the *lower self* comes into existence, and the man identifies with the form.

> "At individualization the two poles are approximated and at their meeting light streams forth, irradiating the cave of matter and lighting the pathway that must be trodden by the Pilgrim on his way back to his source."[12]

The *unfolding human soul* is the "fallen Spark," attending school in the physical, emotional and mental worlds, trying to reach the stage of maturity through the process of evolution and Initiation. When he reaches a certain stage of independence from the glamours, illusions and inertia of the three lower vehicles, he becomes an individuality. He is Himself—truly self-actuated, free and strongly influential. He is one who has achieved continuity of consciousness on the three lower planes and is working toward Intuitional awareness. Having achieved continuity of consciousness, he has won his immortality, his conscious immortality. He no longer dies and enters into *sleep,* but passes from one plane to another with continuity of consciousness.

Such a man keeps his same individuality, but not the same *personality.* The personality is changed from cycle to cycle, just as we change our cars, using different types, different models. In changing our cars we do not change our true selves, nor do we change our individuality when we change personalities. The word personality, written with a small *p* refers to the sum total of the physical, emotional and mental vehicles, aligned and integrated. When written with a capital *P,* it refers to the unfolding human soul, functioning through the physical, emotional and mental bodies. It is also called the lower self; the higher Self being the Solar Angel, and the Divine Self, the Spark.[13]

Most remembrances of past lives by average people are illusions. Only a Fifth Degree Initiate can contact the life film of his earthly existences, and watch His true individuality progressively change his vehicles from life to life; only such an advanced One can witness his lives in many lands, many nations.

Some psychics claim that they can see the past lives of others. This is an impossibility and a great deception. Past lives are impressed upon a very subtle matter, which in occultism is called the second Cosmic Etheric Plane, or the *akashic* plane. Unless a man is a Fifth Degree Initiate, One who has mastered immortality, time and space, he cannot penetrate into that plane.

The distorted reflections of past and present lives, mixed with the records of every person with whom we have had any kind of relationship, can be found in our astral body together with the forms of our day dreams, desires, imagination and phantasies. An honest psychic will never try to fabricate stories out of such an illusive mixture.

Under certain conditions, when the Inner Guide sees that great progress upon the path can be achieved by a disciple, He reflects a part of his past life which has immediate connection with the problem he is facing or with

---

12. Bailey, Alice A., *A Treatise on Cosmic Fire,* p. 345.
13. Patterns of change are described in THE PERSONALITY RAY section in Chap. VI.

the planes upon which he is contemplating. The disciple then becomes able to see it in a vision, in a dream state, or when he is lifted up onto the higher mental planes.

When this happens you have great understanding of the circumstances of your life; you have great enlightenment to help you in carrying out your plan. This is a very rare happening and occurs only to those who really orient themselves toward service for One Humanity.

No one has a right to know about your past lives, even if he were able to see them. Master K.H., in speaking about past lives, says,

> "I have no *right* to look into your *past* life. Whenever I may have caught glimpses of it, I have invariably turned my eyes away, for I have to deal with the present . . . not with ancient man.' [14]

IMMORTALITY

There exists the erroneous idea that man is immortal regardless of his stage of evolution. The fact is that man can be immortal only by gaining continuity of consciousness and continuity of awareness. He is aware of his immortality to the degree that he has developed continuity of consciousness, for immortality is conditioned by continuity of consciousness. When a man does not know who he was, who he is, what he is going to be, he has no immortality. He dies and sleeps; he is born again through the laws of nature, but knows nothing of these processes. He may sleep for an unknown period of time and be born again according to his karma, but he is totally unaware of his continuity—his immortality.

Actually everything *exists*. Nothing can be lost or found. It *is*. Immortality is the process of registration in your consciousness or awareness of your individual existence in Cosmos, upon any plane of creation. If you are not registering your individual existence in relation to the existence as a whole, you are not experiencing immortality, and you have not yet reached the state of immortality, though you exist, as everything exists. We do not say a stone is immortal; we say a stone exists.

Many people express the idea that after a man passes away, he awakens and functions on the astral or mental plane. This also is not true. If he has been able to build his subtle vehicles (perhaps his astral and mental vehicles) through living a life of dedication and service, he can be aware of corresponding planes after death; if not, he continues to sleep.

We are referring here to the unfolding human soul who has fallen into the "labyrinth of ills," into the "world of maya," into ignorance and darkness. It is a seed that must find its own way up toward the Sun. This supports the old Asian tradition that not all men have souls, but only those who through

---

14. Sinnett, A.P., *The Mahatma Letters*, p. 188.

their personal endeavor and effort, "form" it or "create" it. It is after the formation of the soul, after the awakening and liberation of the soul, that continuity of consciousness is established and immortality is achieved.

A Master of Wisdom is one who has been able to build his subtle vehicles and establish continuity of consciousness on the physical, astral, mental and intuitional planes and to register all events and happenings on those planes in his waking consciousness. It is because of this achievement that the Masters are called the "golden bridges" between man and the spiritual world.

Until man achieves continuity of consciousness, he is under the direct supervision of his Solar Angel who watches over the developing human soul while he is in incarnation and while he is out of incarnation. After the man passes away, he is still in the hands of the Angel, but he is not conscious of this fact. When he enters into the process of birth, the Angel hovers above the embryo until he is born. Thus, age after age, the Solar Angel watches, inspires and tries to establish communication with the human soul as He leads him to his destiny.

There is a mysterious announcement in the New Testament, which became the stumbling stone for many an honest person; it says "No man can go to the Father except through me." This is a very occult statement; "through me" means through the Christ, or Christos, the "hope of glory" within man, the "Path." Actually, Christos means the Savior, the Liberator; it also means a state of Consciousness, Soul-Consciousness; no man can pass to the Father-Consciousness, except through Soul-Consciousness, or Son-Consciousness. This Son, this Soul, or the State of Consciousness, is called in the Ancient Wisdom, the *Solar Angel,* the Guardian Light within the man.

No man can enter into conscious immortality except by raising himself to the consciousness of that Inner Guide and becoming fused with Him. It is this state of consciousness that is symbolically represented as the marriage between bride and groom. You will find this symbology in all Sufi literature, and in Christian literature. The Song of Solomon is a great epic about this fusion between the unfolding human soul and the Beloved, the Inner Guide, Whom we call the Solar Angel.

In esoteric literature there are some hints about annihilation, but these hints were unused or distorted by many religious sects and cults. Annihilation does not mean to go out of existence. Whatever exists, *is.* Nothing is ever lost in Cosmos. Annihilation is a state of existence in which the Monad loses His mechanisms which He has built, or was building on the path of evolution, to communicate with the corresponding planes. It causes a loss of opportunity for Him to develop and unfold. We can compare this state of existence with that of a man who was living on an island and building a radio communication system. The man is the Monad, the radio communication system is the level of his development—his unfolding human soul with all his vestures. This radio communication system, or the human soul, is destroyed, and the Monad stands insulated and divorced from the mechanisms that he was using to experience and to communicate. He is now in total insulation or isolation.

We are told that such a state of annihilation comes to those human beings who were acting through many lives as black-magicians, or as criminals beyond redemption. Such a wicked life eventually causes destruction to the "radio communication system," the personal soul. This destruction is called annihilation of the *human soul*, the personality with all its connections.

Let us not forget that the term human soul refers to a state of beingness of the Monad on His evolutionary path. He can lose such a metamorphic state without losing his true Self, but these losses are costly. It will be millions and millions of years before He can have a chance to start anew, to build Himself, to achieve conscious existence and conscious immortality. Wicked people, before they reach such a final stage of annihilation, reincarnate again and again, never having an opportunity to stay in Deva-Chan, and renew their divine urges and drives.

> "Immortality is conditional—it is the reward of the pure and good. The wicked man, the material sensualist only survives. He who appreciates but physical pleasures will not and cannot live in the hereafter as a Self-Conscious entity." [15]

There is another meaning of annihilation to which the Tibetan Master refers:

> "The fire of spirit finally, when blended with the two other fires (which blending commences in man at the first initiation), forms a basis of spiritual life or existence. As evolution proceeds in the fifth, a spiritual kingdom, these three fires blaze forth simultaneously, producing perfected consciousness. This blaze results in the final purification of matter and its consequent adequacy; at the close of manifestation it brings about eventually the destruction of the form and its dissolution and the termination of existence as understood on the lower planes. In terms of Buddhistic theology it produces annihilation; this involves, not loss of identity, but the cessation of objectivity and the escape of Spirit, plus mind, to its cosmic centre. It has its analogy in the initiation at which the adept stands free from the limitations of matter in the three worlds." [16]

THE CYCLES OF MANIFESTATION

"Reincarnation is an aspect of the pulsating life of Deity."

—The Tibetan

Following the period in Deva-Chan, the mental body is destroyed by an act of will and the man stands for a short time before his Solar Angel. He sees the future as clearly as he was previously aware of the past and present. This takes place immediately before the call of incarnation.

In esoteric Teaching the steps of descent are explained as follows:

1. Man takes the first step toward incarnation.

---

15. Blavatsky, H. P., *Collected Writings*, Vol. III p. 295.
16. Bailey, Alice A., *A Treatise on Cosmic Fire*, p. 51–52.

2. His Soul sounds the note of descent which slowly draws the human soul from the mental plane and brings him to the sphere of the etheric plane, where the etheric centers start to form.
3. His three lower permanent atoms radiate, creating a magnetic field upon which the three vehicles are gradually built, according to the records of the permanent atoms.
4. He chooses his parents, if he is a conscious entity, but if not, he is drawn to whoever can provide entrance to the physical plane.

Certain activities are appropriate to these four steps:

1. The first step, which is preparation, is actually a process of detachment from the mental world, from its inhabitants and interests, and a process of making oneself ready for the conditions that are awaiting him on the physical plane.

   This experience is like entering deeper and deeper into limitation and isolated loneliness, which is far more distressing than the passing out of the body. This is true because after a man leaves his body, he meets those who were known to him on the physical level. He is also able to see those who are living in the body, and to feel their thoughts and emotions, but when he reincarnates, he loses both worlds; he is no longer in touch with those who are on the subjective side of life, nor those who were related to him in the objective world, unless he has built continuity of consciousness, the bridge which connects the three lower worlds. The Tibetan Teacher says,

   > ". . . each life is not only a recapitulation of life experience, but an assuming of obligations, a recovery of old relations, an opportunity for the paying of old indebtedness, a chance to make restitution and progress, and awakening of deep-seated qualities, the recognition of old friends and enemies, the solution of revolting injustices and the explanation of that which conditions the man and makes him what he is."[17]

2. The second step, the sounding of the note of return by the Soul, is actually the call of return. This note helps the man to detach himself from Deva-Chan, reminding him of his responsibilities and his karma waiting for him in the physical world. It also puts into action the permanent atoms, which in due time will build the three lower vehicles.
3. In the third step, the physical permanent atom first builds the blueprint of the etheric body, radiating those tiny lines of energy upon which the physical body will form.

   Each permanent atom is like a photographic negative. When the energy of the sutratma strikes them, their contents are projected out as the corresponding vehicles of the man.

---

17. Bailey, Alice A., *A Treatise on the Seven Rays*, Vol. I, p. 300.

4. In the fourth step, the choosing of parents is sometimes done blindly, if the incarnating soul is not evolved enough to discriminate. Concerning this the Tibetan Teacher says:

> ". . . they have also brought too rapidly into incarnation myriads of human beings who were not yet ready for the experience of this incarnation, and who needed longer interludes between births wherein to assimilate experience. Those souls who are unevolved come into incarnation with rapidity; but older souls need longer periods wherein to garner the fruits of experience. They are however open to the magnetic attractive power of those who are alive on the physical plane, and it is these souls who can be brought prematurely into incarnation. The process is under law, but the unevolved progress under group law as do animals; whilst the more evolved are susceptible to the pull of human units, and the evolved come into incarnation under the Law of Service, and through the deliberate choice of their conscious souls." [18]

The whole Cosmos is under the law of cyclic appearance and disappearance. This, being a fact in nature, is also true for each living form in nature—for each atom, each cell and each entity. All and each have their cycles of "going out and coming back," their "nights and days."

Reincarnation is as much a fact for the human being as it is for the great Entity of our planet, our planetary Logos. It also holds true for the Life ensouling a solar system—and so on—and on.

Another point to bear in mind is that the plane in which we all have our existence is the Cosmic Physical Plane. The highest Master on this planet is still in the matter of the Monadic or second Cosmic Etheric Plane. This means that when any being clothes himself on any subplane of the Cosmic Physical Plane, he is performing an act of incarnation. For example, our Kumara, the Ancient of Days, incarnated in the first Cosmic Etheric Plane when He appropriated a vehicle from that plane to help this planet. If another great Entity, living on a higher plane, appropriates substance on the mental plane and uses it as a vehicle, we say that he has incarnated on the mental plane, and thus the Law works on the various planes.

All kingdoms, mineral, vegetable, animal, and human and superhuman, are subject to the Law of Reincarnation. In *Bhagavad Gita* we find reference to these cycles:

"All beings are unmanifested in the beginning, manifested in their middle state and unmanifested again in their end." [19] Manifestation here means the appropriation of matter on any plane ". . . To experiment, to experience and to express." Thus, manifestation is an act of reincarnation, and unmanifestation an act of disembodiment. In the Ancient Wisdom these acts are called days and nights, but if in reference to the planets, chains or schemes, they are called

---

18. Bailey, Alice A., *A Treatise on the Seven Rays*, Vol. 1, p. 272.
19. *Bhagavad Gita*, Chap. II, verse 28.

manvantara and pralaya. All manifestation and dissolution come under the Law of Cause and Effect, regardless of the level, until the "entity" is the master of his destiny.

For further clarification regarding the Law of Reincarnation, we should remember these facts:

– Man has a Solar Angel.
– Three of man's permanent atoms are the seeds of his lower bodies.
– Man is the evolving, unfolding human soul, the Spark in the process of liberation.

In reality it is not the unfolding *human soul* that is incarnating; the incarnating one is none other than the personality, or the records in the permanent atoms. We might say that man is simply getting a new car to gather greater experience in driving and using his threefold vehicle. The unfolding human soul is expanding his consciousness and control over the three worlds, but it is not he who is incarnating. He is the same man, using a new vehicle for each personality. For the threefold vehicle there are many lives, but for the unfolding human soul there is but one life, which is a beam of light passing through days and nights. A great Teacher suggests that rebirth and reincarnation are misleading terms. He proposes the terms cyclic impression, intelligent purposeful repetition, or conscious in-breathing and out-breathing. The latter expression is especially beautiful. As the Soul breathes out, the form comes into existence. As the Soul breathes in, the vehicles slowly disappear. It is the records in the permanent atoms that are creating a new vehicle. It is not the true man, himself, who is incarnating.

Our attachment to our vehicles is so great that we think we are passing away when the body is ready to die, and we think that we are reincarnating when a new vehicle is in the process of being built for our use. As time goes on, when we are able to detach ourselves and build continuity of consciousness through higher planes, we will not be "born" and we will not "die." We will take a new body, use it for special service and education, then leave it and enter into the greater subjective world, until the time that we no longer need a physical body. Then if for some special reason we wish to come in contact with the physical plane, we can create our own *mayavirupa*, or "illusionary body," and use it to perform any service we wish.

In a sense some of the Christian fathers were right when they said that there was no reincarnation, but they were wrong when they thought that man could not have more than one physical vehicle on his journey to his Father's House.

As the soul learns to use body after body, and as he gradually learns to handle them in such a way that he no longer identifies with them, the substance of the three vehicles undergoes transmutation and purification until a stage is reached in which the three vehicles radiate the pure light of the soul. This stage, called transfiguration, is the stage in which the soul is really born. Because of this fact, in occult literature, this transfiguration Initiation is the first major Initiation; it is the true birth into the Kingdom of God.

Life after life the bodies become more refined and more fully utilized for the expression of light, love and power, until man reaches that stage when he no longer needs to be guided by the Solar Angel. At that point he bids farewell to his age long Guide and now works through the Spiritual Triad. At this time he has achieved continuity of consciousness and is no longer caught in the illusion of birth and death, in the illusion of reincarnation.

In the *Upahishads* we read:

> "Man is created by thought.
> What a man thinks upon, that he becomes."

In the Bible we find:

> "As a man thinketh, so is he."

Great Lord Buddha said,

> "All that we are is the result of what we have thought."

We need to learn that we can create better vehicles for ourselves. If we use our minds in the right way, our future life, whether with or without the physical body, will be the result of the life we are living through our threefold vehicle. Our future is the result of all our thoughts, aspiration, faith, desires and actions. Our whole life is a process of building future vehicles, and conditioning our states of consciousness. The great Lord Buddha tells us, "You can no more separate the action from its result than the sound of the drum from the drum." Whatever a man soweth, that shall he also reap.

Thus successive bodily lives are related and linked together like pearls strung upon the life thread; the thread of life is continuous, but the pearls change in color, in formation and in duration. An unevolved man is not aware of this continuum. He passes away, entering into a deep sleep, or a dream state, until he comes in contact again with the physical life, which in a sense is not much different from a sleep, in that it is a life lived with mechanical actions and reactions. Once a man awakens; once he detaches from the illusion that he is one with his vehicles, all life becomes a day and he walks in the sunlight of eternal existence. In the *Bhagavad Gita* we find the following jewel:

> "Verily, there was never a time when I was not, nor you, nor these rulers of men; nor shall there come a time when we shall all cease to be. . . . The Indweller of the body is never born, nor does it ever die. It is not true that having no existence, it comes into being, nor having been in existence, it again ceases to be. It is the unborn, the eternal, the changeless, the Self."[20]

---

20. *Bhagavad Gita*, Chap. II, verse 12, 20.

In all these outgoing and ingoing processes, our ". . . consciousness remains the same, whether in physical incarnation or out of incarnation, . . . development [of consciousness] can be carried on with even greater ease than when limited and conditioned by the brain consciousness."[21]

If we have ten percent consciousness at the present time, the fact of leaving our bodies does not mean that we will then have seventy-five percent. Our consciousness will be the same consciousness which we carry every "day" of our great life, continuously developing and expanding it in greater measure. Each time we acquire a new vehicle we use it more wisely and in closer harmony with the Laws of Nature, until we learn to live in more subtle bodies built of intuitive, atmic or divine plane substance. The Tibetan Sage tells us:

> "Groups of souls come into incarnation cyclically and together in order to further the Plan and permit that interplay to proceed spirit and matter which makes manifestation possible and which extends the working out of the divine ideas as they exist in the Mind of God."[22]

After a man is born, if he is highly advanced, he can see his past lives as easily as he can recall and see the activities of a day. The recollection of past lives does not come to the average person. As we have mentioned in a preceding chapter, there are hundreds of Napoleons, Cleopatras and disciples of great religious leaders, all living miserable lives under pathetic conditions. Besides these, we have thousands of disillusioned ones who claim to know their past lives. The Teaching tells us that no one can really see his past lives until he enters into the plane of total freedom; until his awareness passes beyond the mental plane, the intuitional plane, and is active in the atmic plane. It is only after he has achieved such unfoldment that he can actually see his past lives as they factually were. A man such as this often reaches a state of freedom in which he can no longer sin, and in which he no longer has any desire to continue physical existence.

---

21. Bailey, Alice A., *Discipleship in the New Age*, Vol. I, p. 81.
22. Bailey, Alice A., *Esoteric Astrology*, p. 325.

Chapter XX

PSYCHIC ATTACKS

"A . . . *class of fears*—which aspirants contact more and more as they grow in strength and usefulness in service—is based on the realisation of the forces that are working against the Plan and hindering the work to be done. Occult attacks and occult powers, warring militantly against the aspirant will occur; they may make their power felt in one or other of the vehicles and—in rare cases—where the aspirant is important enough, on all at once.'[1]

—The Tibetan

Possession of individuals occurs today with far greater frequency than is indicated by obvious cases found in asylums. For an aspirant, this is a serious problem. An aspirant invites psychic attack when he:

1. Enters into the path of spiritual unfoldment.
2. Weakens his etheric, emotional and mental vehicles.
3. Cuts his relations with spiritual ideas and beauties or with his Teacher.
4. No longer absorbs the Spatial Fires or psychic energy because of disorders in his head and heart centers.
5. Forces himself into excessive activity because of his pride and vanity, overstimulating his centers and vehicles.
6. Lives a life that wastes his energy through excessive sex or use of alcohol, cigarettes and various drugs or when he is caught by venereal disease.
7. Chooses to follow the left hand path through idle speech, lying, hatred, jealousy, negativity, separativeness, fanaticism, exploitation and possessiveness; by expressing greed and anger, committing crimes and turning his face to the past.

Who are the attackers that take advantage of these practices?

- Very low-level spirits who perhaps were or will be human beings.
- Those who were killed in battle or in the criminal world.
- Suicides.
- Those who were totally enslaved by various vices on earth.
- Those who were totally engulfed in materialism.
- Those who were very doubtful about immortality, and who had no faith in the continuation of life after death.
- Animals that were slaughtered.
- Those whose Solar Angel have left them.
- Astral shells, drawn to a person because of some affinity or relationship.
- Thoughtforms, glamours, illusions.
- Dark forces, or *brothers on the left hand path.*

1. Bailey, Alice A., *A Treatise on White Magic,* p. 346.

Let us look deeper into the seven causes of low psychism.

ONE. *Entering the Path.* When a man decides to turn his face toward the spiritual light and live a life of beauty, service and joy, he becomes a danger signal to the "dark ones." They try, by every means possible, to stop him, to divert him from the path of self-unfoldment. Such a man is generally in good health, and in sound emotional and mental balance, so they try to control him first through his thoughts, interests, fears, inhibitions, pride and vanities. Slowly they contrive to keep him busy on work that is not specifically related to his spiritual path, but which is connected very subtly to his materialistic tendencies, pride, ambitions, fears, and competitive drive. These attacks keep such people from taking their next step in evolution, and gradually lead them away from the main issues of their spiritual interest, causing them to become increasingly lost in those studies, activities, and direction which are in no way related to the true spiritual path. Thus they waste their time, their energy, and decrease their spiritual drive.

Eventually they are led toward materialism, toward self-aggrandizement, pleasure, conflict, worry, ill-health and obsession. Because of this a spiritual aspirant must always adjust his direction to the "north," through self-observation, meditation, service to Great Ones and to great causes. Another way to sidetrack aspirants from their true direction is to induce a process of day dreaming into their lower mind and higher astral level. Dark forces project a chain of images that are enjoyable, soothing, and colorful. Gradually as man watches, they unfold, continuously changing the scenery and action. As the man becomes attracted to and focussed in such an imaginative process, he is led into the lower astral plane where he starts to hear voices, see colors, and receive messages, but all this is done in such a slow and natural way that the man becomes used to it gradually, until finally he is caught in it by his own will. Following this, low psychism with all its traps, suffering, and disturbances enters in, and for a long time the evolution of the man comes to a halt.

Two. *Weakened Vehicles.* The attack occurs more directly when the etheric, emotional and mental bodies are weakened because of:

- Overwork, lack of sleep, not eating right foods and wasting sexual energy.
- Pollution of the astral body through wrong imaginings, jealousy, fear, hatred, and an attitude of constant irritation.
- The misuse of mental energy when a man deceives, lies, and engages in dishonest, criminal and separative activities; activities not in harmony with the path of oneness, of beauty, and of unfoldment.

Such attitudes and activities create an unhealthy condition in the etheric, astral and mental bodies of man, and because of the law of association, entities are drawn to their sphere; entities who want to contact the physical plane through the vehicles of other living people. An attack can be very successful, because the etheric body is weakened and cannot do the needed work of protection, so the attacking one (or ones) finds the weakest spot and anchors there a magnetic thread through which he slowly injects his pollution. Next he controls one or more of the centers in the victim's body, usually the sacral center and the lower part of the solar plexus center. Once these centers are occupied a man is in grave danger. He wastes all his energy in sexual over-activity, and in negative emotional attitudes, such as jealousy, irritation, hatred, touchiness, "nosiness," etc. His mental attitude is also affected. He becomes resentful, stubborn, sarcastic and critical, but all these changes do not come at once. They come very slowly, so slowly sometimes, that the man sees no difference between his former self and his present condition.

The next step is to occupy various minor centers, to lead the man into low psychism, into hypnotism, automatic writing, mediumship, into crime, destruction and probably, eventually to an asylum. Sometimes low entities or elementaries, who are earthbound disembodied human souls, come in contact with living human beings through their pictures, statues, articles they had used, clothes they had worn in their past life. Any object that was important to them or parts of the body such as hair, fingernails, teeth or bones, left by them, can attract these entities to a living human being. Because of etheric and emotional forces attached to these objects, they have a line of communication with the objective world, and often spread their destructive, misleading, offensive, hateful influences through these objects, to those who come in contact with them. We are often warned not to use such objects, particularly if the objects were left by a man who committed suicide, was massacred, condemned to death, died in an accident, or was very earthbound, criminal and anti-evolutionary in his activities and motives.

Some religious groups use a method of communication with the disembodied human beings by keeping their teeth, bones, hair, or objects which they had used. Occultism teaches that unless the departed one is an elementary, he will never be interested in his remnants, and will never come in contact with living beings except when he is a fifth degree Initiate motivated by a great global mission, and drawn to the human sphere through a pure love of the multitudes.

THREE. *Severed Spiritual Relationships*. The attack occurs when he cuts his relationships with his true Teacher, with spiritual ideas, and beauties that were keeping him on the arc of ascent, unfoldment and true service. This situation creates a very dangerous condition in his vehicles. The protective radiation of his Teacher or Master cannot reach him. He is left without a supply of protective energy. His spiritual ideas and cherished beauties, in art or in thought, start a process of decomposition and eventually pollute his aura as decaying materials. This further creates complication in the energy circulation, and the man is ready for occupation by various entities.

It has been observed that such people start hating whatever they have loved and honored, and engage in activities diametrically opposed to those which they seek. Sometimes their downfall starts in extreme fanaticism. A fanatic is an obsessed person who is working against his own interests and ideas. He is not aware of this, and that is his curse. When the fire of his fanaticism reaches its highest point, he unconsciously and slowly reverses himself and engages in activities totally opposite to that which he believed. He becomes cruel, hostile, deceiving, cunning, and loses the path while trying to lead others on the path. We can help such people through special meditations done in the *heart*, to focus their minds on simplicity, humility, truth, inclusiveness and compassion.

FOUR. *Head and Heart Center Disorders.* When the man has any damage in his heart or head center, he is open for obsession. These two centers control the incoming process of spiritual or psychic energy. They are damaged, and become out of order when a man engages in wrong activities, exercises or certain meditations. Stealing, lying, evil thinking and cruelty are activities which damage. Exercises to control the nervous system, the glands or organs of the body, such as Hatha Yoga, hypnotism, mediumism, automatic writing and breathing exercises cause serious disorders. Meditations on centers, meditations to develop the third eye, to raise kundalini fire, to invoke spirits, to penetrate the secrets of others, to control other human beings, all cause serious damage. Such practices petrify the head and heart centers along with the corresponding petals in the Lotus, creating disorder in the form of malfunction of the brain, pituitary body, pineal and thymus glands, and causing imbalance in the man's system which evenutally leads to cruelty and insanity. There are many such people functioning in political, religious, and educational fields, and they represent enormous obstacles on the path of the spiritual progress of humanity.

FIVE. *Excessive activities.* Psychic attacks occur when a man forces himself into excessive activities, due to his pride and vanity, overstimulating his centers and vehicles.

Any time that we force a center or a vehicle we create resistance, weakening and overgrowth, which cause unharmonious conditions within the total man. As an aircraft crashes when it loses its balance because of some damage, so man loses control over his own vehicles when they are out of order, and unbalanced. Excessive activity in the brain, causes damage to various organs. The damage to the organs extends itself to the etheric centers, to the nadis and nervous system, to the blood stream, and thus the whole mechanism is put out of balance. Dark forces use this opportunity to sneak in and occupy the vehicle. They like the chaotic condition, because they cannot survive within a sphere of harmony, rhythm and balance. Excessive activities also lead people into worry. One of the greatest poisons that a man can inject into his mental mechanism is *worry*. Some entities wait impatiently for signs of worry, to start their attack. Worry develops and nourishes the seeds of fear; fear nurses germs of destruction, and invites the invaders to the unprotected and weakened "city." All great spiritual Teachers, who were great psychologists, have warned us against pride, excessive ambition and vanity, for these are the anchors or fishhooks of the invaders. To protect us from such attacks we can develop within ourselves, through meditation and observation, a true spirit of contentment, humility, simplicity, and sharing.

SIX. *Wasted Energies.* A psychic attack occurs when a man lives a life that wastes his energies, through excessive sexual activity, through the use of alchohol, tobacco, and various drugs. Venereal disease creates a great opportunity for obsession. Sexual energy has two parts, the fluid which is concentrated in the ovaries and testes, and the etheric part, which is concentrated in astral and mental generative organs.

When a man has sexual intercourse he usually uses both of these energies. When he imagines intercourse without actually having physical intercourse (or if he has intercourse without orgasm), he uses the energy part, the etherical part from the astral and mental generative organs. This is the reason that sexual imagination drains people of a vital force. Although this activity may satisfy them for a while, it eventually leaves them drained of energy. Obsession in these centers causes over stimulation, over activity and waste of energy. Sexual energy is the substance of lubrication for the total man, or for the whole system, and wasting that energy depletes the creative energy supply of the centers and parts of the egoic Lotus. This creates distortion in the energy field within the aura, and presents an easy door for the invaders.

Alcohol attracts all those earthbound ones who are thirsty and want to satisfy their craving. Once they possess a man, they stimulate his craving to such a degree that he becomes a total slave to his habit. After they have a strong hold on his mechanism, they lead him into criminal activities. This starts first with carelessness, irresponsibility, rudeness, lies and dishonesty, and sinks to deep depression and hopelessness.

Cigarettes and various drugs pollute and crack the etheric body; they build an entrance to the lower astral world where these earthbound entities live and wait for contact. Mass obsession is common for drug users.

Venereal diseases damage various glands, their corresponding centers and the petals in the Lotus; they attract the spirits of professional whores and homosexuals. Victims soon lose their higher interests and become hindrances on the path of others.

SEVEN. *Straying from the Path.* Attacks occur when a man chooses to follow the left hand path through idle speech, lying, hatred, jealousy, negativity, separativeness, fanaticism, exploitation and possessiveness; by expressing greed and anger, committing crimes and turning his face to the past.

It is interesting to note that attacks start in very subtle ways, in ways that you do not suspect at all; it may even seem to you that it is your own interests that are leading you into different situations. For example, when a man cannot sit and talk over a problem with another party for various reasons, he is under attack, because dark forces and lower entities want darkness, confusion, complications, mistrust and doubt. It is under such conditions that their germs have opportunity to spread. They force a man past the limit of his capacity.

They divert your focus and guide you into a secondary interest, so that you do not work upon yourself. They lead you into criticism, and make you feel that loneliness is a curse. They do not want you to be alone by yourself, because they do not want you to have serious thoughts about your life. They foster laziness, frustration and resentfulness, and in these situations you work very hard for self-justification, using it as a door of escape. The greater danger comes later when a man slowly starts to imagine committing various crimes, telling lies, manipulating people for his own personal ends. There is grave danger when his greed, anger, possessiveness, and jealousy deepen.

Imaginations can be the result of projected thoughts of dark forces or earthbound entities. When a person notices a negative change in his mind, he must immediately, by all means, reject such imagination, and clean it away with positive and beautiful thoughts. Another method of attack is; causing you to focus your mind upon your past failures and mistakes. When this happens the best thing to do is to focus your mind on the *future*. Imagine and visualize that in the future you will be the master of your life and the co-worker of the Great Ones. Imagine how you would be, how you would look if you were a Master and a co-worker of Cosmos.

In all the information given here, we can see that we have two forces working against each other; the forces that stand for materialism, totalitarianism, separativeness, involution, inertia, aimlessness and destruction, and the forces that stand for the spiritualization, freedom, unity, evolution, harmony and rhythm; for construction and rehabilitation.

These latter forces work upon a plane motivated by the great purpose of the Solar Life, or by the Solar Angel if considered in the individual field. A disciple, from the beginning, must learn to protect the Divine Plan and the plan of his Inner Guardian. Secrecy and silence are protective shields against dark forces. Dark forces are very anxious to gain information about *plans* that may create unity, progress, transformation and creative living. They are very eager to know when such a plan begins to formulate itself within the minds of men.

In so far as the plan (individual or Hierarchical) is in the intuitional level or in the higher minds of a few trusted people, it cannot be perceived by the dark ones, because the light of the Soul provides a radiant protection around the seeds of the developing plan. The dark forces cannot often tune in to the frequency of these individuals who are contemplating upon a creative plan, whether individual or of group nature.

Danger starts, when those who know the plan speak loudly, mixing the plan with their emotional forces. The real danger appears when one talks about the plan to a man or woman:

- Who is related to the dark forces.
- Who is very emotional about it, and who speaks freely with one who is an open channel for dark forces, though it may be done without bad intention.
- Who, in thinking about the plan, distorts it in his own mind, through his mental and emotional illusions and glamours, and then projects this distortion toward the originators of the plan. When this is the case the dark forces immediately

take action and try to penetrate deeper into the core of the plan. The next step is to attack the originator, in any way possible, to make the plan fail. Often they do not attack the originator, directly, if he is quite healthy in his personality vehicles, but they do try to spread fear and doubts to the minds of those who are going to be useful for the working out of the plan. They also organize astral or emotional urges to make people reveal more and more of the plan, until it is grasped by the opposing group, or opposing line of activity.

Once this stage is reached they mobilize their attacks in as many ways and means as possible, until the plan is exposed, distorted and ridiculed, and the originator or originators are under the heavy pressure of the unthinking masses.

Hence, secrecy is the mark of a disciple, because through agelong experience he has learned the mechanics of the dark ones, and now instinctively he knows that secrecy and silence are the best ways to avoid the dark attacks. He knows also that the possible agents or victims of dark forces are those people who "put their noses" into the affairs of others, and nourish their emotional body with the excitement of their personal or individual plans, thoughts, and feelings. Such people are often approached through fear, doubt or flattery, and are thus encouraged to spread words of destruction.

> "Secrecy is also cautiousness and goalfitness. One may plant flowers in appropriate soil. One should know when and to whom to entrust the seeds."[2]
>
> "You must remember that the enemy tries to enter not through the door but through the smallest cracks."[3]

Master Tibetan emphasizes that:

> ". . . the deciding factor with me is to test out your ability to keep silent until it is not longer necessary to do so. Silence is one of the prime prerequisites for initiation and something which every disciple must perforce learn."[4]

The greatest protection from psychic attack is formulated in these words:

- Let love, humility, a sense of oneness, simplicity, joy and gratitude ever radiate throughout your activities and expressions.
- Let your lips guard your speech and your tongue not move until it is ready to glorify, to sing, and to liberate.
- Let your mind be kept steady within the light, love and power of your Guardian Angel.
- Let your soul firmly renounce the past, and strive toward the Future.

---

2. Agni Yoga Society, *Aum*, par. 149.
3. Roerich, Helena, *Letters of Helena Roerich*, Vol. I, p. 128.
4. Bailey, Alice A., *Discipleship in the New Age*, Vol. I, p. 73.

Morya Sahib says:

> "Many salt pillars are spread upon the face of the Earth. Not only did Lot's wife turn back to the past, but numberless are those who look backwards. . . . Certainly the past chained them for a long time. Thus, one must strive onward for enlightenment and health and for the strength of the future. . . . One should not be disconcerted and mourn over the past. Mistakes are even obvious but the caravan does not wait and the very events press onward. . . . The future is crowded but there is no darkness ahead. Leave all the past to Us and think only of the future. Let us not take anything useless from the past. Let us not burden our consciousness by anything."[5]

---

5. Agni Yoga Society, *Hierarchy*, par. 347, 348.

Chapter XXI

SPIRITS AND MEDIUMS

"There are many aberrant people in the world who, in one way or another, have entered the world of delusion and have been caught there. . . . They are lost in the illusions of the astral plane and it is very difficult to heal them."[1]

Mediums are those people who have a loose connection between the physical and etheric bodies and are able to vacate their bodies for use by other persons. H.P.B. says,

> ". . . we . . . regard the mediumship as one of the most dangerous of abnormal nervous diseases."[2]

One of her great Teachers adds,

> "A medium is but the inn for disembodied liars."[3]
>
> "Verily, a medium has no open centers, and the psycho-vision, for contact with the higher worlds, also is unattainable for him. Man is in error about the power of the medium, and We are often distressed to see how enticing to people are physical manifestations. A materialization attracts them like a magnet. We prefer the channel of the spirit, and for sacred missions We use the channel of the spirit only."[4]

Most of the mediums are not aware of what the possessing entity is doing or speaking through them. They are not aware of the identity of the one acting through them. The unfolding human soul, the real owner of the body mechanism, is out of it, and cannot control it; another "spirit" or "entity" now is in charge.

Some mediums are withdrawn from their body not by their own free will, but by accident, disease, shocks or hypnotism. Others withdraw of their own free will, but cannot keep continuity of consciousness. They cannot register out of body experiences, or control their bodies and senses.

H.P.B. says that there are thirty-three groups of devas, and all together they number 330,000,000. They are classified as those who are good, those who

---

1. Saraydarian, H., *The Fiery Carriage and Drugs*, p. 38.
2. Blavatsky, H. P., *Lucifer*, Vol. III, October-November 1890.
3. Agni Yoga Society, *Agni Yoga*, par. 228.
4. Agni Yoga Society, *Infinity*, Vol. I, par. 106.

are bad, and those who are indifferent. These are the entities who often use mediums to contact the physical plane. There are others; those who passed away with dark sins, those who committed suicide, and those who came to premature death by accident, or were executed for different reasons.

Thus opportunity is given to many entities to occupy mechanisms and come in contact with the physical plane. The dark forces, in particular, search to find every man possible to work on that plane.

An adept can withdraw from his body consciously, keeping continuity of consciousness and protecting his mechanism from any invasion. If he wishes information from higher levels, he raises himself to higher levels and brings down all that he needs at a certain time.

Mediums are like abandoned motels, where many earthbound entities and astral shells rush in and occupy them for a while, to mislead people, to take revenge, or to satisfy their cravings in many forms. The mediums in such cases have no control over their senses but an adept, while away from his body, receives all information from his physical senses and uses it accordingly. Because of the fact that he has full control over his astral and etheric bodies, he can penetrate any obstacle, travel any space, experience and work wherever he is. In addition to this, he can make his astral vehicle visible, exactly as his physical body is, or he can have it assume any shape he wishes. All of this is done under the great Law of Economy and Service, to uplift, to guide and to enlighten groups of people.

The mechanism of an average medium is occupied by entities over which the medium has no control.

In the case of an adept, he can offer his body to a greater Master who is living in subtle levels, and who wants to come in contact with the physical level life. In this situation, the body of the adept is given to him, voluntarily, consciously, and with mutual agreement. At the time his body is occupied by a Great One, the adept is fully conscious of all that is performed through his body by the Great One.

Such instances are very rare, and the effect of the functions of such Great Ones is so powerful that new cultures, religions and civilizations appear as a result. These Great Ones choose extremely pure persons and refined Initiates, who are able to withstand the high voltage pouring through their physical body.

Most of the phenomena of insanity is the result of obsession by many kinds of entities who use the body for manifold purposes, just as some children use telephone lines to contact people in different locations, or pass information that is based on their ignorance or folly.

Mediums, letting their bodies be occupied by various kinds of spirits or entities, build a channel between the astral plane and physical plane. Through this channel, the dark forces that are located in the astral plane, slowly penetrate into the physical plane, and gradually anchor themselves within those who are associated with the medium. They then totally possess them to further their destructive functions.

Hypnotism is one of the methods by which dark forces occupy a human being. A sorcerer is one who opens the gates wide and brings the dark forces in contact with human beings, with the public. Hypnotists and sorcerers are both strongly rejected by true occultism, which is nothing else but the science of Self and the science of becoming Oneself to which these wise words of Delphi referred, "Know thyself."

Necromancy in the ancient world was very popular, and esoteric tradition teaches us that this was one of the main causes underlying the destruction of ancient civilizations and continents. Let us remember that ancient Egypt, Chaldea, Rome, Greece, Central and South America were all countries which started with very high and pure civilizations. Their people built a bridge of wisdom from darkness to light, from the unreal to the real, but as the great Magi, or great Masters passed beyond the veil, ignorant followers tried to practice necromancy, drugs, and various rituals and ceremonies, to reach higher states of consciousness or higher levels of beingness.

The result was that, after they opened a channel between the two worlds, it was impossible to discriminate between good and evil spirits, and because of their level of penetration they attracted the attention of dark forces, who invaded their countries, and eventually caused great destruction. The ruins of such countries are living testimony of this. Experts in this field tell us that through necromancy people do not come in contact with the spirits of their fathers, or the spirits of the dead. Except in a few cases, man comes in contact with a variety of entities, generally with evil ones, whose polarization is toward destruction, materialism, and separativeness.

Exceptions are those human spirits who passed away through suicide, accidents, or in wars. We can add to these those who died at a very young age, those who were extremely criminal and those who were executed. Those who commit suicide, or die a violent death accidentally, stay very close to earth "until the actual period of life decided by the Soul, terminates."

Executed criminals are in general thrown out of life, filled with hate and revenge. These persons are very close to the sphere of earth, and want to avenge themselves by possessing people and their associated fields, causing their destruction. This happens to many persons when they yield themselves to negative, sinful activities. It happens to hypocrites whose behavior invite such elementaries, or "earth-bound disembodied human souls." It happens also to those coming in contact with mediums and lower psychics who act as a communication line between the lower, harmful entities and the person.

The nature spirits often use the astral shells in a way that they appear to be real, logical and eager to help. They also use those who are not on the physical plane, and who are highly wicked or full of revenge and hatred. These are elementaries, which are used by elementals, the nature spirits, and because of their destructive, hateful and revengeful nature, they can be used for many destructive purposes once the link between the subjective and objective worlds is established.

We have also the *elementals*, the forces of nature, "foetal and infant entities," the guardians of animals, vegetables and minerals. They are very sensitive to color, sound, vibrations emanated by certain movements and to our thoughts and emotions.

> "Some of them have a special relation to mental operations and to the action of the astral organs, whether these be joined to a body or not. When a medium forms the channel and also from other natural coordination, these elementals make an artificial connection with the shell [the astral body left in the astral world, or created by human imagination] of a deceased person, aided by the nervous fluid of the medium and others near, and then the shell is galvanized into an artificial life. Through the medium connection is made with the physical and psychical forces of all present. The old impressions on the astral body give up their images to the mind of the medium, the old passions are set on fire. Various messages and reports are then obtained from it, but not one of them is original, not one is from the spirit [the disembodied soul of the person passed beyond the astral realms]."[5]

It often happens that those who attend seances, find themselves extremely tired. This happens when they are in the presence of natural mediums. The reason for this is that mediums and some *elementaries* (half dead human beings) sap the energy of those present. Mediums use this energy for the materialization and building the line of communication between entities and the audience.

Moses, knowing about mediums, and the evil that they were carrying within themselves said, "Thou shall not suffer a witch to live'[6] Of course this was an extreme order to warn his people of the grave dangers that a medium could bring in. There is an interesting passage in the works of Flavius Josephus, in which he says:

> "God, enabled him [Solomon] to learn that skill which expels demons, which is a science useful and sanative to him. He composed such incantations also by which distempers are alleviated. And he left behind him the manner of using exorcisms, by which they drive away demons, so that they never return; and this method of cure is of great force unto this day."[7]

Jesus used His power to cure people, expelling the demons from mediums, or from those who were victims of obsession. He was so successful that the victims, after being cleansed from the obsession, became the servants of the great cause of liberation, as for example, Mary Magdalene and others.

Moses seeing the grave danger of obsession, and knowing the ways through which this obsession was achieved, gave the following command to his people:

5. Judge, William Q., *The Ocean of Theosophy*, p. 105.
6. Exodus 22:18.
7. Josephus, Flavius, *The Works of Flavius Josephus*, printed 1879, Vol. I, p. 263.

"Let no one be found among you who consigns his son or daughter to the fire, or who is an augur, a soothsayer, a diviner, a sorcerer, one who casts spells, or one who consults ghosts or familiar spirits, or one who inquires of the dead. For anyone who does such things is abhorrent to the Lord, and it is because of these abhorrent things that the Lord your God is dispossessing them before you."[8]

Black art, or black magic uses chiefly color, sound, special incense, some movement, feelings, thought and the letters of certain alphabets to communicate with the *elementals*. They use these nature spirits to force their will upon others, to interfere with the karma of others, and to gain personal material advantages. Those ignorant ones who fall into the hands of such people, eventually find themselves possessed by many entities, and become the instruments of darkness and destruction.

Sometimes even a good spirit will possess a man, and the man becomes a new person in many of his expressions, but this does not mean progress for him. On the contrary, it prevents him from exercising his own free will and cultivating self-actualization. The tragedy occurs when this good spirit leaves him; he becomes the same man he was previously with all his hatreds, jealousies and shortcomings. We are told also that the good entity can be polluted to such a degree within the aura of a medium that eventually it acts as an evil force. Our intention is to be ourselves, not to be obsessed by any spirit. We are told that an adept can control these good spirits or angels and render exceptional service through them, at the same time helping them in their evolution. Christ is one of these. In such cases they do not possess the mechanism, but offer their service to the man who knows how to discriminate between good and evil and have total control over the spirits. In the New Testament, these spirits are called angels, and we read in various places that they rendered great services.[9]

The Tibetan Master says that a great number of angels will come with Christ and teach many sciences to humanity, after He reappears among men.

Our own thought builds forms when we come in contact with certain impressions coming from the non-physical world. In most mediumistic cases it is we who give the form and even the content of the message. We are then surprised when the same things are told to us by the apparition or through the medium who acts as an amplifier.

Our thoughtforms can condense to such a degree that we can see them. They talk to us, for our messages can be amplified within the created form and broadcast to us through the emotional and mental aura of the medium. This can be done consciously, also. A person, if he has developed his will-power, can create the form of a man, put words in his mouth and move him in any

8. *The Torah*, Deuteronomy, 18:10–13.
9. John 4:2 and Hebrew 1:14.

way he wishes by remote control, giving the impression that we are in the presence of a true spirit.

It is impossible to contact departed ones on our physical plane, and to make them materialize. However, it is possible to contact them on astral and mental planes if we can uplift ourselves and be conscious upon these planes. True mediums are those people who are able to leave their bodies and consciously penetrate into the astral, the mental, and even into the intuitional plane to bring us true communications from the departed ones and from the great Masters. This may also happen through our dream experience, when it is genuine.

Our beloved ones, when they leave their astral bodies and pass onto the mental plane, do not try to communicate with us by coming down to the physical plane, but their shells can be attracted to living persons through the similarity of desires. They (the shells) seem very alive and self-active, because they reflect the thought of those who respond to their vibration and give them (unconsciously) the power to talk, walk and express themselves.

People who are full of low desires and vices, attract shells that are charged with similar desires and vices, and fall into a greater depth of misery, after being possessed by them.

We become attached to such entities in places where human vice in all its forms, runs rampant; as for example, in places where alcohol is consumed, where people indulge freely in sex and where drug use is abused, because such shells do float in these places and cling to those who synchronize with their vibrations or to those who have cracks in their auras. H. P. Blavatsky very emphatically says:

> "We . . . must never lose sight of the profound axiom of the Esoteric Doctrine which teaches us that it is we, the living, who are drawn toward the spirits—but that the latter can never even though they would—descend to us, or rather into our sphere."[10]
>
> ". . . having been magnetically drawn towards a medium, it is revived for a time and lives in him by proxy so to speak. In the medium's Aura, it lives a kind of vicarious life and reasons and speaks either through the medium's brain or those of other persons present."[11]

It is possible that a person after passing away, can, while in the astral plane, communicate with the physical world through his own Soul or through an advanced disciple. These communications take only a short time, and are possible because of an intense desire to come in contact with the physical world by the departed one, for important connections or messages. The other possibility is that those advanced souls who bypass the astral and mental plane can, for

10. Blavatsky, H. P., *Collected Writings*, Vol I, p. 36.
11. Blavatsky, H. P., *The Key to Theosophy*, p. 90.

some reasons, communicate with persons in the objective world, not through ordinary mediums, but through advanced Initiates.

The Solar Angel leaves the man temporarily, when the person falls into "fright, grief, despair, a violent attack of sickness or excessive sensuality." A sorcerer can enter his body, and use it for destructive purposes. If the person thus possessed were of high level, an executive, you can imagine what power this sorcerer gains in possessing such a person.

> ". . . *sorcery is any kind of evil influence exercised upon other persons, who suffer, or make other persons suffer, in consequence.* Karma is a heavy stone splashed in the quiet waters of Life; and it must produce ever widening circles of ripples, carried wider and wider, almost *ad infinitum.* Such causes produced have to call forth effects, and these are evidenced in the just laws of Retribution." [12]

Occultism is the science of knowing and being oneself. The path of entire evolution is to lead man into his true Self. Benefactors of humanity are those people who try to free man from all their man-made obstacles and hindrances; from all influences that work against the trend of evolution and make a man the slave of involuntionary forces, dependent upon outer wills and mechanical, artifical factors.

Hence, freedom is defined as the process of leading the unfolding human soul to his higher heritage of self-actualization, to the core of his being, actualized only by his aspirations, visions and spiritual inspirations coming from his true Self.

---

12. Blavatsky, H. P., *Collected Writings*, Vol. IX, p. 259.

Chapter XXII

THE WISDOM OF LOVE

"Verily, when one learns to inculcate the emanations of feeling, one will see that precisely love above all attracts the fire of space. He who said, 'Love one another,' was a true Yogi. . . ."[1]

—M.M.

Love energy is the outstanding quality of our Solar Angel, and also the quality that a human soul must develop before he becomes able to penetrate into the sphere of the Spiritual Triad. This quality of Love is the magnetic force of the Soul, Who attracts and heals. Not only does the intellect have light, but the light of Love is tremendous and more penetrating than any light in our created universe. Understanding is a quality of Love. Intuition is purer Love, for Intuition is straight knowledge.

As has been previously stated, Monads are on the three major Rays only. We have Monads of Will-Power, Monads of Love, Monads of Active Intelligence, but we must remember that these three Rays of Aspect are the sub-rays of the Cosmic Second Ray of Love-Wisdom.

Because of the fact that this Solar System was created by the Love Ray, all of its Monads must develop the love quality to its optimum glory throughout the scheme, to the last globe.

The great Sage, M.M., speaking about such a love says:

> ". . . We welcome each transport of love and self-sacrifice. As a lever sets the wheels in motion, so love sets up the strongest reaction. Compared with the radiance of love, the strongest hatred reflects only as a hideous mark. For love is the true reality and treasure."[2]

WHAT IS LOVE?

One day I was sitting on a beautiful, green hill, deeply engaged in study, when a young couple approached me. They were troubled and began to speak to me of their problem. I learned that they were planning to marry, but that the girl had suffered a nervous breakdown and had been hospitalized for three weeks. She had been released only that day, and the young man was anxious that I see her and talk to her. I asked her gently,

"What is the matter? What is troubling you?"

---

1. Agni Yoga Society, *Agni Yoga*, par. 424.
2. *Ibid.*

Without hesitation she replied,

"I went to the Father Confessor and he told me that I will burn in hell because I have loved this man. When I went to my mother, she said, 'I have nothing but disgust for you. I hate you.' Then I turned to my father and he shouted, 'You must leave this house at once!' Now, I don't know what to do. I just hate everybody!"

"Do you know," I said, "you can be happy?"

"How," she cried, "how can I be happy?"

"It is very simple," I answered, "just start loving."

"But whom can I love?" she asked, "Whom can I trust and love?"

"Listen carefully," I said, "and I will tell you about a little drama we are going to have right here on this beautiful hill. First, you are going to run tc that pine tree. You are going to hold that pine tree with both arms, kiss i and tell it that you love it. Next, you will go to that lovely rose and tell i the same thing. After that, you will lie down on the grass and love the grass When you have done all these things, you will come back to me and I wil tell you something."

She paused for a moment and said, "I will do as you say."

She ran to the pine tree and threw her arms around it. I felt that she wa crying because of the length of time she clung to the great trunk of the tal pine.

"Come," I encouraged her, "the next one."

With tears in her eyes she knelt before the rose, the little rose, just opening Holding the blossom tenderly with both hands, I heard her say,

"You know I love you. Do you love me?"

She arose and started to cry as she took a few steps forward and flung herse upon the soft, green grass. Lying there quietly, she uttered these simple word "I love you, grass."

I called to her, "Come here and look at the setting sun. Just cry out t the sun and ask, 'Sun, do you love me? I love you because you are the light!'

The rich quality of her voice was unbelievable. It was joy, ecstasy, freedon It revealed a striving to break through something, to jump forth into realit After a few moments she sat down, quietly, peacefully, and said,

"I love nature. I love everything. I love my mother no matter what sh says or does. I love my father and my priest, but I know that I am not goir to burn."

"No, if everything loves you, how can you burn?"

This is one of the mysteries of Love. I was certain that it would not b necessary for her to be hospitalized again. As they were leaving, she pushe her friend away, saying,

"I am going to drive."

The young man was perplexed. This young woman had changed so much in the matter of a few minutes that he was at a loss to understand it. He did not know what to do about letting her drive the car. I said,

"Give the steering wheel to her. Let her drive."

"Will it be safe?" he asked. "Do you have faith in her?"

"Of course I have," I replied.

Then I said to the girl,

"Before you go, kiss me."

When she kissed me I said to her,

"I, also, love you."

"You do?' she said, smiling.

"Yes, of course," I replied. "From now on everybody will love you—the trees, the birds, the flowers, everything."

The love energy had been released in her. When you suppress, within your heart, the greatest energy in the universe, you burn with that energy, you are cracked with that energy; but if you release it, you are sane and harmonious. You are a rhythmic note in the Symphony of the Universe. Thus you grow and bloom with the Universe, with the Cosmos.

Love is communication, communion and responsiveness. All growth, enlightenment, evolution and progress depend on "the unfolding of a continually increasing power to respond." Life is communication, communion. We are not speaking of the ordinary life which we live, but of Life-energy, which makes us breathe, think and grow. This is communion, itself. It is Love.

Life is oneness. Unless it is one, there is no Life. Oneness means livingness, communion. Separation, a diversity, means death. Closer relationship means deeper Life; less relationship means less Life. All parts are related to the whole.

We can start with man and say, a finger cannot live without becoming a part of the hand; the hand cannot live without the body; the body cannot live unless there is close communication with other parts of the body; the body cannot live without communication with the world as a whole, a chemical world of water, air and sun. Earth cannot support life if it has no communication with the sun. Such relationships are outer communication, or responses.

Responses of a mechanism to a greater mechanism create livingness, but this livingness reaches higher and higher dimensions when you start with conscious responses. Mechanical life will lead you to a certain level, but to continue upward from there to higher levels, you will need to unfold other levels of response—emotional response and mental response. Our livingness depends upon the radius of our emotional response, and upon the width and depth of our mental response.

Emotional response is a process of detecting the emotional needs of a person and fulfilling his needs on the emotional level. Mental response is the process of knowing a person as he stands in his mental activities, and meeting his needs on the mental level. When your ability to respond lifts itself to the higher mental or causal plane, you come into direct realization of the person involved; you see him in the light of the greater whole, greater unity, and your love increases and becomes purer.

In the next step, we enter into the world of pure Love. In esoteric teaching this world is known as the world of Intuition, or the sphere of straight knowledge. It is here that our Love breaks all of its limitations and embraces the *whole*.

Life is communication, an act of loving response and harmonization, a tuning in with higher and higher levels of awareness and beingness.

All wars, all pain, all troubles are due to crystallization. Sometime, somewhere, the flow of energy stops, becomes crystallized and can no longer circulate freely. When crystallization occurs, you have religious, political and social upheavals, bringing great suffering to many. Break the crystallizations, permitting greater responses, and you will have more life, more joy and more happiness.

Religious and political prejudice and intolerance are crystallizations, a "drying-up," in the channel of energy circulation. Hatred and jealousy are emotional level crystallizations which block circultation of energy. Ignorance and illusion are mental level crystallizations. Break through these crystallizations and you have more life. Try to communicate with your Soul and Spirit; communicate with the best in the physical, emotional and mental worlds. Find the inner center of conscious energy. Find your goal in life. Real communication starts when *you are yourself*.

The steps toward reaching that inner core are:

— Discipline
— Concentration
— Meditation
— Contemplation
— Livingness

Only through such steps can you meet yourself and respond to real Love energy. This Love cannot be learned, responded to, or communicated through philosophy, psychology, or by listening to lectures, but through loving. The one way to learn the meaning of Love is to love. Once you have loved, then and only then, can you know Love. It takes you away. It sublimates you, releases you, and instead of becoming a self-centered man or woman, you become Universe-centered, Cosmic-centered; thus is Love energy released.

In our modern world, when people speak of "Love," they usually understand it to be largely concerned with sex. They are not wrong providing they are truly aware of what sex really is. Sex is communication between Energy and matter, between Spirit and substance; communication to carry on the purpose of the Cosmic Being, to give expression to that Cosmic Aim or Purpose for which, by which and through which, this whole Cosmos is created. All of creation is the result of sex; energy and matter coming together. In a religious or philosophical sense, it is said, when Spirit and matter come together, they create all of the universes. Love is all-embracing energy. All atoms, all cells are imbued with it. Actually, it is this love energy which is making greater and greater mechanisms through which to express itself in greater beauty.

The mineral, vegetable and animal kingdoms are vehicles of expression for love energy. We may even say that one of the original long-range goals of this love energy was to create man, who eventually will express love consciously, and then be a co-worker with the Creative Energy.

What is the origin of this Energy? In one occult book, there is a very interesting and picturesque expression of the Energy Source. It states that there are three Suns which give light to the whole Universe. Behind the visible sun, is the Heart of the Sun, which is the source of the Love—the outpouring Love of the Creator. Hidden behind that Sun is the Central Spiritual Sun, which is the Source of Life. It is the second Sun with which we are concerned, for it is the Source of Love. It is all-embracing compassion, and in esoteric literature is called the Great Magnet, or the Great Mother, which continually attracts all Sparks back to Herself. Through this attraction process which we call Love, each Spark, no matter how far away—in the mineral kingdom, vegetable kingdom, in flowers, animals, birds, or in human beings—is attracted to that Central Core, the Cosmic Magnet, which is inhaling it slowly, drawing it back to Its home. This is evolution.

If we review the history of humanity, we see that a man becomes a family, a family becomes a group, a group becomes a nation, and nations become united nations. We know, that no matter what happens, that Great Magnet will pave the way for One Humanity as it attracts individuals, blending them into greater units, greater wholes. Through greater communication, responses, greater harmony and cooperation among the Sparks, among the living souls, all of creation will slowly become a whole Symphony, unfolding the Mystery of Love.

There is only one great science and that science is the Science of Love. Love is nothing but Electrical Energy. If a man has hatred radiations, if a man has jealousy, his vibrations are different, his aura is different, the color of the atmosphere around him is different. If, however, that man is full of Love Energy, he is radioactive, free; whatever he touches blooms, is released, has gained its freedom.

We must know how to use this energy as a good electrician, who knows the laws of electricity, uses them. He very carefully observes and obeys the laws because he is aware of the fact that in working with electricity, he can lose his life or bring lights and many other blessings to us. How can we deal with this Science of Love so that the Love Energy really fulfills the purpose behind it? If a man loves without knowledge of the laws of energy, he can burn himself. Most of our sufferings, our agonies, our pain, our breakdowns, are caused by so-called "love." We may hear such words as: "Oh, that girl rejected me!" "My wife divorced me!" "My son isn't interested in me!" It is all love matter.

All human relationships are based on this great energy, Love, and yet we must educate ourselves to use it as an electrician must be trained prior to attempting to work with electrical energy.

True Love is Life. In loving, you have more life and you give more life. You receive more Life because you are tuning in with Cosmic Love, which is the substance of unity, cooperation, understanding, synthesis, harmony and beauty.

THE PATH OF LOVE

There are seven steps on the Path of Love:

Love Must Be Progressively Expanding

This means that your love must not stop at sex, but must climb upward toward greater unity, progressing toward higher levels of existence, and revealing itself in higher forms of creativity and service.

The downfall of families, of great men and women, of groups and organizations—ancient and modern—is the result of a love that was largely concentrated on the sex level; a love that was not progressively moving from the physical level toward higher levels—emotional, mental and spiritual levels.

The purpose of Love energy is to express Divinity Itself, on all levels. This is what creativity is. In every act of Love, on any level, this uplifting Cosmic Purpose must be realized.

You must always know whether your love limits itself or progresses toward freedom. A loving person must be able to say: "I love myself, but I love you also. I love you as a group of people; but not just all of you, I love your whole nation. I love not only your nation, I love all nations, I love all Humanity. My love does not stop there, I love our Solar System. I stand on the mountain and behold the beauty of the stars, and I say 'I love you'."

If love stops somewhere and you say, for example, "I love, but I love myself—not you," it is a poison. The electrical system has a short circuit somewhere. Because of this one little short circuit, all of your light is gone. By using Love energy in this way, people become dark, poisonous, hateful, jealous, separative. Love must be expanding, expanding, ever expanding. Thus, not only must you love the visible universe, you must also love the invisible universe, divine energies, divine ideas, great concepts. For example, people say, "This is the only way to fly!" This is not true. You are dividing and belittling yourself, narrowing and squeezing yourself. Just be open as a little child is open and embrace the Cosmos. If your love is progressive, you are becoming a co-worker of the great Cosmic Heart, the Great Magnet.

When your love is not progressive, and when your love cannot create something higher than sexual satisfaction, you become weaker and you experience a feeling of dissatisfaction, failure, loneliness, all of which lead you toward carelessness, inertia and death.

True love must start from higher levels, perhaps from spiritual levels, and pass downward to perform creative, therapeutic and releasing work to create unity on the three lower levels, and then climb back to the Source from whence it originated.

If a little chicken says, "I want to stay in my shell, I do not want to grow bigger," that little chicken dies; his life is snuffed out. But if that chicken breaks its shell and says, "I want to crack, to destroy my limitations (those limitations against love, any hindrances to love), I want to crack my shell and get out," then you have a beautiful chicken. It opens its eyes and wonders at the beautiful outside world. If you were a chicken, imagine what you would feel if you suddenly came out of the shell. "My! This is my mother; this is my father. What are these beautiful things—flowers?" Feel the joy! That joy is expansion; joy of freedom, joy of greater harmony, relationship and communication.

Love starts from lower levels also. Let us say, I love a girl, but I love only her body; beyond that I cannot pass, so my love will crystallize. That love will be very short. I try to expand that love toward her heart, then toward her mind, but if I stop there, again the love will stagnate. I must pass beyond the mental and enter into the spiritual levels; and if, in so doing, I can raise that girl and myself together, my love is finding consummation, love is expanding and becoming creative. If at any moment love stops expanding, you can expect trouble from your physical, emotional and mental bodies. That is the Science of Love.

If you say, for example, "I love my nation, but I hate that nation," you must sacrifice fifty or sixty thousand, or a million people in wars. Love bridges all. Love says, "Come let us understand each other!"

Marriage or love is not only the unity of two bodies. We marry with our hearts if we are dedicated to the same goal. We can marry with our ideas, our thoughts, our visions, and receive greater satisfaction than from a marriage based on the physical level. Those who have physical intercourse and do not have intercourse between their higher natures, feel empty and neglected after the lower physical nature has been satisfied. If, however, intercourse is on higher levels as well as the physical level, the result is joy and expansion of consciousness.

There is a story in the Far East that tells of a king who had in his household many beautiful young girls who swam naked in a pool every day. Once each week the king would send his only son down to the pool to bring up a bucket of water. Always, however, when the young man went down to the pool, he was so charmed by the girls that he did not return. The king would have to go to the pool, bring him back, and send him hunting to make him forget the beautiful maidens. One day the son asked,

"Father, why do you not let me stay with them?"

"I am glad you have asked me," said the king. "Until you learn to go to the pool and obey the order by returning promptly; until you can go and return without being swayed by their charms, you will not be allowed to remain with them."

This simple story portrays the principle of self-control, the principle of sublimation, economy and the meaning of purposeful love. Let us remember that the purpose of Love is to take us back to divine unity, into the Cosmic Magnet. This being the case, each act of Love must be a step back toward Home.

The Nature of Love is Sacrificial

There is no love without sacrifice. Love is giving—not taking. There is no expectation in Love. Love must be sacrificial. If there is no sacrifice, it is like bank business or bookkeeping; nothing but dry, cold, unfeeling, selfish action on any level. However, if I say, "I love you," and stand behind my love; if I sacrifice for you, then my love is supported and I am proving that it is a real love.

At one time I was speaking in a private college. As part of the program, another man gave an excellent talk in which he said that we must build fine colleges because they are divine temples. His speech was beautiful and well delivered. When he came and sat by me, I said,

"Write a check."

"What?" he asked.

"Write a check so that we can build that college. You have the money."

"Later," he replied.

"Then," I admonished him, "you are not standing behind your love."

When you say "Love," you must sacrifice. If you do not sacrifice, you are not a lover, no matter what! You may ask, "Sacrifice what?" There is no end to it. In sacrifice, you are giving up your egoism, your separation, your materialism, your self-centeredness; you are sacrificing all that is dear to you for the upliftment of another being who is part of yourself.

That is what Love is. You are, one by one, breaking the bars by which you are imprisoned. You are destroying the crystallized materialism within yourself. You are breaking up the crystallized concept that you are a separated being. Once you have given of yourself, you have proved that you are loving.

Recently a husband said to me, "My wife loves me very much, but when I ask her to make a certain dish, or to prepare a little more food to eat, she says, 'Honey, let's go to the restaurant.' "

Later I met his wife and I said, "You are such a pretty girl. Do you love your husband?"

She answered "Yes, of course."

"All right," I said, "make some sacrifice for him. Start from A–B–C–. Prepare some special dish which he likes. Do little things for him, so that eventually you will learn to sacrifice more, for greater purposes, greater aims, greater destinations, and without expectation."

Every time you "love" without sacrifice, you create a complex situation in your inner world. You create congestion. This can be avoided if you will stand behind your love and express it through your *practical* sacrifices. If you love and do not express your love with sacrifice, the fire of Love burns your mental, emotional and etheric centers, creating in them insensitivity, dullness, ulcers, and many other unwholesome conditions. Every time you love and are not making sacrifices for it, you are touching electrical energy which may burn you. It is said that our God is burning fire.

If you say to a beloved one, "I love you," but refrain from performing sacrificial acts for him to meet his various needs, your love is selfish. If you fail to make sacrifices necessary to lift him to a deeper stage of understanding and creativity, your love is selfish. Selfishness is a state of mind in which the channel of love is congested. The Love energy cannot circulate and communicate with the greater whole. Selfishness stops the transmutation of matter. Love causes transmutation of matter. The matter of your vehicles must be transmuted into higher sensitivity, enabling you to create under higher spiritual impulses.

The goal of a human being, of a nation, of humanity, is not survival. Survival is a station on the eternal path of spiritualization. The ultimate goal of any living being is to express Beauty and to be beautiful. There is a great Symphony in the mind of Cosmos. Each act performed to increase our capacity to "feel," to be "impressed" by that Symphony, and each effort to express it in our individual and global life, is an act of touching the Beauty, a step toward the realization of Beauty. This is accomplished only through the acts of creative loving.

The true Love energy emanates from the Heart of the Sun. This energy cannot be contacted until a man actually enters into the Intuitional level of awareness through real acts of sacrifice. Oddly enough, mothers, because of their nature, have access to this energy in their dedication and sacrifice. When dedication and sacrifice are withdrawn, they lose the true contact with Love. Once Love is lost, ugliness starts. No man or woman is handsome, pretty or beautiful without Love. *Love is the midwife of Beauty.*

There are three active energies—light, love and power or life. The life and love and light of our three bodies are given by the visible sun. It is the source of our light, electricity, love and life on three levels. On the fourth level, the Intuitional, the Heart of the Sun becomes active for us, and a higher love starts to penetrate into the heart of the human being. On special occasions, a certain extra quantity of such love is given to the individual. For example, a woman receives her higher love energy at the time of conception, and an additional amount at the time of delivery. The father receives higher energy at the time of the first intercourse with the mother, providing the act is sacred, conscious and accepted. The child receives it through breastfeeding and the love of his mother. At puberty, another quota of higher love is given to both sexes.

The amount of love is occasionally increased through acts of sacrifice or conscious suffering, but a human being truly starts to love when he comes into conscious contact with the reservoir of love on the Intuitional level. The brotherhood of humanity will be possible when the majority of men contact the Intuitional level. For this reason we are urged to expand our consciousness, because in expanding our consciousness, we will become more brotherly and closer to the concept of the brotherhood of man.

When light and life energy are used without love, the trend is toward materialism, possession, separation, all of which are forms of hatred.

Love energy given to animals, to trees, to insects, at certain times, is used largely in procreation, or in cooperation with nature. It is like a heartbeat which is distributing love energy in cycles to lower kingdoms, and to the human kingdom.

Because the greater portion of humanity is oriented physically, emotionally and mentally, love energy is translated through the contents of these levels, and used for satisfaction on these three levels only. This indicates that man can increase his quota of love energy by the performance of special acts and through self-exertion. The greatest way to increase love energy is through the labour of responsibility which results in sacrificial acts.

The Unconditional Nature of Love

The unconditional nature of love stands behind these beautiful words spoken by Christ: "Greater love hath no man than this, that a man lay down his life for his friends." You love, not because you are expecting hundreds of dollars, great fame and glory, or a great reputation, but because the fulfillment of the purpose of the Cosmos is that you, as a drop, give yourself and love more. People say, "If you love me, I will love you." This is not Love. Can you love a man who hates you? Can you love a man who has blackened your name, slandered your reputation? Can you still say, "I love you and I am going to stand by you and help you in any way you may need my help." This is *unconditional* Love.

As you become Love, you become stronger, more magnetic, more understanding, more powerful and influential, and slowly, very slowly, others will see that you are a rich, radiating beauty. You inspire them; you take them from the low state in which they are living; you crack their self-centeredness. If you save only one man, only one woman, you have done the greatest work in the Cosmos because, as is said in the scriptures, great joys are witnessed and recorded in heaven if a man turns toward the Light, toward Love. All over the world we are short on Love; hence the many kinds of sorrow, pain, suffering, debts and crimes.

When Love, pouring down from the Heart of the Sun, is assimilated and used to build a path toward the Cosmic Magnet, that distorted noise which we call the universe and humanity, will slowly change into a great Symphony, and every man everywhere will love, will understand. When this glorious change comes to pass, this planet, instead of being a planet of sorrow, a planet of pain and suffering, will be a planet of Joy, Freedom and Liberation. Those who are moving toward greater blooming are sensing the greatest joy, even though their physical, emotional and mental natures are passing through strain or stress. They have great joy because they are communicating with the Source of Divine Joy, the Great Cosmic Love.

In real love, the lover is lost in the loved one. He or she exists for the loved one. Thus is unity performed. Such love is not an emotional outpouring, but the result of an intuitional urge in which one feels that whatever he is doing is absolutely the right thing to do. It is not a blind, emotional drive, a desire, but clear reason and identification with the lover.

When our love increases in spite of conditions, we become able to touch the life-saving energy. If it decreases because of existing condtions, we have not yet tasted the joy of real love, which is all-giving under all conditions.

Responsibility Is One of the Laws of the Science of Love

Love performed without a sense of responsibility, leads us to sorrow and suffering. Responsibility means that you will sustain the unity once created, and work for the progressive advancement of that unity toward more love, more light and more life. Responsibility teaches you that other people's failures and sorrows are yours, and that you must try to eliminate them physically, emotionally, mentally with freedom and joy, as if they were yours.

Ask yourself, "Am I ready to face my responsibilities?" If you can face them, you are really loving, but if you are escaping, you are degenerating. It is a very difficult thing because Love is our Life. Wherever we go we meet it. It is everywhere. If you make a selfish move, you will suffer; you will cause suffering. It was because of this that in olden times, one of the ancient races used to teach the subject of Love to people before they entered into marriage. What a beautiful idea; that man must know what Love is—spiritual Love, unity, beauty, understanding, cooperation, harmony, great sacrifice—before he is able to lift someone up to that level in his marriage or love.

The Non-Separative Nature of Love—
Man Is Not Really Loving if He Leaves Out Anything in Creation

This is surprising? Everything must be loved, even your ugliness or your beauty. Nothing must be left out—trees, birds, fish, sky—everything in the universe must be loved until you feel that YOU ARE LOVE ITSELF. This is very important, because many people think that they love if they say, "I love you, dear" or a person may say, "I love you so much, but I hate your neighbor." Here, you are short of love. Love must be a unified, cosmic, all-embracing Love.

I know a medical doctor who wrote a beautiful article about love. After reading it I said to him,

"Doctor, you really know the biology of love, and I assume that you really do love, too?"

"Of course," he said, "I love my wife."

"I didn't mean that." I said, "Is your love really as all-embracing, all-forgiving as the sun?"

"Hum," he said, "I guess so."

Later, on a very stormy night, at two o'clock in the morning, he called me.

"Oh, H—, I have killed my wife! Come quick!"

"You are crazy!" I said.

I hurried to his home. It was true. He had shot his wife, because he had found her talking to another man. Now this man may know the biology of love, but he does not know what Love is.

If you read the newspapers all over the world, you can see and feel and intuitively understand what jealousy does; what a miserable, unhappy life it brings to wives, children, husbands and friends. I do not think the universe can be changed by armies. It has never been done that way, but the universe can be changed only by Love. No matter what we do, or do not do, the love energy pulls us toward unity, through suffering.

One hundred years ago we were so separated in the world. What do we have now? We have the United States, United Kingdom, United Republics, and now, United Nations. Then why not think that the next step will be United Humanity? All these unities are the result of the human response to that outpouring Solar Love.

You cannot have real love in your heart if you love one person and hate another person, another race, another religion, another nation, another culture; because Love is the current of energy taking you toward unity, toward the Great Synthesis.

The Sixth Step or Characteristic Is Joy

Anytime you think about or sense Love, you think about Joy. There is no Love if there is no Joy. Any sacrifice, any act of love, will be an act of joy, because physically, emotionally, mentally and spiritually, when you are loving you are in great joy. You are radiating joy, because joy and love are the same energy. If at any time you see that in your love there is no joy, there is something wrong. You must adjust yourself, adjust the conditions and try to find the focus; when you have found the focus, you have found the joy.

In one of His greatest, most critical moments, Jesus, looking at the people who were crucifying Him, said, "My Lord, forgive them, for they know not what they do." Imagine this outpouring Love! What great Love this is—that in the last moment, when there is almost no blood left in His veins, He is saying, ". . . forgive them."

The Seventh Is Gratitude

Gratitude is so beautiful. Are you grateful? If in your love there is no gratefulness, there is no love. This is one of the greatest problems in our lives, in our social, family, and international life. Gratitude is the appreciation, the recognition of Love. Let us be grateful to trees, to flowers, to birds, to sunshine, to the rivers, to the oceans, to all men, known or unknown, who have helped us, who have created our culture. Let us be grateful for our suffering, for our harsh lessons, for existence as a whole, because all is love, essentially, and all must become love again. If we are blind to the offerings of Nature, to the hands that have helped us, to the conditions that have made us grow and unfold, we close ourselves to the life-giving current of love, and invite pain and suffering.

Gratitude is a higher form of communication. It is a way to radiate our blessings. It is a way of showing appreciation for the Fountainhead of all joy, of all love. A grateful man becomes healthier, more magnetic, more enduring, more patient, and all of his acts become creative. Only in gratitude is the Love energy of Cosmos assimilated and changed into creative and uplifting energy.

Gratitude is a state of being in which man communicates with the energy of the will-to-good, with the energy of right human relations. It is a state of being which enables man to see the working of Karma, and to trust himself to the arms of the Divine Love.

All those who are striving for the common good, for the upliftment of humanity, eventually will be drawn together by the energy of love, will be galvanized by the power of love, and will act according to the Law of Unity, through cooperation and understanding. Thus will be created a new culture, a new civilization in which man will live in sacrificial service for all humanity.

True love will be recognized as a process of diminishing the flame of our separating selves, and increasing the fire of the great Whole within ourselves. This is the way to clear our path for the glorious Future.

All our past debts, which have accumulated because of our wrong deeds, emotional reactions and mental activities, can be paid in a life of more loving. This means that Love leads us into more freedom on the path of return. This means that loving increases our joy, our bliss, our understanding, and our health on all levels. To love, means to tune into our Self, the greatest creative power "from Whom all things proceed and to Whom all things return." Thus a man becomes a Creator and a Fountain of Life.

"The Word that issues from the heart saturates the space."[3]

3. Agni Yoga Society, *Hierarchy*, par. 105.

Chapter XXIII

BEAUTY

"In Beauty we are united
Through Beauty we pray
With Beauty we conquer."
—Nicholas K. Roerich

One of our recent philosophers said that the purpose of life is survival. It seems to me that survival sub-stands all phenomena and that Life does not pursue survival, because no matter what form Life is in, *It ever is.* It is the form-side of life which tries to keep itself as it is, and which struggles to survive. This approach to survival is a hindrance on the path of Life, in the long run. The form tries to prevent the free flow of life and its progressive unfoldment which is accomplished through the process of building and destroying the form.

It seems to me that the purpose of life, on any level, is the expression of Beauty, and this is especially true of the human kingdom. Man is created to manifest beauty. Man is created to enjoy the beauty of lower kingdoms, to be inspired by the beauty of higher kingdoms, and to synthesize these two beauties. In so doing he becomes a path between these two worlds of beauty.

Each life is supposed to radiate itself. Radiation is the expression of the beauty within each life. Flowers, birds, trees, animals and even tiny insects have a tremendous drive toward beauty. Actually they are attracted to each other through expressed beauty.

You feel that a lily or a rose is proud of its color and form; you feel that the pine tree is proud of the beauty of its branches, its fragrance, its color, its psychic radiation.

A bird with its colorful feathers, pouring forth its own melody . . . a tree blossoming in the springtime and laden with fruit in the fall . . . a girl with her crystal purity and striving . . . a mother with her child . . . a man with his drive to serve and sacrifice—all are expressing beauty, radiation—but beyond these . . . I feel that the Great Lives of the stars and galaxies are labouring to produce symphonic beauty in Space.

Inspired men tell us that God sings and all comes into existence as manifestations of His Song. What a magnificent way to say that Beauty is the act of the manifestation of God's Purpose! Beauty is the result of the progressive adaptation of the form to the *divine intent.* All flowers, birds, trees, men, solar systems, galaxies are the result of the manifestation process of His Song.

It is only man who can be a conscious expression of Beauty, or a distorter of Beauty. As he harmonizes all his life to the divine intent, to the law of evolution and to the achievement of perfection; as he passes from glory to glory, from partial beauty toward total Beauty, he becomes a conscious expression of Beauty. This can be accomplished by first establishing communication and then fusing with the Source of Beauty within himself. It is his Soul, the Solar Angel, that is the true reflection of Beauty. The Solar Angel is reflecting the innermost Sleeping Beauty.

In our physical, emotional and mental consciousness, we distort the beauty in nature with which we come in contact. We distort it because of our glamours, our illusions and our selfishness.

Beauty evokes a synthetic response from all parts of our nature. This response may be joy, an expansion of awareness, a feeling of freedom, or a sense of synthesis and unity. It may surge through us as a feeling of deep gratitude, admiration, and a fiery aspiration toward purity.

Beauty works and stands only for unfoldment, release, evolution and spiritualization. It expands our consciousness, enabling us to contact the Soul. Soul is the embodiment of beauty, as far as the human kingdom is concerned. Its nature is Love-wisdom, and Beauty can be totally enjoyed only through the sense of Love-wisdom. Just as our body needs food, water, air and light, so our Soul needs Beauty to unfold and to radiate. *Beauty is the path to Cosmos.*

Once we enter into the Soul Consciousness, we will begin to see things as they really are. This means that we will see the archetypal blueprints of the existing crystallized forms. Beauty is the archetype, the divine blueprint, the idea conceived in the Mind of God.

Our Solar Angel with Its own body is a mechanism which tries to bring into our consciousness the sense of beauty, and to establish the rhythm of beauty within us. To manifest beauty we must expand our consciousness into the Soul consciousness and contact the beauty in the Soul through the soul. As we grow toward Soul Consciousness, we manifest more beauty, because we harmonize our life-expression with the existing archetypal beauties. Each time a man contacts his Soul, he is charged with a stream of beauty which bestows upon him joy, upliftment, peace and serenity.

The Soul is only a path leading us to deeper beauty, which exists in the sphere of the Spiritual Triad and beyond. There, we are closer to the divine melody and to divine energy.

True beauty inspires in us the qualities and activities which lead us into striving, expansion, self-observation, harmony, gratitude and sacrificial service. All these are flowers on the tree of beauty, or notes in the symphony of beauty.

I once said that Beauty is materialized love. Love is the essence of Life. Any time, anywhere, when true love expresses itself, you have beauty. Love becomes beauty through manifestation of the archetypes, and the expression of love is the process of the adaptation of matter to Spirit, the expanding love.

The Solar Angel within us is the tuning fork (the keynote) of Beauty. A life lived in harmony with that keynote is a life of beauty. A life lived out of tune with that keynote is an ugly life in which life-energy has difficulty in forming better ways of expression. This is the cause of all suffering. Whenever we suffer, we must strive toward more beauty. This will create a healing process within our bodies. Health is the externalization of inner harmony, which is achieved when a man steps into the fifth Initiation, the door to the world of endless Beauty.

Each time a man strives and records an achievement, he manifests more beauty. Beauty is the manifestation of our ever-widening field of achievement or unfoldment.

When I was a boy my mother read a story which I have never forgotten. It tells of a great artist who wanted to paint The Last Supper. He was seeking a man who could be used as the model for Jesus. At last he found such a man, a man of radiant beauty, and asked him to be his model. The man agreed and the painting was begun. Years passed and the same artist, wishing to finish his painting, sought this time, a man to pose for Judas, the betrayer. He searched for many days without success, until one evening he entered a place of revelry. There he discovered a man who reflected the psychology of a betrayer, and asked him to be a model for the painting of Judas. He agreed to go with the artist to his studio. As they entered, the man began to cry bitterly. The painter asked,

"Why do you cry?"

Pointing to Jesus in the unfinished picture, he said,

"A few years ago, I was Jesus, and now I am Judas! I betrayed the beauty that was mine. . ."

Living according to the inner standards of simplicity, truth and beauty makes a man the model for a great image. Living with an opposite attitude toward beauty, simplicity and truth makes a man the model for a traitor.

Beauty is touched on a gradient scale. We may say that on the first level, the expression of Beauty is a melody; on the second level it is a duet; on the third level it is a chorus; on the fourth level it is a symphony. On the fifth, sixth and seventh levels, beauty enters into the domain of eternity. It is about such beauties that mystics speak, describing them as ". . . beauties which cannot be expressed by words, but can be known only through direct experience." On all levels we have beauty, but the beauties found on the lower levels are constituent parts of greater beauties on higher levels. The search for beauty leads us to our inner Self. The steps of the path leading to the inner sanctuary are built of living beauties. The Real Man is the Beauty, and eventually it is this real Beauty that will absorb the outer, suffering, faltering man into Itself. Then will the age-long labour to create Beauty reach a new height leading to greater Beauty.

Each beauty is a center of energy. Every time we create, unveil, or identify with beauty, we build a radioactive source of healing, uplifting, unfolding and purifying energy. We experience an amazing realization once we know that Beauty is a charge of tremendous energy. It is as lightning, charged with the energy of the sun. Because of this, all creative people are filled with energy and radiation. This energy and radiation reach optimum expression when the inner Sleeping Beauty, the Real Self of man, starts to awaken and shed Its light upon the surrounding world.

It is this awakening beauty which eventually forms the bridge leading to eternity. After a man becomes a Beauty unveiled, he has overcome death, and the matter side of life no longer has control over him. He passes from the inside to the outside to shed his rays of beauty, and to be a path which will lead men toward achievement. On this path he keeps his continuity of consciousness, and whether in the form or in the formless world, he stands as an ocean of Beauty.

Striving toward beauty leads us to the Future. Let us converse with our Solar Guide through words of beauty, and transform ourselves to a chalice of beauty.

Chapter XXIV

THE SACRED WORD AND THE SOUL

"There are . . . great points of tension from which the Sacred Word . . . goes forth. Let me list them for you:

1. *The creative point of tension—a tension achieved by a planetary Logos . . . thus creating the manifested world . . .*
2. *Seven points of tension . . . produce the seven planets, the seven states of consciousness, and the expression of the seven ray impulses. . . .*
3. *The A.U.M. itself or the Word made flesh; this creates finally a point of tension in the fourth kingdom in nature [the human kingdom] . . . an accumulative tension arrived at through many lives. . . .*
4. *Then comes a point of tension from which the man eventually achieves liberation from the three worlds and stands as a free soul; . . .*

"From tension to tension the initiate passes just as do all human beings, aspirants, . . . from one expansion of consciousness to another they go . . ."[1]

—The Tibetan

We are told that three great Lives came together and created a Solar System. According to *The Secret Doctrine*, these three great Lives were called the Three Logoi. Each Logos has a special function in building a Solar System. Manifestation requires three principles in order to become objective.[2]

The Third Logos gave His principle of Intelligence and all substance of that particular system was charged with His Light-energy, infused with the principle of Intelligence. The Second Logos acted as Form Builder in the Womb of Space, and the globes, chains and schemes began to take form. The First Logos, the Separator of the Solar System, gave it birth, bringing it into manifestation. Thus, the First Solar System was created. We are told that a great cycle of *our* evolution will end with the Third Solar System.

These three great Lives, acting as Unity in Trinity, contribute to the creation of each Solar System, but each Logos qualifies His System by His own Ray. For example, the first Solar System was the System of Intelligence. The Second Solar System, the one in which we live, is the Love System. The Third Solar System will be the Will System, with the quality of Will dominant over the qualities of Light and Love, just as Love must eventually be the major note in our system.

---

1. Bailey, Alice A., *The Rays and the Initiations*, pp. 55–56.
2. Blavatsky, H. P., *The Secret Doctrine*, Vol. I, p. 89.

After the First Solar System disintegrated and entered into pralaya, the Second Solar Logos attracted to Himself the substance left in Space, and with the help of the other two Logoi, produced the Second, our Solar System. The substance used by the Third Logos was charged with Intelligent energy. Our Logos charged it with Love energy.

The First Logos will gather the substance left by the Second Solar System after its disintegration, to form the Third Solar System. He will charge with *Will* this substance which has previously been charged with Light and Love in the First and Second Solar Systems. Thus, the atoms of substance in the Third Solar System will have three charges—Light, Love and Will, placing them higher on the scale than the atoms of the two previous Solar Systems.

In our Solar System there is intelligence, the Light of the Third Solar Logos, in each atom. There is also affinity, the Love quality of the Second Logos, in each atom, which builds variety in Cosmos. For the Third Solar System, in addition to intelligent affinity, there will be *Will*, when the atom receives the charge of Will from the First Solar Logos. Eventually this Third Solar System, too, will be disintegrated by radioactivity and its essence will enter into a higher dimension. Thus will the three Solar Systems enter into the great Night of Brahma.

Figure 4 shows that each Logos has His own Solar System, and demonstrates the fact that each Logos is acting upon each Solar System.

We are told that at the beginning of each Creation, the Logos of the System sounds a Sacred Word and manifestation of the System begins. The Tibetan Master says:

> "The great WORD that peals through one hundred years of Brahma or persists in reverberation throughout a solar system, is the sacred sound of A U M. In differentiation and as heard in time and space, each of those three mystic letters stands for the first letter of a subsidiary phrase, consisting of various sounds. One letter, with a sequence of four sounds, makes up the vibration or note of Brahma, which is the intelligence aspect dominant in matter. Hence the mystery hidden in the pentagon, in the fifth principle of mind, and in the five planes of human evolution."[3]

Thus, the substance in space responds to the vibration of the AUM, which is charged with Purpose, Plan, and the Will of the Solar Logos. The electromagnetic energy of the AUM creates great whirlpools which attract responding atoms from space and create a nebula. Ages and ages later the nebula becomes a solar system upon which life forms and kingdoms eventually manifest, unfold, and reach their Solar destination.

This means that the initial AUM is vested in matter and continues to vibrate until the end of the manvantara, because, we are told, once the sounding of

3. Bailey, Alice A., *A Treatise on Cosmic Fire*, pp. 217–218.

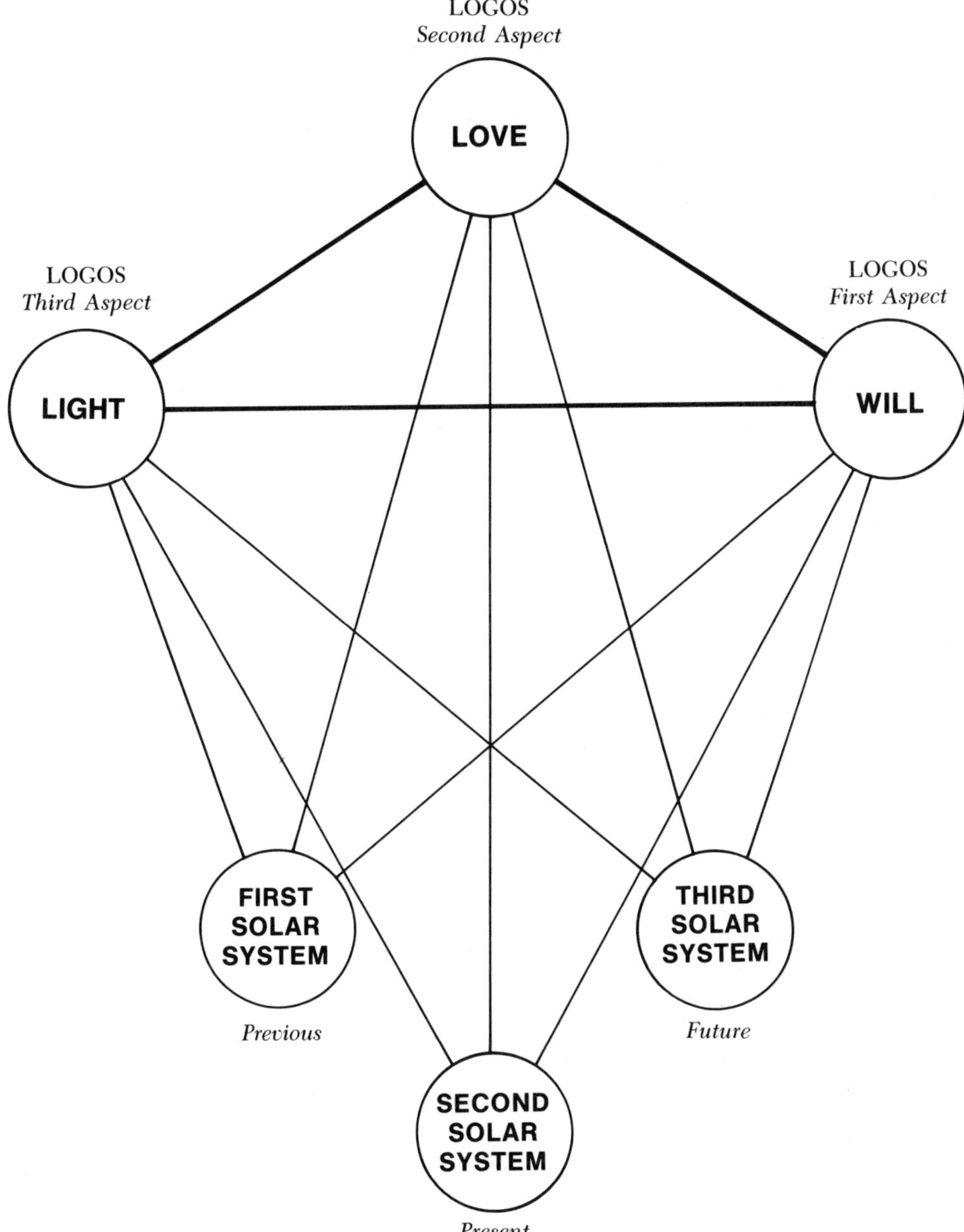

FIGURE 4. SYSTEMS IN FORMATION—THREE LOGOI IN ONE

In reality these three Logoi are not separate beings, but one Being with three aspects. We find this true also in Christian mysticism. Father, Son and Holy Spirit are considered to be one unit. The same is true in many other religions, but in some occult books these aspects are spoken of as separate "persons." The Ancient Wisdom teaches that we have seven groups of Cosmic Logoi; each group being composed of seven Solar Logoi. Our Solar Logos belongs to the fourth group of the seven groups.

the AUM ceases, all creation will disappear in a moment and the substance of the Solar System will return to merge with its oceanic Source.

In the act of creation, the great AUM differentiates into *fifteen notes*, because, as the Tibetan Teacher says, each letter is followed by four other letters, forming a *Word*. We remember what the Beloved Disciple wrote: "In the beginning was the Word, and the Word was with God, and the Word was God; . . . all things were made by him, . . ."[4]

The Word is the vibratory expression of a meaning or a thought. When we think and verbally express a thought, we create a thoughtform in space. This thoughtform gradually condenses, attracting appropriate matter from space, and creates a form. Thus, all of creation is a result of vibration or Sound which slowly condenses and changes into material form. The Word differs from Sound in that it serves as a bridge between the Sound and manifestation or creation.

This bridge carries sound in two directions—out-going and in-going. The out-going Word changes to *AUM*. The in-going Word is the *OM*. The first Word, the AUM, differentiates into specific tones or notes and carries the purpose and the plan of the originator into manifestation. The second Word, the OM, is the bridge of *Return* which releases the Spirit from matter and leads it back Home, back to its Source. When creation reaches its lowest degree of objectivity, its involution is completed and it starts to turn back toward dematerialization as it enters upon the path of evolution. These two Words keep the manifestation of the Solar System in motion and form a way for cyclic manvantara and pralaya in all kingdoms. In a sense they are the yin and the yang within the wheel of Sound. Thus, the AUM expresses itself as the basic principle, energy, the fire which perpetuates existence.

The OM is the pilgrim engaged in the process of leaving the not-self behind and climbing the ladder of evolution. This is the time when the human being strives to change all involutionary tendencies in himself and to enter upon the path of evolution, discipleship and Initiation. Prior to this stage, on the arc of involution, the Spark was on the current of out-breathing. Now on the arc of evolution, He is on the current of in-breathing. At first He was an AUM. Now, He is intended to be an OM. Thus the "three" become "two" and the "two" become "One"—the Sound.

In man, the Spark sounds a triple note and draws seven layers of matter around Himself, creating a seven-fold vibration. Eventually He becomes imprisoned on the lowest plane of manifestation. The Solar Angel performs similar work, and in sounding certain words, brings the lower man, the physical, emotional and mental man, into existence. To release itself from its limitations, the human soul seeks to find and sound the *lost Word*. As man progresses on the path of evolution, he learns the secrets of the Word and finally succeeds in

4. John 1:1.

tuning his instrument, making it a fit instrument through which the Cosmic Beauty expresses Itself.

A man is like a musical instrument with seven strings. He has a central *Artist* Who plays, or attempts to play, this mysterious harp, that He may contact the Cosmos and reach out to express and actualize Himself. He first tries to play on the lowest string and comes in contact with the physical universe; but the sound coming forth is lacking in variety and beauty. Later, His music becomes more complicated and more beautiful as He learns to play on the higher strings of His instrument. When He has mastered all seven strings, He creates His Symphony which is His mode of *communication*. To communicate means to *expand into* and *fuse with* the object of communication, at the same time, preserving one's individual center of registration and awareness.

This communication, or radioactivity, is in a state of confusion at first, but as the Artist, the Inner Beauty, begins to master the science of music and the technique of plucking the strings, He creates a beautiful Symphony of Communication, of response, a great field of radiation which touches the Cosmos, bringing back to Him, Cosmic awareness. He is flooded with new awareness of Beauty, Goodness and Truth—the Reality behind the created Cosmos.

The seven strings represent our vehicles of expression, each of which has its own note. In the beginning the notes are not clear, but are fluctuating and changing constantly, depending upon the outer conditions and inner states of our being; until one day when, one by one, the notes have been purified and brought in tune with the other strings by the touch of the Inner Musician.

These seven bodies are divided into three parts which are often designated by various symbols. They may be called Spirit, Soul and personality. The Soul is the Inner Conductor who holds the tuning fork, the *Word*, the *note* with which the personality must be in tune if it is to create a channel for the spiritual energies of higher planes, the higher strings.

A man is a note in the great Symphony of Creation, but that note is not yet fully expressed in his own individual life and through his unfolding human soul. This means that man is not yet able to hear his own note. Once he hears his true note, he will be able to create immense changes within his vehicles and environment.

The Word of the unfolding human soul is the OM, the Word which was lost as man entered into more objective and separative living. One of the great tasks of man is to find that Word and its true Note and use it to release the spirit within the three bodies, making him conscious of the three worlds.

The average man cannot find the true note of his Angel, and even though he may find it by chance, it will cause him more difficulty than it will be of help to him. After he has refined his triple personality, the note of the OM can be imparted to him for magical work, because through the sounding of the OM, he can channel energy, heal, transform, regenerate, and bridge the many and varied cleavages which occur.

Sometimes there is confusion in distinguishing between the Soul note and the sub-tones of the physical, astral and lower mental planes. These planes being separate units and an aggregate of lives, have their own sub-tones. It is possible that people may pick up these sub-tones at times, creating a constant buzzing in their heads, which often leads to a state of bewilderment. A ringing in the ears bears some relation to this fact, but more often the cause is biological. This note heard in the head is probably one of the sub-tones of the personality vehicles which is being confused with the real note of the Solar Angel or the real note of the unfolding human soul.

The tone of these sub-notes changes as the subject changes his level of consciousness and the level of his being. For example, if he is focussed in his physical consciousness and is hearing a note in his head, this note changes into a different note or vanishes for a long period of time.

Man loses the note when he is in the process of transferring his focus of consciousness from the physical to the emotional plane. When, however, his consciousness is settled in the emotional body, he starts to hear the note in a clear tone. He continues to hear the note until he begins to shift his consciousness from the emotional to the lower mental and from the lower mental to the higher mental. Here on the higher mental plane he discovers that both his and his Solar Angel's notes are fused into one.

Usually the average man sounds a sub-tone of his physical note, and then gradually by experimenting, he finds those notes which bring changes in his emotional and mental realms. There comes a time when these three notes are harmonized and a chord is born. This chord is the chord of Personality. It is the note of the unfolding human soul, which must eventually tune in with the note of the Solar Angel and fuse with the Monadic note of his essence, finally settling the age-long battle between the higher and lower selves. In this process there is a period when the note of the unfolding human soul, identified with the personality, conflicts with the note of the Solar Angel. This conflict endures for a time because man thinks that fusion with the note of the Solar Angel will cause him to lose whatever he is or has. This is the rich man confronting the Christ.[5]

It is possible also that when a man is astrally polarized and focussed he may hear many different notes, words, even direct conversations. These are communicated to him by astral entities to deceive him, and to lead him into darkness. People often follow such guidance and even record in writing whatever information has been conveyed to them. They call such communication the genuine teaching. The fact is that they are being led into darkness and confusion which very soon will unveil itself as total frustration. Symbolically speaking, these voices will lead them into a forest of darkness and when they are deep in the forest, the voices will cease, the guidance will be gone, and they will be lost.

5. Matthew 19:16–23.

The true *Soul Note* has a powerful transfiguring effect upon your personality and bestows upon it the power of the true Will. It is through the power of true Will that you control your energies, forces and bodies, using them for creative purposes, and in the performing of sacrificial acts.

Let us not forget that sound is fire, and all that is related to sound is fiery. All your words, songs, chantings and prayers are fiery in nature, and when you are dealing with them, you must know that you are dealing with Fire. Fire is the agent of Cosmic Creativity, the agent of purification, and the agent of destruction.

In sounding the OM at the aspirant stage, we let loose a new vibration throughout the personality to reach the cores of the cells and atoms of the three bodies, making them radioactive and in tune with each other, and opening a channel for the circulation of Soul energy.

As the Initial Space, caught in the whirlpool of energy, changes chaos into a Cosmos, so the Spark, caught in the seven layers of the human mechanism, eventually changes the chaotic condition in the atmosphere of man into Cosmos—into an integrated, aligned, transfigured and organized mechanism, a mechanism in communication with the Solar systemic planes in which the greater Life is performing a corresponding activity.

Imagine, if you will, that each of our bodies is a musical note. These seven notes must be, first of all, clear notes. Each vehicle and all parts of each vehicles must sound a pure note. The totality must be a well-tuned instrument through which the Inner Light will express its creative beauty on all levels of life. If we had a highly sensitive "electro-ear" which enabled us to listen to all parts of the body, we would hear the vibration of each part. If noise were coming to our ear, it would mean that a certain part was not healthy. If the whole body, or the principal organs, were noisy, not working harmoniously with each other, it would mean that the body was ill and moving toward disintegration.

We must remember that most of the noise or disharmony in our body is the result or echo of the noises reaching us from our emotional and mental spheres. If our emotional sphere is filled with negative and contradictory emotions, such as hatred or jealousy, these accumulations will create great disturbances and noise in our astral body, expressing themselves on our physical body as ulcers or as many nervous and glandular diseases. Similarly, our mental plane can be a poison producer, or a well conducted symphonic orchestra.

If our thinking is clean and in harmony with the tide of evolution, with the laws of Nature and the beauty of the Cosmos; if there is great good in it, goodness toward which all the subtle atoms and rays of the mind are polarized, we have health and beauty—a symphony. If, however, there are destructive, criminal, selfish thoughts and contradictory ideas and worries, we have a battleground, a terrible, noisy situation where energies are striking and consuming each other. This condition will eventually reflect down to the physical body, creating psychosomatic illnesses.

This is the reason that all *strings* of our nature must be in tune with the inner beauty, goodness and truth, thereby creating a great symphony of light love and strength. Your music and beauty cannot be concealed once they star to radiate. People will draw light, love and power from you if they communicate with you in any way, physically, emotionally or mentally. You will pour into them symphonies of light, love and power which will restore health in thei three bodies; symphonies which will gradually, but steadily, turn their chao to Cosmos.

We must understand that all the disturbances of our three bodies are highly contagious. They poison and create complications in the atmosphere of othe people, making their lives miserable by creating depression or violent agitation Man, himself, is a *word*; man, himself, is *music*!

A mantram is a word or sentence put together in a way that when sounded the vibration of each letter or each word of a sentence, will cause creation liberation, release, purification, and will bring light, love, power and deepe insight.

We have seven vehicles, each with its own original note. If you can fin the note of the body concerned, you can control that body by chanting on tha note. You will be able to purify, to restore, to expand or to heal. The not of each of our bodies can be flat, natural or sharp. The whole problem is matter of attunement, not only within ourselves, but also with Planetary an Solar Symphonies. Through attunement a channel is opened for the inflow c great energies, for divine communication.

Before you can profit from sounding the OM, you must have reached th level of the OM, which brings you into the light of the Soul on the ment plane. This means that your mind, emotions and physical activities must b carried on with a sense of responsibility and loyalty to the law of evolutio under the guidance of the Inner Light. When this is done, you will know ho to sound the OM because you will be on a level which enables you to hea the true note of your own *human soul*.

It will be possible in the future to form healing groups which are on th Soul level. Such groups will be able to discern the true notes of other people bodies and, by sounding the OM, cure them of many complications in the physic or subtle bodies. These complications may start in the subtle bodies—etheri astral and mental—and express themselves as many kinds of illnesses in th physical body. They can, through infection or accidents, start in the physic body and create disturbances in the subtle bodies. The OM not only harmoniz the bodies, but it also releases energy from higher sources, from great huma and divine centers.

We must unite with the OM and imagine that we are liberating ourselv from our physical, emotional and mental bodies, but at the same time, crea harmony in them so that the Soul-life can pour through them and create beauti in our environment. To liberate ourselves, to detach ourselves from these bodie does not mean to leave them, to cut ourselves off from them; it means to rid ourselves of disturbing, inharmonious conditions, from the glamours, illusions and maya of the lower vehicles.

To find your soul note you need not search for it in your three lower bodies, but when you have purified and aligned these bodies, you will find that one day when you sound the OM, you will hear an echo, or a different note inside your head. That echo may be your soul note which must be used for redemptive purposes. When you clean the atmosphere of the lamp, the light will shine forth.

After a period of time, when you are sounding your own soul's note, you will hear the major note of your Angel, and the two will form a chord, or vibrate in unison, uplifting the focus of your consciousness to the higher mental planes.

If your ear is not clear of the noise of physical urges and drives, from the noise of physical complications and material values; if your ear is clogged with the noise of negative emotions, conflicting thoughtforms, habits, selfishness, pride and many kinds of vanities, you cannot expect to hear the Voice of Silence, the OM. The OM is the magnetic pull of your Angel calling you back to your Source through detachment, release and freedom.

When your ear is cleared of the noises, you are ready to hear your Soul note, the note of liberating energy. The question may be asked, "Should we sound the OM before we reach such a state?" The answer is, "Yes," because it is through striving toward the core of your being, and through the effort to reach your Source by cleaning poisons from the outside by sounding the OM, that eventually the inner OM and the outer OM meet and synchronize.

Knowing your need, you can sound your note on the plane of that need. It can be sounded on the physical, emotional or mental planes, but the real help comes when you find and use your Soul note; the note which gradually unveils the plan of your Soul for this life.

On the ladder of evolution we have:

The Purpose—the will
The Plan—the idea
The Sound—the creative agent

We are told that by using the proper notes, we can control the forces of earth, water, air and fire through AUM or OM. The OM is the fire of the true alchemist, the fire through which he performs work of energy transmutation. By sounding the OM a magnetic, fiery sphere can be created on the higher mental plane, causing all atoms of the lower planes of the human vehicle to polarize toward the higher levels. Thus, the atoms of inertia or motion enter into a rhythmic relationship with the central core of a human being and are transmuted, transformed and transfigured. This is accomplished on a gradient scale.

When a man finds the true note of the word on the physical plane, he can control his physical body and his physical environment. When he finds his astral note, he can not only control his emotional reactions, but is also capable of finding the notes of other human beings and can help them to grow. When he finds his higher mental note, he has found the note of his Solar Angel and the note of the group in which he is working. Here, he can use that note to increase his light, to synchronize himself with the Inner Presence, and to be of tremendous service to his group. On the buddhic plane, we are told, he finds the note of the planetary Logos and thus expands his consciousness toward the Universe. Later, on the atmic plane, he discovers the note of the Solar Logos and expands his consciousness toward the Cosmos.

Thus, in using the Sacred Word, sounded on the right notes, he establishes communication between himself and his Solar Angel, his Master, humanity, the planetary Logos and the Solar Logos. He expresses this communication as creative living and in the form of great service rendered willingly to the whole of Creation.

We must sound the OM three times before meditation. The following steps are suggested for the sounding of the OM:

- The first OM is very soft, almost a whisper.
- The second one is a little louder.
- The third is still louder.

As the first OM strikes the mental unit and the mental permanent atom, it builds a bridge of light between these two units so that the lower mind and the higher mind become in tune to some degree. It purifies and pushes away all surrounding thoughtforms—thoughtforms left in our homes by our friends, children, newspapers, radio, television, neighbors, or thoughts which are being sent to us by other people. The OM builds a protective, mental wall around our mind. If seen clairvoyantly in our mental aura, it appears as a golden spark at the center and spreads out to the periphery of the egg-shaped atmosphere, forming a magnetic shield around us. It also purifies thoughtforms which we, ourselves, have created earlier. Another effect of the first OM is that, as it touches the lotus, a flame springs forth from our aura. Masters of the Wisdom do not watch our physical body. They watch only the flame, and when They observe that the flame is growing larger and shining more brilliantly, They create a magnetic line of communication between Themselves and us. The next effect of the first OM is that, as the head center receives stimulation, it becomes magnetic and sensitive to higher impressions.

The second OM, sounded a little louder, stimulates the astral permanent atom, cleans our emotional atmosphere, creates a protective wall against dark forces, and stimulates the heart center, from which love energy begins to flow. When emotional purification is under way, the emotional body becomes magnetic to intuitional energy, or intuitional impressions.

The third OM affects the etheric and physical bodies. It stimulates the physical permanent atom and the etheric body is purified. It forms another protective wall around the physical body. Thus, we can see that sounding the OM is actually a process of alignment with higher bodies, giving protection and purification.

If one is emotionally upset at any time, he should not sound the OM, because it can have a reverse effect on the emotional, mental and physical bodies. Those who are irritated during the daytime cannot easily pass to higher dimensions while asleep at night; if any instruction is given to them by high Initiates or Masters, it will not be remembered, or if recalled, the teaching will be distorted and become degenerated. An irritated man is like a fireball when he leaves his body.

How must we sound the OM?

1. For the first OM the mind must be concentrated, but relaxed. The lips must form an "O" and the full, round "O" sound must be sent forth. This "O" must rise as if you were pushing the sound to the roof of your mouth, on up to the middle of the top of your head, and out. As you are doing this, you must visualize your mental vehicle as becoming purer and more subtle.
2. The same visualization will be used for the second OM, but this time for the emotional body. Try to see the emotional body as a fine mist around you.
3. When sounding the third OM, relax the physical body completely, and imagine that your aura is becoming a golden color.

The duration of the OM is divided into two parts, the "O" and the "M." The sounding of the OM must be preceded by taking a deep breath. Its true effect starts after it has been sounded. We must allow an interval of silence as we end it, and in that short period of silence the effect of the OM enters deeper and deeper into the bodies. This effect can be compared to the effect of a stone thrown into a lake. Rings begin to form at the point where the stone enters the water, and continue to radiate outward long after the stone has sunk to the bottom. Similarly, in sounding the OM, a purifying influence spreads around us, and gradually rises to higher levels.

When you feel any pressure in your head while chanting the OM, change the tone and the note of your voice. This may help to remove the pressure. It will take a little time to find the correct note, the note which gives you peace, clarity of mind and sensitivity to in-going energies.

The time duration is important for both letters, O and M. Duration time of exhaling the breath in sound will be divided into two periods of ten or fifteen seconds for each letter, O—M. This time period, if filled with thoughts of the power of the OM when sounded, will form a strong foundation for future, advanced breathing.

In this process, the note, the waves of sound or the vibration, does the cleaning, refining and expanding work for the vehicles and centers. The breath brings into these vehicles and centers the energy from the level on which you are focussed in your consciousness.

The OM is sounded in different keys, because every man has a different note, according to his constitution. Your physical body has one note, your emotional body another, your mental body has its note, and your Solar Angel still another. If you are an integrated personality, the physical, emotional and mental notes are harmonized or united into one chord. There then remains the task of playing this chord in harmony with the Soul note.

How does one find his *own note*? Finding one's own note is one of the secrets of initiation which has not yet been given. Instinctively you may sound it correctly, or when you take the Third Initiation, your Master will tell you how to sound your OM. You will hear it and recognize it. Sometimes, while you are meditating, your Soul will give the note. When this happens, from then on, you must use it. It will be a very subtle tone, but once you experience it, you will recognize it by its soft, bell-like tone resembling that of a tuning fork.

Our Solar Angel is in continuous, deep meditation from our birth to our death. Meditation for a Solar Angel means absorbing the Divine Plan, digesting it and radiating it out to the world. Thus, we can see the importance of regular and rhythmic meditation. Through meditation we slowly enter into the sphere of vibration or radiation of the Soul, where we are gradually purified, sublimated and transfigured, until one great day when we become *one with our Soul*; this union is called the mystical marriage. The Spark slowly blooms and moves closer to the Source. When It reaches the Solar Angel, Its vibration and the vibration of the Solar Angel become as one, completely unified. It is like two violins being tuned together. A quarter of a degree difference in tone can be detected by a sensitive ear, but if the two instruments are perfectly in tune with each other, no difference can be heard by the most sensitive ear. The two violins have become as one. In like manner, the Soul and the One becoming a Soul, unite and become as one. This can be accomplished only through meditation.

All three personality bodies have three subdivisions, each of which is affected by each OM. We have formulated the following table to show the subdivision of the three bodies:

THE MENTAL BODY—
1. **mental mental**
2. **mental emotional**
3. **mental physical**

THE EMOTIONAL BODY—
1. **emotional mental**
2. **emotional emotional**
3. **emotional physical**

THE PHYSICAL BODY—
1. **physical mental**
2. **physical emotional**
3. **physical physical**

The correspondences of these subdivisions are:

THE MENTAL BODY—	**mental**	**1. thoughts**
	emotional	**2. mental stuff**
	physical	**3. brain**
THE EMOTIONAL BODY—	**mental**	**1. emotions**
	emotional	**2. feelings**
	physical	**3. touch**
THE PHYSICAL BODY—	**mental**	**1. brain**
	emotional	**2. glands, blood**
	physical	**3. bones**

When the first OM is sounded, the mental correspondences of each body are tuned in and affected. The coarse atoms of these subdivisions are pushed away and finer atoms are attracted. They are aligned with each other, and integrated as a whole, making them ready to be impressed by the incoming energy and then ready to radiate it, without obstruction.

The OM is sounded on various levels, according to the level and awareness of a person. If a man's consciousness is not beyond the physical level, his OM will have very little effect. If his consciousness is advanced and the OM is sounded on the mental plane, the effect will be stronger. If it is sounded on the Soul level, as a Soul, the effect will be very potent. It is here that the OM can be used for magical purposes; for the creation of subtle forms to further the expression of the plan and purpose of God; for cooperation with the law of evolution through transformation, transfiguration, and alignment with greater sources of energy and awareness.

Sound and words are either creative or destructive agents, depending upon the motive behind them. The influence of the voice differs from person to person, not only because of the difference in motives, but also because of the difference in the focus of consciousness, the interest level of a person. In this regard we will divide people into three groups, according to the three stages of development:

- Those people who speak from the level of Soul consciousness.
- Those who speak from the level of their aspirations, visions and dreams.
- People who speak from the level of their physical urges and emotional drives.

Whenever a person sounds the OM, or speaks on any subject, he charges his voice with the force of the level upon which he is functioning. It is important, therefore, that before a person sounds the OM or gives a speech, he must deliberately raise his level of consciousness to the higher mental plane through alignment and visualization. It is possible to climb a mountain and for a short time enjoy the beauty of the heights, but when in that short time, you become able to touch your Soul and sound the OM, or speak the words of your Soul, you raise your own level of being tremendously and you release greater energies into your system.

Through such alignment, upliftment and effort the day will come when you will hear an echo from within, and eventually this echo will become a clear note, the note of your soul. You will have found the lost Word which was You. You have been lost, but when you have reached the right tonality in your being, you are found. After a man has found his soul level and then sounds the OM, his voice is a synthesis of etheric, emotional, mental and spiritual forces and energies. He is a creative agent. This fact is illustrated in figure 5. The circle represents an object and the arrow, forces and energy.

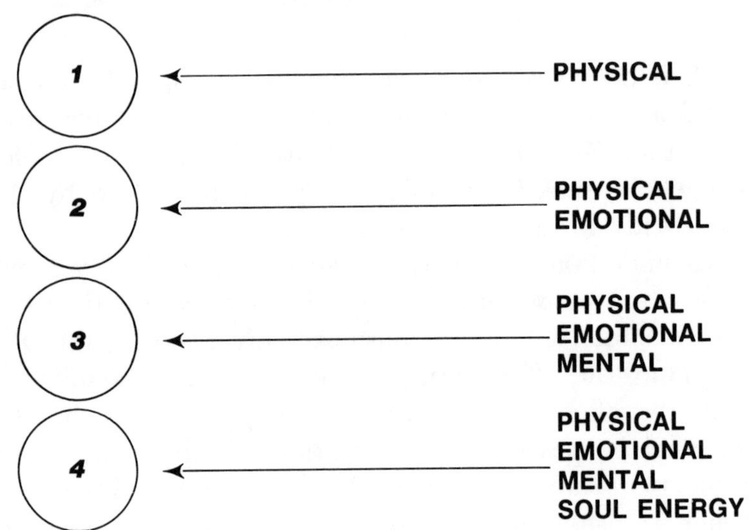

FIGURE 5. FORCE AND ENERGY CHANGES THROUGH ALIGNMENT

In number one, man is influencing through physical energy.

In number two, his words have more power, being a combination of physica and emotional force.

In number three, his words have still more power, being a combinatio of etheric, emotional and mental forces.

In number four, his words are most powerful, and he deeply impresse his vehicles or other people, because his voice is charged with three forces plu soul energy.

This shows how diverse is the effect of speech, especially the soundin of the OM. In view of this diversity, the average man or beginner can expec only very slight effects from sounding the OM or from his speech.

When a man has identified himself with the OM, the next step is to procee toward the Source of the Sound. This step belongs to the realm of the Spiritu

Triad. It is the path of an Agni Yogi, a Disciple of Fire, who after cleansing all of his lower vehicles, is ready to tread the path of sacrifice for the ultimate good of humanity and to work for the fulfillment of the Divine Purpose on earth.

To sum up, we can say that the AUM is the note of involution, creation and manifestation. It is related in the microcosm to his personality. It is a magical word which when adequately pronounced, brings the ideas and energies into objectification, materialization, or manifestation. The OM is used mostly for evolution, or let us say, spiritualization and liberation, for contact with the higher sources of energy and for unfoldment and blooming. Sound is the highest potency. It creates in out-breathing and annihilates in in-breathing.

The music of the spheres is not a fantasy. Millions of *divine singers* form the chorus of the Almighty One, and as they sing the great Song of Creation, each on his own level brings forth his own galaxy, his own system, his own comet.

Thus space is filled with the music of colors, with the music of globes, and with the music of evolving or unfolding Sparks, each with its own song, its own radiation and glory.

The creative agent of our three Solar Systems is the A U M which is divided into three sounds, one sound for each Solar System. Each note has seven sub-tones called "breaths." With each sub-tone of the Logos, one of the sub-planes of the cosmic physical plane came into existence. For example:

- The first sub-tone gathered together the atomic substance of the Solar System.
- The second sub-tone created differentiation in substance and charged the substance with love energy.
- The third sub-tone charged the substance with the energy of intelligence.
- The fourth sub-tone brought out the intuitional plane, the Fourth Cosmic Etheric plane and charged it with the qualities of harmony and bliss.
- The fifth sub-tone brought out the fiery world, the mental plane.
- The sixth sub-tone brought out the sphere of water.
- The seventh sub-tone brought materialization of energy and the dense physical plane came into existence.

In the same manner, the Monad sounds its seven notes and collects the substance for manifestation in seven planes.

The unfolding human soul is a reflection of the Monad. When he finds the true note of his essence, he conquers plane after plane, and ultimately reaches his Source. Thus the reflection becomes one with its own Essence.

On each plane he finds the Monadic sub-tone for that plane, and controls it through sounding the Sacred Word. Eventually he finds the major note of the Monad (of his Essence) and through using that major note, he steps into the path of major Initiations which lead him toward great at-one-ment with his own Essence.

Chapter XXV

SPIRITUAL SOURCES OF ENERGY

"A vessel brimming with spirit! . . . 'Could one call a great toiler in the spiritual realm a Leyden jar?' Verily, thus is the outer energy accumulated, and in due time a discharge follows."[1]

—M.M.

The Real Man is his essential Self, a fountainhead of energy. We are told that this energy is distributed to the tiny lives of all vehicles through a thread extending from the essential Self to the heart; to the physical, etheric, emotional, and mental heart centers. It extends through the heart to the millions of tiny lives composing all of the vehicles of man. Ancient sages called this thread the life thread or sutratma. Man has three main sources of energy:

- The etheric, astral and mental centers.
- The causal body or the chalice.
- The Spiritual Triad.

The Self is the principal source of *life* energy for all of man's vehicles. The Solar Angel, dwelling in the causal body, is the main source of *intelligent* energy and the manipulator of the energy of the Spiritual Triad, a field of light, love and power composed of the radiating fields of *manasic, buddhic,* and *atmic* permanent atoms. A thread extends from the Solar Angel and is anchored in the brain, physical and etheric. The intelligent energy, or light energy, is carried throughout the vehicles by the nervous system, nadis or etheric nerves, making the vehicles a functioning whole. In occult literature we are told that the spiritual side of man is the Spiritual Triad, the vehicles of which are built with atmic, buddhic and manasic substance, or light substance.

Man has three main motivators; energy, consciousness and force.

- Energy radiated from the Self is called *electric fire*, the purpose of which is to align all tiny lives of the vehicles according to the *divine purpose* of evolution or the path of perfection.
- Consciousness is the result of action of the Solar Angel on the mental plane, the purpose of which is to align all the atoms of the vehicles, thus building a path of light for the returning pilgrim as he endeavors to work out the *divine plan*. This energy is called *solar fire*.
- Force is radiated from the lower bodies. Its main purpose is to provide vehicles for higher energies and to establish a channel of communication between the man and the triple worlds. This force is called *fire by friction*.

1. Agni Yoga Society, *Agni Yoga*, par. 144.

The material side of man is formed on the physical, emotional, and lower mental planes. These planes express force. The higher planes express energy. The spiritual side of man uses the material side as its mechanism, but strives constantly to transmute that mechanism, making it capable of expressing the spiritual life.

During man's lifetime, force is largely used; the force of his lower vehicles with which he is identified. As he begins to focus his consciousness on the higher mental planes and is in touch with his Solar Angel or the Spiritual Triad, he begins to express energy instead of force. The difference between energy and force is relevant to the difference between the arc of evolution and the arc of involution. Energy is used in evolution, promoting spiritualization and synthesis, while force is used in involution, promoting materialization and separation. Energy is the power which is oriented toward man's center, the great Magnet, by treading the path of spiritual striving and unfoldment. Force is the power of matter which moves away from the center, causing contraction, creating disharmony and separatism.

SOURCE AND EXPRESSION RELATIONSHIPS

The relationship between the sources of energy and the expression of energy on the fields of our daily life is shown in figure 6.

The numbers 1, 2, and 3 label the main reservoirs of energy.

Number 4 constitutes the lower vehicles and is the reservoir of force.

Number 5, the aura, is formed of physical-etheric, astral and lower mental matter plus soul substance and will accommodate either energy or force. It may be called the motivator. The aura resembles a film through which light passes, producing a picture on a screen. The "film" contains all of our glamours, illusions and motives. When pure light (the light, love and will energy) passes through it, the picture is affected by the content of the film. It regulates, hinders, obscures, changes or distorts the pure light. The state of the aura *conditions* the health of the body and the relation of man to his environment. It is important that this atmosphere be kept clear of illusion and glamour and that it be enriched by lofty images of great aspiration and beauty. Until unreality in the aura is replaced by reality through higher aspiration, the inner sources of energy will not have opportunity to shine forth in their full beauty and will be unable to create a life of light, love and power.

Number 6 is the expression, the result, the effect, or the picture projected on the screen of life.

We have referred to number 7 as the actor, the "man," the unit of consciousness, the evolving human soul. Much depends upon the state of this unit for it indicates man's level of development, his relations with energy reservoirs, his ability to manipulate force or energy, his education, karma, his responsibilities, and above all, his aspirations and striving toward the spiritual goal. All that a man is, is reflected on number 5, the aura, and it becomes the conditioning factor of all expression and the state of his personality vehicles.

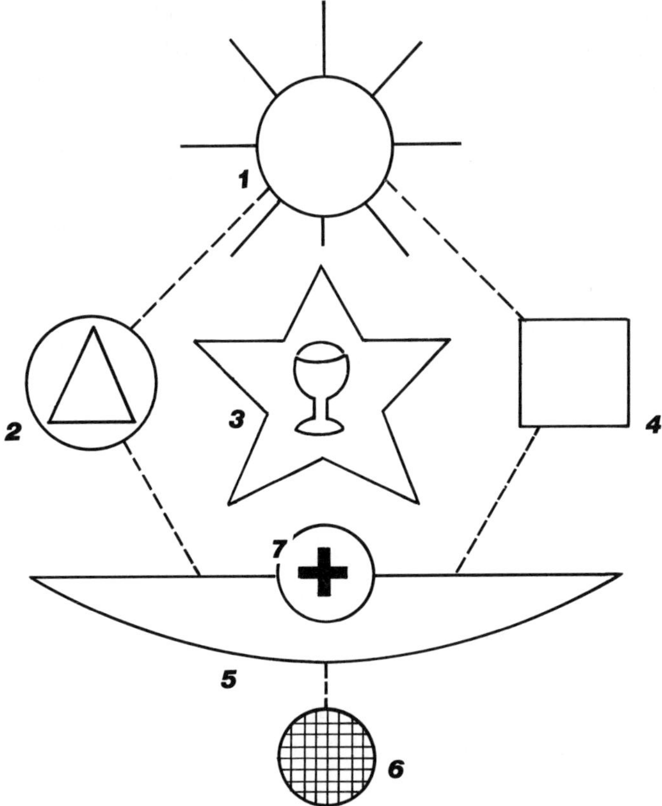

FIGURE 6. OUR DAILY LIFE—SOURCES AND EXPRESSION OF ENERGY

1 — Self, the fountainhead of energy.
2 — Spiritual Triad.
3 — Causal body, the chalice and the Solar Angel.
4 — The sum total of etheric, astral and mental forces.
5 — Atmosphere through which the energies or forces pass for expression; the aura.
6 — Expression, the result or effect.
7 — Actor, the "man" at a given time, level or condition; the unit of consciousness; the developing human soul.

The progress of the pilgrim depends upon the developing of his ability to wield energy rather than force. He is free to drift with the current of force toward involution and enter into more separation, crystallization and materialization, or he may strive to row his boat against the current of involution and follow the river of evolution toward inner unfoldment, blooming, radiation, unity and synthesis.

THE SEVEN ENERGY-PROCESSING TECHNIQUES

There are seven main techniques through which energy is produced, absorbed and used to further the conscious evolution of man and nature. We have formulated them in the following terms or concepts:

1. Energy is produced when one of our higher bodies comes in contact with one of the lower vehicles and brings it into perfect rhythm and harmony through alignment, integration, and fusion.

2. Energy is produced when we check a certain outgoing wave of force on lower levels and sublimate it to its higher counterpart on spiritual levels.
3. Energy is produced when we control our mechanical activities and use our vehicle consciously.
4. Energy is produced when the lower atmospheres of the Soul have been cleared of crystallized forms, allowing the light of the Soul to shine forth.
5. Energy is produced when we release creatively the "locked in" inpressions from our lower mind.
6. Energy is produced when we visualize certain forms or symbols, or when we create thoughtforms.
7. Energy is produced when we come in contact with higher individuals, Initiates or Masters through our higher nature.

Let us now study these techniques in more detail.

Energy Is Produced when One of Our Higher Bodies Comes in Contact with One of the Lower Vehicles and Brings It into Perfect Rhythm and Harmony Through Alignment, Integration and Fusion

In the Ancient Wisdom we are told that there are seven planes of existence in which man "lives and moves and has his being."Most people are conscious upon only the lowest plane; advanced indivuduals are conscious on more planes, and Great Ones are conscious on all planes. These seven planes are:

1. First etheric or Divine Plane.
2. Second etheric or Monadic Plane.
3. Third etheric or Atmic Plane.
4. Fourth etheric or Buddhic Plane.
5. Mental or Manasic Plane.
6. Emotional or Astral Plane.
7. Physical or dense Plane.

The higher planes are represented by the numbers 4, 3, 2, 1, while the numbers 5, 6 and 7 represent the lower planes. By studying this table given in numerical order, we find application of the Law of Correspondence, each plane having its counterpart on a higher plane. The physical plane is a reflection of the mental plane (7–5). The astral plane is a reflection of the intuitional plane (6–4). The mental plane is a reflection of the atmic plane (5–3). The buddhic plane is a reflection of the Monadic plane (4–2). The atmic plane is a reflection of the Divine plane (3–1). These Seven Cosmic Physical Planes, combined, are a reflection of the Cosmic mental plane.

These seven planes of consciousness and being also have correspondences in the seven vehicles. The nerve ganglia and a system of nerve fibers make up a network of nerves called the plexus. In the following tabulation we are giving the correspondences in the force centers, the lotus, the plexus and the glands of the lower vehicle.

FORCE CENTERS	PETALS	PLEXUS	GLANDS
Head	1000	—	Pineal
Ajna	2	Cavernous	Pituitary
Throat	16	Laryngeal	Thyroid
Heart	12	Cardiac	Thymus
Solar Plexus	10	Epigastric	Pancreas
Sacral	6	Prostate	Gonads
Base of spine	4	Sacral	Adrenals

This table furnishes us with a clue as to how we may transmute, transform and transfigure our lower vehicles. For example, the transmutation of the physical body or forces is accomplished by the power of the mind; the transformation of the physical and emotional bodies is carried out by the light of buddhi; and the transfiguration of our physical, emotional and mental body is achieved through light from the *atmic* plane.[2]

Our higher or spiritual nature is heavily charged with electricity on the evolutionary arc. Our material or lower nature is a unit of force on the involutionary arc. Its vibration is slow or violent. It is composed of our physical-etheric body, our emotional body and our mental body. Most of the time these bodies work mechanically. The fact that we may do good works through them makes no difference, they may still be acting as automatons. For example, a preacher may deliver a fine sermon, but if there is no energy behind it, we do not feel it; we are not impressed by his words. A man may paint a picture, sing or dance, but we are not inspired and we receive no impression, because something is lacking; we feel no energy. He is not drawing from an energy source. There is a lamp, but no light. We see his actions, we hear his words, but there is no transmuting, burning energy behind them. His bodies are working mechanically.

On the other hand, when a man is drawing from an energy source as he speaks, the words are impressed upon our mind. They are not only impressions, but they also serve as a continuous source of energy within our being. They lead us. They protect us. They enrich our life. When a person views a truly beautiful work of art and is filled with inspiration, it changes his level of being; he enters into another plane of living. Something opens within him. He feels released as this new energy comes and draws him to a higher level of existence, greatly expanding his consciousness.

You observe another man walking and you feel energy from his action. When he waves his hand to say, "Good morning" or "Goodbye" a wave of energy comes to you. He smiles and the energy is increased. You feel the energy coming to you because this man is in contact with his higher, spiritual side. He is fused with one of the power-houses of his being and all of his thoughts, words and activities are charged with high potential electricity.

2. For further information, read *The Science of Becoming Oneself* by H. Saraydarian, Chap. XIV, p. 130.

If you can control your physical vehicle through your etheric body or higher mind, your emotions through your intuitional plane, your mind by the Soul or atmic energy, your vehicle is fused with a source of energy and energy is manifested in all your activities, you are fused with a power-house of your being and you are charged with high potential electricity.

Most of us lack energy regardless of how well we sleep or rest. When this is so, it is because the energy lost from or used by the physical vehicle is not replaced by energy from the etheric and higher mental reservoirs. The secret of the abundance of energy is successful alignment and integration of the lower and higher bodies and the infusion of all vehicles with the Soul; and later, infusion with the Spiritual Triad.

Energy Is Produced when We Check a Certain Out-Going Wave of Force on Lower Levels and Sublimate It to Its Higher Counterpart on Spiritual Levels

The seven centers are divided by the diaphragm. The four centers below, being in immediate contact with the physical universe, spend energy absorbed from the inner and outer suns. Often the sacral and solar plexus centers expend tremendous amounts of energy, leaving the physical and etheric bodies weak and exhausted. This condition can be avoided and the energies saved, by controlling our negative emotions, wild imaginations and sexual urges.

The throat center is the higher creative center above the diaphragm and corresponds to the sacral center, the creative or reproductive center below the diaphragm. By elevating the sexual energy to the throat center, man can become extremely creative in many of the arts. The same is true of the solar plexus center. Energy from this center can be raised to the heart center, thereby changing individual love to true group love and compassion. When we have succeeded in elevating energy from these two centers to their higher counterparts, we have not lost our sex power or love for individuals. We have simply controlled the sexual urges of the sacral center and used the energy goal-fittingly. By controlling the urges of the solar plexus center, we have used the energy to expand our resources of love, from individuals to the group and to humanity.

If energy leaks from any of the centers, its corresponding gland and physical organ lose their sensitivity and their true functions. When such a condition exists, any forceful pressure upon the center creates further organic difficulties.

All higher energies are refined forces and materials found on denser levels. All kinds of energy are eventually assimilated by the petals of the chalice and used for the building of the higher vehicles of man, filling the chalice with purest energy. This transmutation process is carried on through our aspirations, dedication, devotion, meditation, contemplation and renouncements.

On whatever level our consciousness or awareness is focussed, there, we are located; that is our level. Our level of expression indicates that level of consciousness or awareness with which we are identified. As we raise our consciousness to higher levels, we expand our horizon of understanding and increase our ability to raise forces and energies through the process of transmutation. Forces can be converted to energy. Just as ice can be changed into water and water converted to steam, in similar manner, forces or energies on lower planes can be elevated to higher planes, creating more power. Thus, a sexual urge, sublimated, produces powerful creative energy.

As a unit of energy passes to lower levels, it loses its power, becoming force and then matter. Matter, sublimated, changes to force, and force, sublimated, changes to finer and finer energy with extremely creative powers.

Sublimation is most often brought about through points of crisis or shocks. The energy unit is released from lower to higher levels. As energy accumulates on higher levels it exercises certain pressures on the physical, emotional and mental bodies through the centers and glands. At this point, there is danger of overstimulation and misuse of energy. The greatest protection against this danger is to think in terms of one humanity and to find a field of service in which we can perform some kind of creative work, without expectation of reward in any form. An attitude such as this transforms all of our vehicles and brings them into harmony with the Great Nature, which finds in us a co-worker to further the work of creation.

Energy Is Produced when We Control Our Mechanical Activities And Use Our Vehicles Consciously

Some of our energy is wasted through those activities which we call mechanical or habitual. This is true not only on the physical plane, but also on the emotional and mental planes. Physically, we perform some activities or make certain movements, not intending to do so, but because of some kind of reflex action. We may move our feet, our fingers, our facial muscles or shoulders with no purpose behind the action. When we find the cause of these involuntary movements and check them, we save a great amount of energy on the physical and emotional planes. Behind such involuntary actions is found a thoughtform, a post-hypnotic suggestion, or an engram. All these causes can be cleared away by observing the movement, the mechanical expression in any form, the time and conditions under which it occurs. In this way we observe ourselves more closely and draw ourselves toward the inner reality from which we can exercise our will, our intellect, to stop all mechanical expression.

A habit is the result of a force circuit in the lower mind, commanding certain nerves, muscles and organs, and pushing them into monotonous activity. When this circuit is broken, the flow of energy is established between the conscious mind and the enslaved part of the body, and man is more self-actualized. Alignment and direct communication between the Conscious Center and its vehicles guarantees the flow of energy from inner sources. Habits and involuntary actions are like short circuits in an electrical system. They prevent power from the main source reaching all parts of the organism. A man of habit and involuntary actions lacks fiery energy in his system. He behaves as a crystallized being and is unable to absorb shocks of events in his life.

We have been speaking of involuntary *actions*, but we may also be victims of involuntary *attitudes* in our emotional and mental worlds. One may feel hatred toward another for reasons unknown even to himself. His attitude is the result of a blind and artificial impulse or stimulus, which must be recognized, analyzed and cleared from his emotional and mental spheres.

Our system lives within an energy field which is composed of the substance of love. Any act against this love-field brings unhappiness, suffering and weakness. The cleansing of any negative wave from this field results in more love, more happiness and better health. Hate burns and exhausts our fuel supply. Love increases it. Love is energy and, surprisingly, it increases as we share it with others in working for their highest good.

Another habit which is disasterous to the love-energy field is the habit of complaining. If we listen to the average man, we will find that his words express no more than a long succession of complaints. Complaining disturbs the love-energy field and robs it of its magnetism. We must remember that love is a magnetic substance. Those who are victims of the habit of complaining lose their magnetism and are automatically repelled or rejected by others, even though they may make themselves outwardly attractive.

Most of our creative works receive their nourishment from the love-energy field, which is none other than the energy field of the Solar Angel.

Another way to increase control over the mechanical nature is through the development of will-power.[3] Fasting is a good method for developing the will to control the lower vehicles, their appetites, urges and drives. Extending fasting to the emotional and then the mental planes will enable you to control your negative emotions in all of your expression, to develop your power of discrimination, and to withdraw deeper into the inner Sanctuary of the Soul.

Energy Is Produced when the Lower Atmospheres of the Soul Have Been Cleared of Crystallized Forms, Allowing the Light of the Soul to Shine Forth

The Soul, one of the main inner energy sources, is like a sun within us. In most people, however, there is a thick layer of clouds between phenomenal man and the Soul. The first step in gaining contact with this inner source of energy is to exercise observation and discrimination between "you" and your vehicles on the three lower planes. Observe the world around you. For a long period of time do not think about what you are seeing; just observe things as they are. Then start to use your power of discrimination and see both the illusion and reality; the constructive and the destructive; the time killer and the builder. After exercising your discriminative ability, you will choose those ways which are constructive, saving yourself much time, energy and money. The saving of time, energy and money will help you more and more to go deeper in the

3. Saraydarian, H., *The Science of Becoming Oneself*, pp. 146–156.

right direction in the accumulating and the using of energy. Every right step upon any level of your being evokes the light of your Soul.

The next step is clearing yourself of illusions, glamours and the many attractions of the material plane. Let us understand that the Soul is a nucleus of fire within us. As we succeed in clearing the atmosphere of the Soul, Its radiation increases proportionately. Every word, thought, action or emotion that obscures the radiation of the Soul, or is out of harmony with the Soul vibrations, decreases the vitality of our body in the long range, and gradually dims the light of our mind, causing illness and disease.

The clearing work begins with the process of detachment. The real Self within man starts to detach himself from every factor that has control over him. He cuts the threads of identification on the physical, emotional and mental levels, and assumes the position of a detached observer. He observes all of his activities on three levels. When his central Self is in deep sleep, illusionary or momentary selves impose themselves upon him. As his observation deepens and he continues to detach from the false selves, he moves ever closer toward finding himself, his true Self.

Detachment greatly increases our energy because everything to which we are attached draws energy from us. Even material objects sap our energy if we are closely attached to them. We detach ourselves automatically if we observe clearly. Clear observation opens a cleavage, a gap, between the Self and that which is not the Self. The moment that this cleavage occurs, the real side of man increases in power. To the extent that his power increases, the gap widens and the observation becomes clearer. This cleavage must be created on the three lower levels.

On the emotional level we have hundreds of negative emotions which are controlling our whole being. They are like cracks in a jar through which water leaks. Our emotional world is like a sea on which every wind creates a corresponding wave and every voice its echo. The man who lives in the emotional sea is all but lost in the fog of glamour, or he floats about as a piece of wood upon the waves. The moment he tries to observe, he invokes the light of the mind and the fog begins to lift. The light of the mind increases upon this emotional sea and, proportionately, the fog grows lighter . . . lighter, and one day the sea appears as it is. At this point man knows his situation, but he says, "I cannot help it."

This is the critical stage, the critical moment, the crisis. We can pass this obstacle by continuing our observance, studying the direction of the winds and the formation of the waves. Gradually we will note that the winds will quiet and the sea will sleep, motionless, reflecting great beauties. In this stage we have full control over the emotional world. New winds will blow and new waves will rise, but the mind is active now. We will be able to control the waves by causing a different wind, a high level wind, to blow upon the waters creating harmonious motion, harmonious vibration upon the sea.

We must now observe and detach on the mental level because the mind is the prison where the Self is chained. The Self has lost his individuality through attachment and identification. The mind is like a portion of space in which clouds begin to form. These cloud formations are those thoughtforms which may wander about in the mind and gradually dissolve, degenerate or grow stronger and stronger until some of them condense and become a hindrance or an obstacle in the mind itself. All superstitions, doctrines of any kind, and fixed opinions are formed in this manner. When such formations take place, it is difficult for the mind to think creatively. These thoughtforms may crystallize to such a degree that a man cannot think, and he becomes the slave of other minds. He will take extreme measures to create his own thoughtforms. All fanatics belong to this category of people. Their thoughtforms crystallize to the degree that, in due time, they become obsolete and pose a powerful obstacle on the path of progress for the individual and for humanity. To prevent crystallization of thoughtforms in the mind, we must exercise detachment on the mental level. The first step is clear observation on the mental plane.

How should we begin? We can start by looking at our mental activities, our predominating, narrow or limiting thoughtforms and opinions. As we observe them clearly their pressure upon us will gradually lessen, because, as we have learned, *observation creates a cleavage between the observer and the object observed.* This cleavage starts when we try to change our point of view, our point of observation, from negative to positive, to neutral, to indifference; from the past to the present, to the future. It becomes more pronounced when we are able to widen our viewpoint on a larger scale, from personal to national, to universal, to cosmic.

Each time we change our opinion or take a different position, we decrease the power of the thoughtform to control us or to put pressure upon us. Slowly it disintegrates and, eventually, there remain only those aspects which are particles of divine principles.

Not long ago many religions were fighting bitterly against each other. There were wide cleavages among religion, science, politics and psychology. Thousands of thoughtforms from each field were battling with thoughtforms of others. Now, thousands of bridges are extending from one field to another, because life is so constructed that we are forced to change our position and look at our object from different angles, from different viewpoints. After we have weakened the power of any thoughtform to control us, we feel a deep release and with the release, a deep joy; these are forms of energy.

If any thoughtform crystallizes in a man's mental space, it blocks the transmission of energy from the Soul realms. It not only blocks, but also absorbs energy and becomes a tumor in the mind; a self in the mind, a sensitive wound in the mind. If anyone from the outside tries to "touch" it, to change it, it is so painful that the man may lose all of his reasoning power. We are told that such a man was once debating with Socrates who was trying to help him by dispelling the mental cloud. The strain of having his thoughtforms with which he was identified, destroyed, was too great for him to bear. It was as though he were being killed inwardly, and some time later the man took his own life.

We all have our thoughtforms. They may be beautiful, ugly, harmonious, noisy, strong or weak. It is almost impossible not to have a thoughtform. The differences among them are based upon the following:

- Some thoughtforms control the total mechanism of a human being.
- Some thoughtforms are easily built and easily dissolved.
- Some thoughtforms are very elastic and sensitive to change. They grow as a simple melody grows to a symphony, having bridges or connecting links reaching out in every direction.

The latter kind of thoughtform differs from the other two in that it is under the control of a man and the man is not identified with it. He is detached from the thoughtforms, but he uses it in every practical way to serve his fellow man. Such a man is known as an educated man, a man of high and limitless culture.

When a man knows the differences in thoughtforms and the effect of thoughtforms upon his life, he begins to become a different person. The first indications of this are greater tolerance; a spirit of forgiveness, of search, of understanding; the ability to integrate, to explain, to see the essentials, to discover principles and to use many keys to solve the same problem.

A man, moving freely in the mental world, can extend a line of communication toward the Soul, releasing Soul energy to the lower fields of his vehicles, to bring in more alignment, integration and, eventually, fusion with the Soul. Such a process heals the gaps, removes obstructions from the path of the circulating divine flow, and establishes health, beauty and radiation.

Energy Is Produced when We Release Creatively The "Locked In" Impressions from our Lower Mind

There are few words that can be substituted for the word, *impression*. For as long as man lives he receives impressions from the world above and from the world below. Impressions coming from below are usually registered and acted upon by our five senses. Impressions coming from the world above are energies released from great lives acting through constellations, systems, planets, great Centers and from Initiates and disciples.

Man is like a harp, capable of producing harmonious music, but for the majority of people the strings of the instrument are not drawn taut enough to produce a reaction when struck by higher impressions. We are under constant bombardment by higher impressions, but few of us are able to translate them into sensation, action, thought or creative living. Thus, the majority of impressions come and sink into the layers of our higher vehicles, awaiting the time when they may be called to life through a conscious contact or attraction, and be used creatively. Most of these higher impressions are not registered by our five senses, our waking consciousness, but they are not lost forever. They reach the higher atmosphere of our being and leave there a mark, a sealed treasure for future use, which will serve as a continuous source of inspiration, enlightenment and power when contacted through meditation and used in creative expression.

Impressions coming from below, through the five senses, can be divided into two classes; those which are in harmony with the unfoldment of man's inner beauty, and those which are hindrances to it. Many of us are of the opinion that impressions are not effective if they do not produce immediate action. The fact is, that every impression is registered in our being by one of our vehicles. There it remains and at any time, through an association or restimulation, it may become active and control us, even against our own will, causing suffering, complications, problems, and waste of energy and matter.

Imagine the millions of impressions loaded upon our children through television programs and motion pictures, depicting crime and violence, activities on the battlefield, degenerated literature and associates. We may read a book or hear a lecture and fail to grasp the real meaning because our reading or listening is colored by our previous impressions. Actually, we read and hear our own impressions, restimulated by what we read or hear at that moment.

For these reasons it is important that we create a beautiful atmosphere for our children; an atmosphere of love, harmony, beauty and striving, instead of an atmosphere of crime, war, bloodshed and misery. In so doing we can help them to grow and reach sources of greater beauty within themselves.

To learn something new or to enlarge our horizon of consciousness, we must first clear our minds and view the ideas as they are presented. Our judgment and discrimination are based upon what we have previously learned, or what we *are*, because of the impressions which have molded us consciously or unconsciously in the past. This clearing process can be accomplished by a man who is expert in meditation and who can easily shift his level of observation into higher levels, and thus deal with new situations without being hindered by previous impressions which could obscure his vision.

New ideas enter into our being easily if there is a welcoming point within us which vibrates and draws the new idea in. When we clear our mind for a short moment and detach ourselves from our mental furniture, we give an opportunity to our *Inner Light* to observe. Within the human being there is a *source of light*, the source of freedom and beauty. This means that we actually have within ourselves a powerful magnet; a magnet of light, freedom and beauty which *can* draw all to Real Beauties, Light and Freedom *if* the space between the magnet and the object is clear.

The energy of the Sun pours through more potently when the cloud layers are cleared. It shines through the atmosphere, penetrating into all living forms, energizing and vitalizing them. *The same thing happens when "locked in" impressions are transmuted and released creatively.* Every impression in our mental world is a condensed, "bottled" force which can generate uplifting energy. For example, suppose a man falls in love with a a young woman who has impressed him deeply. This impression and his emotional and mental response create a whirlpool of force within his mind. He can use this whirlpool of force *creatively* to produce uplifting and transmuting energy within himself and within the young woman, if she responds to it. This whirlpool of force will be recharged every time he thinks of her or sees her. Here, he has a tremendous opportunity to channel this force field into a field of higher vision. This can be accomplished by thinking along these lines—

> ". . . I love her. She is really beautiful. I want to love her forever. I want her to be attractive to me forever. I want her to love me forever, and I want to be attractive to her forever. It can be this way if, apart from our physical communication, we seek a path upon which we can travel together toward a peak of achievement, see new horizons and aspire to higher and higher peaks; so let the intention of my love be to elevate, uplift and transform her from beauty to beauty through active work and sacrifice, and let me be wise enough to evoke a similar vision in her for me . . ."

Through such thinking, the inner pressure, the locked in force is used creatively and a potent energy is produced for upliftment and radiation. In this case energy is not flowing on the path of least resistance, but is raised to a higher rate of vibration by passing through a transmutative center, such as a vision, an idea for the future, a sublime aim, a high purpose, an intention, or a strong aspiration toward love, light and beauty.

On the other hand, higher impressions can be contacted and released when we reach them through meditation and contemplation, or when we invoke them through our aspirations and by living a life of dedicated service. Once we have made contact with a spot of beauty within ourselves, it becomes a fountainhead of inspiration and energy, which causes our field of life to bloom with rare beauties. Of importance is the fact that translation and utilization of these energies become more accurate and expand to wider fields as we raise our level of being.

Actually, the true Teaching is a technique for contacting the higher fields of impression within us and for releasing them in creative living. It is also the technique for building some miraculous "tubes" which will transform noise into music, and crime and hatred into striving toward love and cooperation. Thus, a flood of muddy water can be channeled to irrigate the field of lilies.

Energy Is Produced when We Visualize Certain Forms or Symbols, Or when We Create Thoughtforms

The Tibetan Master gave a wonderful definition of the word *symbol* when he said, "A symbol is an outer and visible sign of an inner and spiritual reality, carried out into expression upon the physical plane by the force of the inner, embodied life"[4] Thus, symbols are keys which can unlock stupendous energies

4. Bailey, Alice A., *The Destiny of the Nations*, p. 119.

within ourselves and within the higher realms. They can open the doors of light, of love and power; charging our life, our expressions, making of us, influential human beings. The symbol can also serve as a means of "tuning in" through which we are immediately placed in contact with higher sources. If a man uses symbols consciously and with pure motives, he can become a manipulator of energies. If, however, his motives are mixed, he can not only destroy himself and his mechanism, but he may also harm others.

In higher creative activities the creative artist builds special "stations" to pick up or collect the rays of energy from higher realms. These instruments are constructed in the space of the mind by the mental stuff. The act of building the stations is called the art of visualization.

Visualization is that process in which the unit of consciousness, through meditation and contemplation, attempts to bring down, through symbols, the archetypal forms existing on intuitional levels within the man and the universe. On the intuitional levels are found the keys to all of our problems; the solutions to our problems. Through visualization we build those subtle forms in mental space which gradually draw a vibration from their higher correspondences through attunement. As soon as this communication is established between the higher archetypal form and its reflection, the symbol, a flow of energy begins to pour down from the higher to the lower, and man experiences pure energy from a new source flowing into his being and activities. It is light, love and wisdom, and peace. A man who is under the flow of such energy, becomes a synthesizer, a man of broad tolerance, a man who lives in eternity and looks down upon the world from that high level of peace, timelessness and eternity. He is a man of serenity.

This flow of energy gradually wipes out all the unclean, infectious forms which are found in our mind and in the atmosphere of our bodies, and creates a high level of integration. The same is true for a group. If a few of such people are to be found in the group, the flow of pure energy integrates them, creating group-consciousness, tolerance, freedom, respect and love.

Every thoughtform in our mental space is a transformer and a transmitter. If the thoughtform is of high order and in tune with the higher worlds, it is a power station in the mental world and it draws life, inspiration and illumination from the intuitional world.

Visualization is a science, an art by which we build symbols in the mental world to serve as bridges to link the everyday life with the Life eternal. Every form or every thoughtform in the mental world transmits a different kind of energy according to its nature and substance. If the form is of higher quality having finer substance in its make-up, the energy pouring down through it will be of very high order.

Powerful symbols are: the five-pointed star (pointing up), the cross in its various representations, the torch, the lotus or lily with a flame in its center, a flying arrow, original Tarot cards, signs of the zodiac, etc.[5] If your intuition is awakened, you can create your own symbols and thus manipulate energy for furthering the actualization of the Divine Plan.[6] These symbols serve as accumulating and distributing agencies between the world of need and the world of answers; between the manifested world and the great ocean of energies beyond man. Symbols can also be used as protection against dark forces or entities. The energy produced by the symbols pushes away such entities, and often burns their vehicles which are largely built on the astral plane of astral substance or of lower mental matter. The flaming sword, the five-pointed star and the cross, when visualized properly, are powerful weapons against such forces.

Energy Is Produced when We Come in Contact with Higher Individuals, Initiates or Masters through Our Higher Nature

Every contact is a giving and taking process. There is no isolation in the universe. Everything is under the influence of everything. All life influences everything existing in it. The tiny leaf on the tree is the result of numberless influences from the universe and Cosmos. It is possible, however, to change our reactions and the effects of influences by changing our level of beingness, allowing us to come in contact with higher levels upon which we can communicate with advanced beings. Man, like the little leaf, is subject to the effects of all influences until he has learned to practice discrimination. When he has reached this level, when he is able to discriminate, he will choose the influences which he can utilize for his immediate or eternal purposes. The advanced, conscious man is the only mechanism that can perform the metamorphosis of assimilating higher energies and transforming them into creative science, art, religion and leadership.

Man is a sensitive mechanism. He changes when his location, climate and relationships are changed. Every location, every climate and every relationship creates in him different reactions, stimulates different centers within him, and leads him into different kinds of activities. Gradually, however, man builds a permanent center within himself; a center having permanent aims, permanent direction, permanent intentions. When he has reached this level, he can choose among the influences and come in contact only with those influences which suit his purpose and help him to bring it into actualization.

A man, a book, an idea are sources, which if rightly chosen, can elevate your consciousness, your mind, your heart and even your physical body. There are people who weaken your vitality, create disharmony in your emotional and mental worlds, never casting a single beam of light. There are writings and books which obscure the channel between you and light, love and power. There are thoughts which lead you into confusion or destruction.

---

5. Saraydarian, H., *The Science of Meditation*, Chap. XXIII.
6. *Ibid.*, Chap. XXX.

On the other hand, there are individuals whose influence helps in the upliftment of humanity. If you come in contact with them, you are raised in your being, in your feeling and consciousness. Because of the fact that they are in contact with higher levels of being, they radiate constructive, creative energies which flow into your being. When you talk with them, or perhaps just sit by them, you are elevated into your higher realms of consciousness or awareness. Their ideas can inspire you and become a source of power in your life. Their ideas are real ideas, created upon higher levels and charged with high voltage energy. They transform your whole being, your life, your environment, your nation.

Study the lives of those great sons of man who were inflamed with a new idea. Observe how the idea grew, how it destroyed obstacles and created civilizations and culture. If a man is charged with a real idea, he is unconquerable. He is a flaming bush, a flaming sword, and everything in opposition to his idea serves only to increase its power, beauty and influence.

There are individuals who are in continuous contact with higher sources. These people are like mighty magnets who draw to themselves the ready, worthy people and make of them magnetic sources; radioactive sources of love, light and power. Such advanced men not only pour into us their blissful energies, they also stimulate and awaken latent energy centers within us. If the man coming in contact with them is an advanced man, he becomes radioactive, shining and creative, but if he is a low level man, he destroys himself because this contact stimulates the evil or lower tendencies, and he becomes an agent for destructive forces. When a man is polarized toward vices, hatred, jealousy and gossip, these vices will become stronger and stronger if he comes in contact with such energy sources or centers. The time comes when he loses all control over his lower vehicles and he becomes the victim of released energies. Just as weak or damaged wires should never be connected to a huge dynamo, so the low level individual should not be exposed to the high voltage energy of a spiritually advanced man.

In olden days the centers of spiritual education were hierarchical in their functions. A newcomer was not allowed to see the great teachers until he had been trained by "little ones" and had reached some degree of purification, making it safe for him to come in contact with advanced teachers. Contact with the true teacher was very rare, occasional and short. These contacts were intended to give only the needed impetus on the path of the aspirant.

The same is true in occult teaching today. We are told that the real Masters communicate directly with Their initiate disciples, but They communicate with the world through their disciples and aspirants and through Their written word. Most average people who claim that they are in contact with the Masters, are in illusion. A true Master cannot be contacted until a man establishes conscious contact with his Solar Angel. When he has met his Solar Angel face to face, he is led into the presence of the Masters. Before this time, any real or illusionary contact can have disturbing effects on his vehicles and on his way of life. This is the reason that reaching the Masters is not made easy. It is the reason that humanity is passing through so many long years of "preparation" for the reappearance of Christ.

IMPORTANCE OF GENERATION AND CONSERVATION OF ENERGY

The health of our body, the beauty of our heart, and the clarity of our mind depends on the generation and conservation of energy. Through every physical action, through every emotion or feeling, through every thought, we spend or generate energy. When we are cut off from the Inner Light, inner purpose, we become debtful, for we are spending or wasting energy. We generate energy if we are always conscious of our Inner Light which is a Spark of the One Light. It is important to keep a detached attitude and try not to identify with passing time and space. It is the only way through which man connects himself with the dynamo of the universe, making it possible for the universal vitality to pour through him day and night in every activity. Thus, he brings joy, health, wisdom, happiness, light and love to everyone around him, for he is an ever radiating center of pure energy from whom everyone can draw what he needs.

There are people in the world who are living on such great heights of beingness that they not only radiate, but know how to stop the flow of radiation for a time. Their greatest emphasis is placed upon speech because speech is like fire; it burns and destroys if not used properly. Speech molds our character; we become what we think and speak. The results of our speech can create a path toward the Great Ones if it is charged with the energy of truth, love, harmlessness and expressed as service for our fellow human beings. People, capable of using speech in this way, can enter into the aura of the Great Ones and become radioactive centers of light, love and power.

The destiny of every man is to become a living Soul, eventually making it possible for his Divine Guide, the mysterious Sacrificial One within, to be released from His age-long labour with us, to perform His cosmic duties.

He has led us

From darkness to Light,
From the unreal to the Real,
From death to Immortality,
From chaos to Beauty.

Now we must strive beyond and enter the path which leads

From the individual to the Universal,
From the many cycles to the One Life,
From manifestation to Space.

INDEX